ective development> <WMLS n> <cost-effective development> <WMLS
ment guidelines> <ASP> <ci > <development guidelines> <ASP> <cir
ntegration> <cost-effective de <database integration> <cost-effective de
LScript> <development guide ment> <WMLScript> <development guide

que®

201 West 103rd Street
Indianapolis, Indiana 46290

Chris Tull

9/02

48467195

WAP 2.0 Development

International Standard Book Number: 0-7897-2602-5

Library of Congress Catalog Card Number: 2002100461

Printed in the United States of America

First Printing: *March 2002*

05   04   03   02   4   3   2   1

Trademarks

Warning and Disclaimer

Publisher
David Culverwell

Executive Editor
Candace Hall

Acquisitions Editor
Loretta Yates

Development Editors
Bryan Morgan
Sarah Robbins

Managing Editor
Thomas F. Hayes

Project Editor
Tonya Simpson

Production Editor
Megan Wade

Indexer
Eric Schroeder

Proofreader
Andrea Dugan

Technical Editor
Allen Thompson

Team Coordinator
Cindy Teeters

Interior Designer
Karen Ruggles

Cover Designer
Bill Thomas

Page Layout
Rebecca Harmon
Cheryl Lynch

Contents at a Glance

Table of Contents

About the Author

Chris Tull is a Web applications developer and Internet technologist based out of the Dallas/Fort Worth area. Besides immersing himself in the design and development of leading-edge Internet applications, Chris also balances his time writing on a variety of topics. He is a regular contributor to AnywhereYouGo.com, a site designed to help developers further their expertise in the realm of wireless development.

Dedication

This book is dedicated to my family.

Acknowledgments

If you're like most people, you'll look at this section for a moment and then quickly flip past it. I beg you not to flip. In many ways, this section is the most important in this book. Without the help of the people listed here, this book would have never been.

I'd like to give thanks to my parents, Tom and Carole Tull. Their love, guidance, and support make all things possible. I'm also deeply indebted to my wife, Niki. Her support in everything I do is beyond value. This book is for you all.

I'd also like to thank Matt Tull and Peter Thoryk. Both have helped me in more ways than they realize. Also, thanks to the Theriot family. Their Thursday night dinners gave me the strength to write.

Many thanks also go out to my editors at Que Publishing, including Loretta Yates, Cindy Teeters, and Tonya Simpson. They work harder than anyone has any idea and are the best at what they do. Their hard work has truly brought this book up to another level. Also, many thanks go to the other folks at Que who worked behind the scenes on this book. Forgive me for not knowing your names, but know that I am deeply grateful.

In addition, I'd like to thank my technical editor, Allan Thompson, my copy editor, Megan Wade, and my development editor, Bryan Morgan. Their comments and suggestions have improved this book immensely. They also kept me from sticking my foot in my mouth on more than one occasion. Any errors you find within this text are mine alone.

Finally, thanks to Stacey Johnson, Devin Pike, and the team at www.anywhereyougo.com for introducing me to WAP and the world of wireless development.

Tell Us What You Think!

As the reader of this book, *you* are our most important critic and commentator. We value your opinion and want to know what we're doing right, what we could do better, what areas you'd like to see us publish in, and any other words of wisdom you're willing to pass our way.

As a publisher for Que, I welcome your comments. You can fax, e-mail, or write me directly to let me know what you did or didn't like about this book—as well as what we can do to make our books stronger.

Please note that I cannot help you with technical problems related to the topic of this book, and that due to the high volume of mail I receive, I might not be able to reply to every message.

When you write, please be sure to include this book's title and author as well as your name and phone or fax number. I will carefully review your comments and share them with the author and editors who worked on the book.

Fax: 317-581-4666

E-mail: feedback@quepublishing.com

Mail: David Culverwell
           Que Publishing
           201 West 103rd Street
           Indianapolis, IN 46290 USA

Introduction

In the last 20 years, technology has changed the way the world communicates. Take the revolution of the Internet. In less than a decade, the Internet has transfixed itself into our lives, becoming a viable social and business entity. The Internet has come a long way from its humble beginnings as nothing more than a type of electronic billboard.

Today, technology and communication continue to progress hand in hand. However, progress isn't limited to only the world. As is evident from the millions of wireless phone users in the wired world, people love mobile communications. As a result, the telecommunications industry is beginning to extend its services to meet these growing needs, providing a variety of mobile communication possibilities for users.

Mobile communication includes wider possibilities than simply keeping in touch through voice. Wireless devices, such as mobile phones and PDAs, allow users to view and manipulate data on the go—providing a cost-effective and easier method of communication in comparison to traditional computers.

This book explores the development of wireless applications for mobile devices. The technology you'll use for wireless development is the Wireless Application Protocol (WAP). WAP is a wireless standard, supported by most of the world's telecommunication companies. Learning to develop with the languages associated with WAP is an excellent way to become familiar with one exciting area of wireless development.

A great need exists for developers who can provide the types of wireless applications users want and need. This book teaches the skills necessary for developing wireless applications in the quickest and easiest manner possible.

The Purpose of This Book

The purpose of this book is to teach both new and accomplished developers how to develop applications for WAP-enabled devices. This book walks through the variety of tools available for wireless development in WAP, the programming languages best used for WAP development, and where to go after tackling the subjects in this book. This book uses real-world examples to present concepts and principles of WAP development.

As you progress through this book, you'll see that WAP development contains many similarities to Web development. WAP uses markup and scripting languages similar to those used in Web development. It also incorporates familiar Web developmental concepts, such as client-side and server-side development. If you're already familiar with Web development, you'll have no problems picking up WAP development quickly.

However, if you haven't had any experience with Web development (or any development for that matter), this book provides an excellent starting point. It not only teaches new developers how to develop WAP applications, but also provides a foundation for other types of development.

What This Book Covers

This book introduces new developers to the foundation skills of WAP development and then builds on these skills. By the end of this book, you'll find yourself equipped with an understanding of WAP development, as well as a number of other popular Web development skills.

The following is a summary of the topics presented within this book:

- **An introduction to WAP**—You'll learn how WAP applications work, the technology behind them, and the types of applications you can expect demands for in the coming years.

- **The variety of software tools required for WAP development**—The tools necessary for WAP development differ in complexity and price. You'll look at a sample of these tools, so you can choose which best fit your preferences. All examples within this book use software tools already installed with your operating system or available free on the Internet.

- **A thorough understanding of WML, one of the most widely used programming languages in WAP**—WML handles the display of content within WAP devices and contains a number of similarities with HTML, the language used to develop Web pages. Thus, by learning WML you'll also begin building a foundation for pursuing other development areas, such Web development.

- **The incorporation of images and timers into a wireless application to provide animated sequences and splash pages**—Splash pages are introductory pages that display at the beginning of an application. This book familiarizes you with the WBMP format, the only graphical format available within WAP devices today. Converting existing images into the WBMP format is also discussed.

- **All areas of WMLScript**—WMLScript is a programming language used to enhance the functionality of WAP applications. WMLScript stems from JavaScript, one of the most widely used Web development languages. By learning WMLScript, you'll also increase your understanding of JavaScript.

- **Advanced WAP development techniques**—You'll learn several advanced development techniques, such as accessing and retrieving information from a remote server using Active Server Pages. Active Server Pages is a server-side technology used widely throughout both the wired and wireless worlds.

Development Tools

WAP developers will find a variety of software tools available at their fingertips, ranging in various complexities and pricing. In this book, you'll use the most widely available tools—most are already included within your PC's operating system.

The following is a quick summary of the development tools used in this book. These tools are not the only tools available for development, but they're used here simply because they're the most easily accessible tools. Throughout this book, other development tool options are also presented, in case you want to try other development software.

Test Environment

In this book, you'll develop WAP applications on a test environment using a PC and WAP device-emulators. The examples in this book assume you're using a PC that contains a Windows operating system.

You can use one of the following development platforms for the majority of this book (Parts I–III). In Part IV, "Dynamic Wireless Development," you also can use any of these platforms; however, the examples in Part IV use ASP 3, which is available only with the Windows 2000 products. The following is a summary of the acceptable operating systems you can use for your test environment:

- Windows 95, 98, or Millennium (Me)
- Windows NT 4.0, XP
- Windows 2000 Professional, Advanced Server, or Datacenter Server

Text Editors

This book uses Microsoft Notepad for all application code creation.

Two other products that work just as well are TextPad (by Helios Software Solutions) and HomeSite (by Allaire). Both of these products are available for a reasonable price, but you also can obtain a free trial version of both. See Chapter 2, "Tools of the Trade," for more information regarding text editors.

WAP Device-Emulators

Device-emulators are software simulations of a WAP device. They provide developers with a test environment in which to test code before moving it over to an actual wireless device and Web server.

Most WAP device manufacturers provide their own emulators, available free to developers. Some excellent emulators that are available include Openwave's SDK, Nokia's Mobile Internet Toolkit, Ericcson's WapIDE, and Motorola's Mobile ADK. Again, check out Chapter 2 for more information about device emulators. Figure I.1 shows the Openwave SDK Emulator.

The examples and images in this book have been tested and verified to work with a variety of emulators. All examples and screen images within this book have been done with the Openwave SDK.

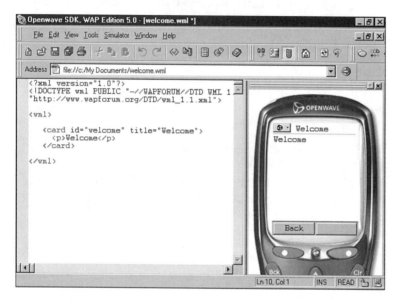

Figure I.1   *Image of SDK courtesy of Openwave Systems, Inc.*

WBMP Image Tools

Starting in Chapter 7, "Working with Images," you examine converting images into a format usable by WAP devices. You then learn to incorporate these images into your WAP applications.

To use images in WAP applications, you must use some type of image editing tool. A number of image tools are available, including the following:

- Image converter programs
- Online converter pages
- Plug-ins for existing graphic software

Figure I.2 displays examples of image tools available for WAP development.

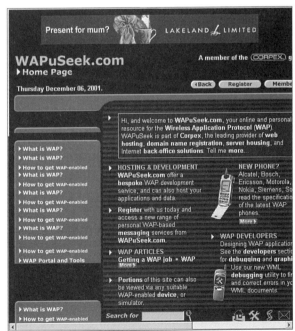

Figure I.2   *WAP image editing options.*

Web Servers

In Part IV, you create WAP applications that use Web server technology. Although several Web servers are available on the market today, this book uses the Windows Web servers in all examples (Microsoft's Personal Web Server or Microsoft's Internet Information Server). Both are available for free download from www.microsoft.com. In addition, setting up a Web server as a test environment is discussed in Chapter 13, "WAP Development with ASP." Figure I.3 shows the Microsoft Personal Web Server in action.

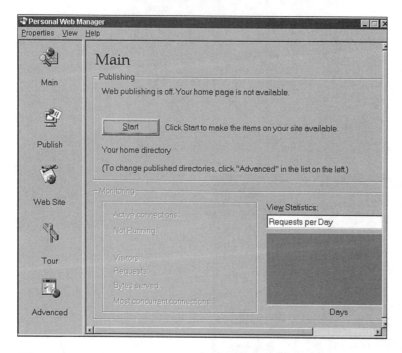

Figure I.3   *Microsoft's Personal Web Server (PWS).*

Text Conventions Used in This Book

This book uses several text conventions to help you more easily understand information and concepts. The following summarizes the conventions used throughout this book:

- `Monospace regular font`—Represents a portion of code. It also represents keywords of the programming languages, variable and function names, and language element tags.

- **`Monospace bold font`**—Represents an area of the code to direct your attention toward. It also indicates text the reader should type in when following along with the examples.

- *Monospace italic font*—Represents a portion of code where the user or developer should supply some sort of value.

Graphical Conventions Used in This Book

In addition to text conventions, this book also uses graphical conventions to help present information more clearly. The following is a summary of all graphical conventions used within this book.

Notes

NOTE

Note boxes represent additional notes associated with a subject on the page.

Tips

TIP

Tip boxes represent any helpful tips or suggestions associated with a subject on the page.

Caution

CAUTION

Caution boxes represent potential trouble areas associated with a subject on the page.

Coding Examples

Most coding examples within this book are preceded by numbers. These numbers are for reference only and are present as a means to refer to individual lines of codes during explanation of the code. Line numbers should not be typed into your code:

```
1 <?xml version="1.0"?>
2 <!DOCTYPE wml PUBLIC "-//WAPFORUM//DTD WML 1.1//EN"
3 "http://www.wapforum.org/DTD/wml_1.1.xml">

4 <wml>

5    <card id="firstcard">
6      <p>First Card</p>
7    </card>
8 <wml>
```

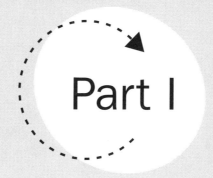

Part I

Introduction to WAP Development

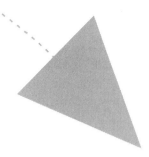

What Is WAP Development?

Welcome to the world of WAP development! In the past couple of years, you might have noticed the increase of wireless devices around you. Go to any shopping mall and you've probably noticed the majority of people have a mobile phone with them. Or, next time you're at work, sneak a peak at your co-workers' desks. I'll bet you see more than a fair share of personal digital assistants (PDAs). Wireless devices are everywhere.

Even more exciting is that many of these devices now contain the capability to access and manipulate data—bringing the concept of mobility to a higher meaning. The accessing of e-mail, personal data, and business information from wireless devices is only the beginning of possibilities for this new industry.

The need for developers in this new arena of technology is at an all-time high. This book aims to get you up to speed quickly, familiarizing you with the developing wireless applications using the Wireless Application Protocol (WAP). You'll learn more about the possibilities of WAP in this chapter.

This chapter gets you started with WAP development by tackling the following:

- The state of the wireless world.

- The types of devices available for WAP development

- An introduction to the technology of WAP, and how this exciting technology fits into the spectrum of wireless development

- Design principles to keep in mind when developing WAP applications

- Future business perspectives for the WAP technology

The State of the Wireless World

According to estimates by several groups, there are roughly 800 million mobile users in the world. By 2002, the number of these mobile users is estimated to reach one billion.

Obviously from these figures, it's no doubt that people love mobile devices. In fact, people love their mobile devices so much that it's also estimated that by 2002, the number of mobile users will finally overtake the number of fixed Internet subscribers worldwide.

As the demand for mobile devices grows, so does the desire for services. People want more than simply the ability to communicate by voice.

Today, users want the ability to access mobile data, be it services such as e-mail, messaging, or up-to-the-minute business and financial information. The simple fact is that people want the services of the Internet available to them anytime, anywhere. And they like the idea of mobility.

So, what's wrong with PCs and laptops? Don't they supply this mobility users are looking for?

The answer is yes. PCs and laptops are more powerful and functional than any wireless device today. In addition, technologies such as Bluetooth are brining the capability to wirelessly access data from a PC or laptop. However, mobile devices do have several advantages over PCs and laptops. Perhaps the most important is cost effectiveness.

Consider the price of a PC or laptop computer. PCs and laptops have not come down in price over the years. In fact, if anything, their prices have risen. The reason is the effectiveness of computer hardware companies. Computer hardware has constantly improved. Anyone who owns a PC or laptop realizes that the hardware that was "state-of-the-art" when it was purchased becomes almost antique within three years.

For the most part, wireless devices have not hit this type of price plateau. Perhaps it's time for the Internet, e-mail, and all the services users love from our PCs to move on. This is what the wireless world is about: bringing the services users know and love into a wireless device.

A Wireless Device Primer

Before you delve further into the topic of wireless, it's important to familiarize yourself with the types of devices for which you'll be developing. In this book, you learn wireless application development using the WAP technology (more on WAP in a moment). Essentially, the Wireless Access Protocol (WAP) is a technology that enables the transfer of data to wireless devices.

NOTE

WAP offers several advantages over other competing wireless technologies. The following are some of the most important aspects of WAP:

- · WAP is an open standard (and therefore vendor independent).

- · WAP is network-standard independent.

- · WAP contains a transport mechanism, optimized for wireless data bearers.

For mobile phones to be WAP-enabled, the device must contain two key characteristics:

- **A micro-browser**—This is embedded software within the mobile device that enables users to view information, such as Internet information, company data, e-mail messages, and so on, from the mobile phone.

- **A method for users to input data**—Most WAP-enabled devices provide user input through the number buttons. However, higher-level devices now incorporate more advanced input methods, such as touch screens or folding keyboards.

WAP-Enabled Phones

In this book, you'll use WAP phone emulators to build and test your applications. WAP-enabled phones provide a good place to start for the budding WAP developer, perhaps for no better reason than the number of challenges they present. WAP-enabled phones do not allow for robust user input because they have small display screens. They also do not readily support multimedia, such as sound, or sophisticated text-formatting functionality, such as complex tables, large and color graphics, and frames.

By the very nature of this development environment, developers must start small. This is a good thing because it avoids information overload and the distractions of developing too much too soon. As you progress through this book, you'll tackle more and more advanced developing topics, coupling WAP development with a number of other Web development techniques. By the end of the book, you'll find yourself developing an advanced database application that accesses information wirelessly from a WAP device.

Figure 1.1 displays an example of a WAP-enabled phone from Siemens. This type of device is similar to the devices you'll develop applications for within this book.

Figure 1.1 *The Siemens SL 45 WAP-enabled mobile phone.*

NOTE

This book focuses on development of WAP applications for mobile phones. However, all the concepts and applications within are also applicable to PDAs.

PDAs do differ from WAP-phones in that they use an operating system. Working with devices that have operating systems offers developers a lot more flexibility. However, working with operating systems also means you must familiarize yourself with a more robust programming language, such as C++ or Visual Basic.

What Exactly Is WAP, Anyway?

Now that we've examined the WAP-enabled devices that are your development environment, let's focus now on what exactly WAP does.

WAP is the technology this book uses to develop wireless applications. It is a set of *protocols* (more on these in a second), which are rules that designate how computers should interpret WAP data.

WAP was developed by the WAP Forum, a consortium that consists of some of the world's largest wireless vendors and manufactures, such as Siemens, Nortel, Lucent, Vodaphone, Motorola, Nokia, and Ericsson to name a few. Today, more than 500 companies have joined the group, which is responsible for defining WAP's standards. To find out more about the WAP Forum, go to www.wapforum.org.

As a WAP developer, you won't need to know the intricacies of how this technology works. However, it is a good idea to have a general idea of how the technology operates. The following is a summary of the various components behind the WAP technology.

How WAP Works

WAP applications use an application architecture known as the *client/server model*. The client/server model is used widely on both PC and WAP applications.

To understand how this model works, let's first look at how PCs use the client/server model. After you understand this model in the wired world, you'll be able to easily translate these concepts to WAP applications.

THE WIRED CLIENT/SERVER MODEL

The PC computer sitting in your living room or at your place of business more than likely is a client in some client/server application. In the client/server model, clients receive a plethora of information (such as Web pages or sales information from a company database) from larger, more powerful computers called servers. Servers contain enough processor speed, internal memory (RAM), and disk storage to serve the clients that are accessing it. Clients and servers are connected by many networks.

In the case of some client/server models, such as the Internet, a client might actually access several remote servers. For example, your company might have one server that allows you to access business information; your favorite e-commerce or Web site might have another server. The beauty of being on the client side of things is that accessing one server or another is effortless and seamless. You simply type a network address (such as the name of a Web site) and you're there. What is happening behind the scenes is that you are accessing different Internet protocols. Each time you access a different network address, you might actually be jumping from one remote server to another. Figure 1.2 presents a graphical representation of the wired client/server model.

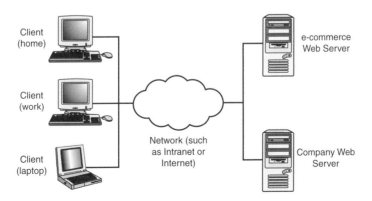

Figure 1.2   *The wired client/server infrastructure.*

This client/server architecture enables users to perform a number of actions. Users can view Web sites and Web pages, get company information, and run reports from their databases. Users can also play games with other users, whether they are half a block or half a continent away.

THE WAP CLIENT/SERVER MODEL

The WAP client/server model is in many ways similar to that of the wired client/server model. However, instead of a client being a PC, in the world of WAP the client is a WAP-enabled device. WAP devices contain a micro-browser (similar to browsers such as Microsoft Internet Explorer or Netscape Navigator found on desktop PCs) that enables users to view applications and content hosted on remote servers.

For WAP devices to communicate with a remote server a couple of inter-mediary steps must first occur. When a WAP device accesses (or sends) information to or from a server, the request is first sent from the WAP device. This request then travels through a mobile operator's network.

NOTE

A mobile operator's network is the company or organization that provides carrier services to its subscribers. More often than not, the company that you're paying your mobile telephone bills to is your mobile operator.

Depending on your location in the world, mobile networks can use a variety of wireless communication technologies and standards, such as CDMA, CDPD, GPRS, GSM, iDEN, PDC, PHS, and TDMA. For the WAP developer, these technologies and standards work equally well with WAP. Don't worry about the details of these standards; they won't take precedence in your development efforts.

After sending the request for information through this network, a WAP gateway (which is a computer that sits between the WAP device and the server), intercepts the request. WAP gateways translate data into wired network protocols, where a server receives the information, acts on it, and then sends back a result. When a WAP gateway receives this result, it converts this information into a data format that is viewable on a WAP device. Figure 1.3 summarizes the WAP client/server infrastructure.

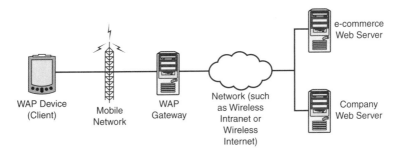

Figure 1.3 *The WAP client / server infrastructure.*

What Are Wireless Protocols?

Protocol is a technical networking term that means the series of steps used to transfer data. Most developers shy away from in-depth discussions about networks; however, it is a good idea to familiarize yourself with the protocols that make up WAP.

The term *Wireless Application Protocol* is in some ways misleading. The term is misleading because the WAP technology is actually made up of not one, but five, different protocols all working together. You'll often hear the entire set of WAP protocols referred to as the WAP stack. The WAP stack covers the whole process of wireless content delivery, including the creation and layout of the content, specification of security, and transportation of data. Figure 1.4 illustrates the WAP stack.

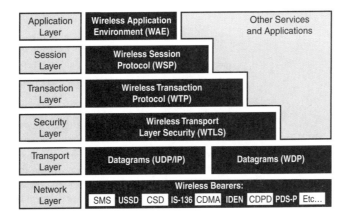

Figure 1.4 *The WAP stack.*

These five protocols provide several advantages when working together. They help to reduce unnecessary data transfers by using a binary code to reduce the size of the data. WAP devices have a slower connectivity time than PCs; because of this, the transfer of data needs to be as efficient as possible. The WAP stack works toward accomplishing this goal.

Table 1.1 summarizes the five protocols and what each does. Don't worry about memorizing these—understanding the WAP stack's overall functionality is what is important.

Table 1.1   The WAP Stack

Layer	Name	Definition
Presentation Layer	The Wireless Application Environment	This layer, also known as the Wireless Application Environment (WAE) layer, provides an area where WAP applications and services can be used. This layer also defines the user interface (the method by which users interact with applications on their WAP devices).
		Graphics (in the Wireless Bitmap format) can also be present within this layer. The Wireless Bitmap format (WBMP) currently is the only graphic format available for WAP applications. WBMP is a single-bit plate graphic interchange format that defines single bits for basic black-and-white images. However, as the specifications and technology developers, you can expect that WBMP will eventually support grayscale and color images.
Session Layer	The Wireless Session Protocol	This layer, also known as the Wireless Session Protocol (WSP) layer, links the WAE to two services. These services control how content is exchanged between client/server WAP applications.
Transaction Layer	The Wireless Transaction Protocol	This layer, also known as the Wireless Transaction Protocol (WTP) layer, provides different methods for performing transactions, suitable for low-bandwidth mobile networks. This layer's main job is to reduce unnecessary transactions between a client WAP device and a remote server.

Table 1.1 *continued*

Layer	Name	Definition
Security Layer	The Wireless Transport Layer Security	This layer, also known as the Wireless Transport Layer Security (WTLS) layer, contains similar security layers as those found in the wired Web, these being the Secure Session Layer (SSL) and the Transaction Layer Security (TLS) protocols. The WTLS layer is optional and is independent of the layers above and below it, and provides a number of security features such as authentication and data integrity checks.
Data Transport Layer	The Wireless Datagram Protocol	This layer, also known as the Wireless Datagram Protocol (WDP) layer, is a datagram-oriented, network layer protocol modeled on the User Datagram Protocol (UDP) used on the Internet. In essence, this protocol controls the general transport of WAP protocols.

NOTE

For more information about the WAP architecture specifications, visit the WAP Forum site for additional reference documentation.

WAP Application Design Practices

To date, the greatest demand for WAP applications has been within the business world. As a result, applications—such as real-time programs that access corporate LANs, intranets, or databases; e-mail; and messaging applications—are the first types of development efforts you might face as a WAP developer.

Of course, it's safe to say that the demand for WAP applications goes far beyond the corporate world. Real-time delivery of content is a type of application that all users will find beneficial. Applications that provide up-to-the-minute stock quotes, traffic alerts, and weather information are helpful for a variety of users.

There are some key points developers must take into consideration when creating any type of WAP application. The four main questions you should always ask yourself as a WAP developer are as follows:

- Can the data be displayed logically on a small display page?

- How much data can be transmitted to the user quickly (these being bandwidth and processing power issues)?

- What type of cellular data coverage does the user have (is he dealing with poor connections)?

- How much battery life does a device have?

As you work through this book, keep these points always in the back of your mind.

Business Perspectives

The WAP Forum estimates that by 2004, wireless subscribers will top one billion. Of these, approximately 800 million subscribers will be mobile data subscribers. The number of WAP devices capable of accessing information is staggering. But what types of market opportunities exist for wireless applications and services? What types of information will users need to access?

Let's look at some of the most popular, and necessary, applications WAP developers will find themselves creating in the next couple of years.

Corporate Applications

One area in which WAP developers can expect to find a huge demand is within sales and service. Sales and service personnel typically spend the majority of their days away from a PC computer. In many cases, many of these users might not even have a computer.

By using a WAP application to access company information, WAP devices could provide new options for sales individuals. A salesperson could use a WAP application to access the latest pricing and competitive data regarding a particular sales product. Delivery and service users might use a WAP application to view and update progress in the field. Such applications would also enable personnel who are in-house to spend more time dealing with customers rather than their own service staffs.

Online Services

Real-time applications and services such as stock prices, news, weather, and travel are always popular with users. In the world of WAP, you can expect to see these types of services being taken one step further, as the use of a mobile operator's network now allows for the actual delivery of location-based information. Location services provide a way of delivering location-dependent information and advertising to users, such as the nearest bank or the closest hospital.

Personal Productivity

E-mail services have always been important to users, and providing such services to WAP devices will be in high demand for the WAP developer. These types of wireless applications can enable users to contain information such as a real-time copy of an address book and a calendar that allows several individuals to view changes simultaneously.

Summary

This chapter has looked at the Wireless Application Protocol, the technology accepted by the WAP Forum as the standard method of wireless data transfer. WAP is the technology you'll use to develop applications within this.

You also learned about the types of devices you'll develop application for, as well as information about WAP—the technology that makes this type of development possible.

This chapter concluded with some important design guidelines to consider as you work your way through this book. With the information learned in this chapter, you should now be familiar enough with the technology to begin creating WAP applications. However, you'll first need to set up the tools you'll use throughout this book.

In the next chapter, you learn where to find the necessary tools to begin your development efforts, all of which are available for free download from the Internet. By the end of the next chapter, you'll have set up a test environment that will serve you throughout the course of this book. You'll then be ready to get down and dirty with your first WAP development application.

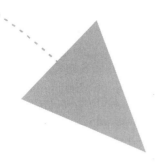

Tools of the Trade

Before you can begin to write WAP applications, you first must create a work environment in which to write and test your code. In this book, you use device-emulator software available free from the Internet. The only things you need to create a test environment are a Microsoft Windows operating system and an Internet connection (to obtain the device-emulator software).

A number of tools are available for the WAP developer, ranging from freeware available from the Internet to major software packages that cost hundreds of dollars. This chapter presents some of the most popular tools available to the wireless developer and where to obtain them.

This chapter looks at the following:

- The tools you need to get started in WAP development

- Text editors—what they are and why they're used

- The various device-emulators available today and where to obtain them

- How to install the device-emulator used in examples throughout this book

- How to configure your test environment for WAP development

The Text Editors

Text editors are what developers use to write the code for their applications. Text editors come in many shapes and sizes today. Microsoft FrontPage and Macromedia Dreamweaver are two popular commercial text editors that essentially create files for you. Even though these products are great, they also contain a number of bells and whistles that can distract you from truly understanding WAP development. Besides, these commercial products are not free, nor necessarily inexpensive.

A better solution is to stick to a simple text editor. You need to know how to build applications from the ground up, writing every bit of code yourself. The only way to learn any kind of programming is to do it hands-on.

Figure 2.1 shows a couple of examples of text editors you can use.

Microsoft Notepad

One of the easiest text editors to use is Microsoft Notepad. If you are working on a PC that is using a Windows operating system then Notepad is already loaded on your PC and ready to go.

To access Microsoft Notepad, go to your Start menu. Then, select Programs, Accessories, Notepad.

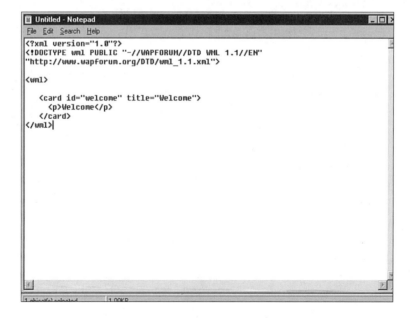

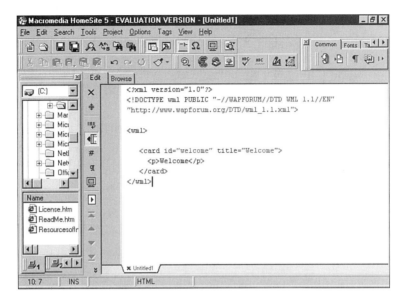

Figure 2.1 *Various text editors available for WAP development.*

NOTE

The location of Microsoft Notepad can differ from one Windows operating system to another.

This book doesn't spend a lot of time discussing Notepad—most of you are more than familiar with the program. However, if you haven't played around with Notepad before, take a few minutes to familiarize yourself with it before moving on within this book.

Helios TextPad

Another popular text editor favored by many developers is TextPad, developed by Helios Software Solutions. TextPad provides a number of functionality advantages over Notepad, such as the ability to edit multiple files at once and a warm start feature that lets you restart a file exactly where you left off. However, perhaps the biggest advantage of TextPad is that it understands the syntax of several programming languages.

TextPad is available for around $30. However, you can obtain a shareware copy at `http://textpad.com`. Figure 2.2 displays an example of TextPad in action.

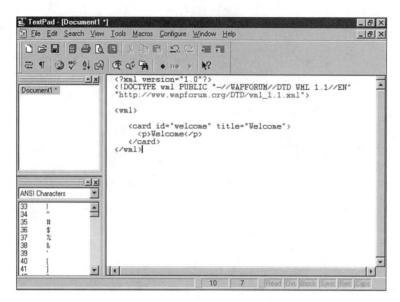

Figure 2.2   *The TextPad text editor in action.*

NOTE

Shareware simply means that you can download the product free. However, each time you start shareware, you're reminded to register the program.

Allaire HomeSite

HomeSite is another excellent text editor, developed by Allaire (the creators of ColdFusion). HomeSite contains many of the same functionality as TextPad, but takes things one step further by incorporating tools that actually help you write code for several programming languages. HomeSite contains a number of wizards and even provides some tips and reference information regarding the code you're writing.

Of course, all these features come at a price—HomeSite retails at around $90. You can get a free, 30-day trial version from the Allaire Web site: Go to http://www.allaire.com and select the Products link on the title bar. A Product page displays. From here, you can select the HomeSite link to obtain your free trial version.

Device-Emulator Software

Now that your text editor is in place, you're ready to install your device-emulator software.

Device-emulator software is a great tool in learning to develop WAP applications. These programs run on a PC, enabling developers to develop and test applications while sitting at the same computer.

Device-emulator software is also useful in that it provides a cost-effective, easy, and fast way for developers to create, test, and debug applications. Consider the alternative of not using device-emulator software. Without these tools, a developer would need to

1. Write code on a PC.

2. Upload the code into a live Web server.

3. Run the application from an actual WAP-enabled device.

4. Debug the code on a PC.

5. Upload changes to the code into a live Web server.

6. Run the application from the WAP-enabled device again.

Imagine trying to learn WAP development using such a method.

Many WAP developers create their applications by first using device-emulators to make sure their applications work the way they want. After their applications are tested numerous times on a device-emulator, they're moved to live Web servers for testing on a real device. Figure 2.3 displays some of the device-emulators discussed in this chapter.

Figure 2.3 *The Openwave and Nokia device-emulators.* (Image of SDK courtesy of Openwave Systems, Inc. Image of Nokia Mobile Internet Toolkit courtesy of Nokia Corporation.)

Openwave's SDK

The SDK is a standalone application that runs on Windows, and it is available for free download. Figure 2.4 displays the Openwave SDK.

NOTE

The SDK also contains a text editor if you want to write and then view your code all within this one program.

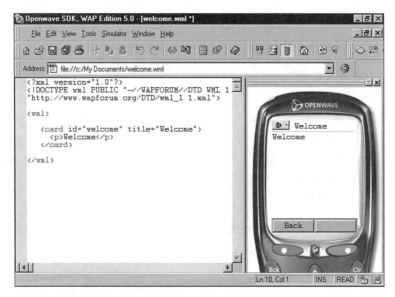

Figure 2.4   *Image of SDK courtesy of Openwave Systems, Inc.*

DOWNLOADING THE SDK

To download any of the Openwave products, you must first register for a free developer's account. You can do this by accessing the Openwave developer site at `http://www.developer.openwave.com`.

After registering your free developer account, you can download the SDK. If you're not already there, return to the developer site at `http://www.developer.openwave.com`. Once there, do the following:

1. Select the SDK hyperlink, underneath the Downloads section on the Contents bar.

2. Select the most recent version of the SDK available. At the time of this writing, the latest version is around 23MB.

NOTE

The SDK 5.0 is the first Openwave version to support Windows 2000 products.

3. Select the appropriate executable to download according to your operating system.

4. Openwave has a self-extracting executable to install the product. Follow the instructions on the executable to install the product on your PC.

CAUTION

SDK 4.1 or earlier have a known bug that creates problems if you use the product without an Internet or network connection. To resolve this problem, reinstall Internet Explorer 4.0 or higher after installing the SDK. This problem seems to be resolved in later versions.

Starting the SDK

To start the SDK, click the Start button, and then select Programs, Openwave SDK *version_number*, Openwave SDK. Depending on the SDK version you've downloaded, the name of the application might differ slightly.

After you select the application, a device-emulator displays. In recent versions of the SDK, a Device-Information window and a text editor also display.

The Device-Information window displays information regarding what occurs behind the scenes (such as where a file is loaded from and error messages that occur).

The text editor is similar to those discussed earlier in this chapter. The text editor allows users to work with their code and then compile and run it all without switching from one program to another. Figure 2.5 shows the various parts of the Openwave SDK.

SDK Documentation

The Openwave SDK provides excellent reference documentation, including

- **A Getting Started Guide**—Discusses the installation of the SDK. This document also provides a good reference in regard to using the product.

- **A WML Developer's Guide**—Provides advanced information about the many services available with WAP and WML. Don't worry too much about this documentation right now. You might want to look through this material after you've worked your way through this book.

- **A WML Language Reference Guide**—Provides a great reference to all areas of the WML language.

- **A WMLScript Developer's Guide**—Provides an overview of using the WMLScript language. This documentation does not provide information regarding the WMLScript's built-in functions. You might want to refer to this information as you complete Part III, "Advanced Wireless Development," which deals with the WMLScript language.

- **A WMLScript Reference Guide**—Provides information regarding the elements of the WMLScript language. This document includes WMLScript's Library of built-in functions.

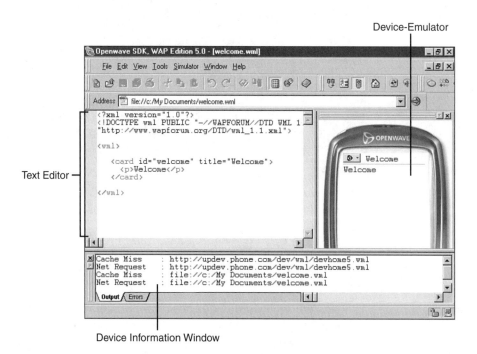

Figure 2.5   *The parts of the Openwave SDK.* (Image of SDK courtesy of Openwave Systems, Inc.)

Depending on the SDK version you've installed, additional documentation might also exist, such as guidelines about how to style your applications. Although this documentation is good, you probably won't use it as much as the documents listed previously in this section.

The Nokia Mobile Internet Toolkit

Just because this book uses the Openwave SDK in its examples doesn't mean that it's the only available option for developers. Let's look at another excellent device-emulator software package, in case you want to try some other software tools with your development efforts.

The Nokia Mobile Internet Toolkit is another development tool, provided by Nokia (www.nokia.com). The Nokia Mobile Internet Toolkit is available free to all users who register as a developer at its site. Like Openwave, registering as a developer is also free of charge.

To register as a developer at the Nokia Web site, go to http:// forum.nokia.com/main.html and follow the Registration hyperlink on the right side of the page.

After you have registered, log into Forum Nokia and enter the WAP Developer Section. Perform the following to download the Nokia device-emulator software:

1. Select the WAP hyperlink, located underneath the Technologies section to the right of the page.

2. Select the Nokia Mobile Internet Toolkit link, available from underneath the original WAP hyperlink.

3. The Nokia Mobile Internet Toolkit has a self-extracting executable to install the product. Follow the instructions on the executable to install the product onto your PC.

4. The Nokia Mobile Internet Toolkit comes with a couple of default devices. However, users also can download additional Nokia device-emulators from this area of the developer site.

NOTE

The Nokia Mobile Internet Toolkit requires the Java 2 Standard Edition Runtime Environment. The Nokia software detects during install whether this environment exists within your PC.

If the Java 2 Environment does not exist, the install asks whether you want to install the Java 2 Standard Edition Runtime Environment. Click the Yes button to install—this software is required for the Nokia software to run correctly.

---

5. After it's installed, you can start the Nokia software by clicking the Start button and then selecting Programs, Nokia Mobile Internet Toolkit, Mobile Internet Toolkit. Depending on the version of software you've downloaded, the name of the application might differ slightly. Figure 2.6 displays the Nokia Mobile Internet Toolkit in action.

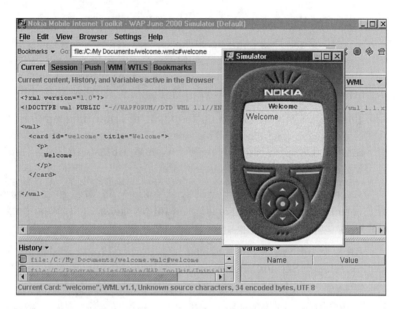

Figure 2.6 *Image of Mobile Internet Toolkit courtesy of Nokia Corporation.*

Commercial Software Development Tools

In recent years, a number of Web development applications have begun to include WAP development tools within their packages. You can expect within the coming years that the number of commercial WAP development tools will increase.

Nevertheless, the following sections discuss some of the popular WML development environments available from some popular commercial development software.

Dot WAP

Dot WAP is an excellent text editor for WAP, provided by Inetis Ltd. Dot Wap 2.0 enables users to utilize a number of built-in tools and references dealing with WAP and WML. The product is available as a free trial version from http://inetis.com/freeware.asp. The Dot WAP product runs under any Windows operating system.

After it's downloaded, you can use the self-extracting executable to install the product. Then, follow the instructions on the executable to install Dot WAP onto your PC. Figure 2.7 displays some WML. Check out Dot WAP to see whether this is a product you like.

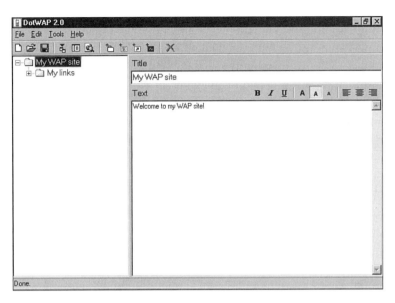

Figure 2.7　*Image of Dot WAP courtesy of Inetis, Ltd.*

Yospace's SmartPhone Emulator Developer Edition

The SmartPhone Emulator Developer Edition is a product made by Yospace (www.yospace.com). It is a standalone software product that enables users to develop and test WAP applications from a PC computer. SmartPhone contains a friendly user interface; is reliable; supplies excellent error reporting; and is available for Windows, Unix, and MacOS.

A single-user license for the complete version of SmartPhone Emulator is $99. However, users can download an evaluation version by first registering at the site. After registering, go to the Downloads page at http:// www.yospace.com/cgi-bin/resources.pl to download a trial version of this product. Figure 2.8 displays the SmartPhone emulator.

TIP

The first time you log in, you'll need to enter the trial licensing information sent to your e-mail address. Be sure to type in the information exactly as it appears within your e-mail. This includes any parentheses that might follow the license name.

Allaire ColdFusion Studio

ColdFusion is one of the world's leading cross-platform Web application servers. ColdFusion works equally well on Windows and Unix platforms. Specifically, ColdFusion's claim to fame is its ease of integrating databases into Web applications, especially across platforms.

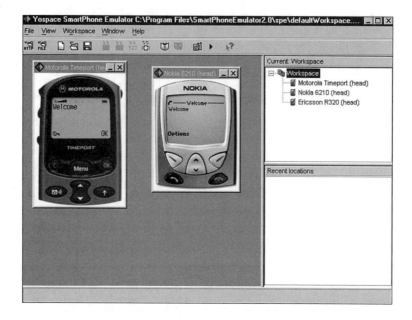

Figure 2.8 *Image of SmartPhone Emulator courtesy of YoSpace.*

The ColdFusion Studio product by Allaire (www.allaire.com) is one of the most widely used and successful HTML editors today. ColdFusion supports several Web content languages besides HTML and WML, such as DHTML, VTML, XML, HDML, SMIL, and a variety of scripting languages.

A single-user license for the complete version of ColdFusion Studio costs about $500. However, users can download or have sent to them a free evaluation version of ColdFusion 4.5. To obtain any kind of evaluation software, though, you first must register with Allaire. To do this, go to the Login page at http://commerce.allaire.com/Ecommerce/Forms/LoginForm.cfm.

After you're registered with Allaire, you can download or order evaluation products at http://www.macromedia.com/downloads/ by following the ColdFusion link. At the right side of the page is a link to evaluate this product. Be sure you're selecting ColdFusion Studio and not ColdFusion Server.

Figure 2.9 shows the ColdFusion Studio Text Editor.

ColdFusion Studio contains a number of features, including a tag chooser that provides information about a number of markup language tags. Figure 2.10 shows some of the ColdFusion Studio Tag Chooser's functionality.

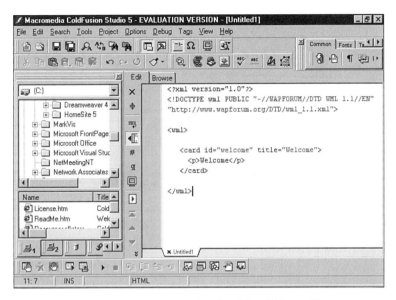

Figure 2.9   *The ColdFusion Studio Text Editor.* (Image courtesy of Allaire Corporation.)

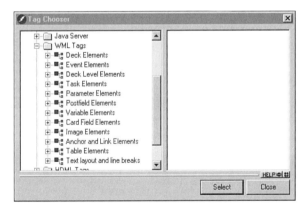

Figure 2.10   *ColdFusion Tag Chooser.* (Image courtesy of Allaire Corporation.)

In discussing ColdFusion's and WAP development, I've only scratched the surface. The real advantage and power of ColdFusion comes from the ease of incorporating capabilities into your WAP applications, such as

- The ability to query and update virtually any database (such as SQL, Sybase, Oracle, Access, and many others)

- The ability to integrate with other objects on a server (such as COM, COBRA, and Java)

- The cross-platform portability among multiple operating systems and Web servers (on both Unix and Windows)

- The support for state management, error handling, load balancing, failover, and much more

Although these topics provide too wide a scope for the purposes of this book, ColdFusion is definitely a product to investigate should you consider delving further into both Web and wireless development.

Getting Ready to Develop

At this point, you've gotten your text editor ready and your device-emulator software installed and ready to go. You're almost ready to begin creating your first WAP application.

However, first you must set some simple configurations on your PC. These configurations ensure that your test environment interprets wireless files correctly. Specifically, you'll need to configure the MIME content types on your server.

What Is MIME?

MIME stands for multipurpose Internet mail extension. In the Web context, MIME is a piece of header information that comes with every file sent from a Web server to a browser. MIME is a specification for the format of data that can be sent over the Internet.

So, how does a Web browser know the difference between an HTML file, image data, audio files, or video files? The answer is through MIME. Table 2.1 lists some of the common MIME types that exist by default within Web servers.

Table 2.1   Common Web MIME Types

File Type	MIME Type
HTML	text/html
GIF	image/gif
JPG	image/jpg

How MIME Works

To understand how MIME works, let's think back to the Internet infrastructure. The Internet works by clients and servers communicating through each other. Typically, a client first sends a request to a server. The request is a question, also known as a *query*. Figure 2.11 displays a graphical representation of the Internet infrastructure.

When a Web server receives this request, it replies with an answer, also known as a *result*. This result is sent back to the user, and the user views this result through a Web browser.

When results are sent back to the user from the server, a MIME type is also sent. The server uses the file extensions to associate the correct MIME type with the result, and the browser uses this MIME type (not the file extension) to know what to do with it.

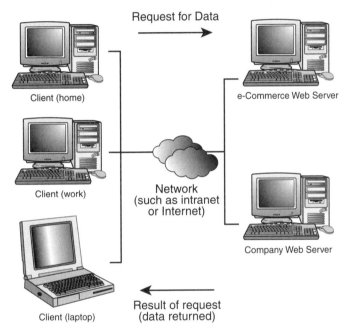

Figure 2.11   *The Internet infrastructure.*

Setting Up the Web Server

WAP files also have their own special MIME types. WAP MIME types enable servers to know what to do with the data when it arrives.

Most Web servers already contain the correct MIME types for common file formats (such as those listed previously). However, because WAP is a new technology, most Web servers are not set to include WAP MIME types. For the time being, developers must configure their own servers. Table 2.2 lists the WAP MIME required for WAP development.

Table 2.2   Common WAP MIME Types

File Type	MIME Type	File Extension	Typical Use
WML files	`text/vnd.wap.wml`	`.wml`	These files define the look and basic functionality of WAP applications (see Chapter 3).
Compiled WML files	`application/ vnd.wap.wmlc`	`.wmlc`	These are the compiled versions of WML files (files must be compiled before real-world use).
WMLScript files	`text/ vnd.wap.wmlscript`	`.wmls`	These files add functionality to your applications and are not available from WML (see Chapter 9).
Compiled WMLScript files	`application/ vnd.wap.wmlscriptc`	`.wmlsc`	These are the compiled versions of WMLScript files (files must be compiled before real-world use).
WBMP files	`image/vnd.wap.wbmp`	`.wbmp`	These files are the graphical format for images used in WAP applications (see Chapter 7).

Adding MIME Types

Chapter 13, "Introduction to ASP," covers adding MIME types to a variety of Web servers. However, for now, the following steps will get you up and running. These configure your PC to recognize WAP MIME Types correctly:

1. Go to Windows Explorer. Then, from the Explorer toolbar, select View, Folder Options. The Folder Options screen displays.

TIP

Depending on the version of Windows you're using, the View menu might contain either Folder Options or Options. Both provide the screen you want to access.

2. An Option screen displays. Select the File Types tab. Figure 2.12 displays an example of how your screen might look.

3. Scroll down the list of Registered file types. You should add all MIME types listed in Table 2.2 if they don't already exist on your PC. If these types already exist, double-click them and go to step 5.

4. Click the New Type button on the right side of the screen.

5. The Edit File Type screen displays. Check that the appropriate MIME types exist in the Content_Type (MIME) field. Refer to Table 2.2 for the list of MIME types to add. Figure 2.13 shows the Edit File Type screen.

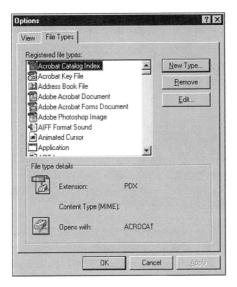

Figure 2.12 *The Folder Options screen.*

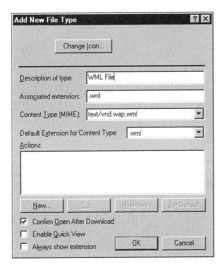

Figure 2.13 *The Edit File Type screen.*

CAUTION

If you're using Windows Me, Microsoft has removed the ability to modify MIME types. When you access the Edit File Type screen in Windows Me, you can only define extensions for files.

Microsoft is edging away from supporting development efforts within its operating systems designed for "home" use. Because of this, you might find it difficult to use Windows Me as a development platform for WAP, or for that matter, any type of Web development.

Summary

Now that you've gotten your text editor ready, your device-emulator software installed, and your PC configured to recognize WAP MIME types, you're ready to begin developing. You'll jump into WAP development in the next chapter, looking at the Wireless Markup Language and how to build WAP applications.

This chapter introduced you to the WAP development tools used throughout this book. You looked at what text editors are and where to obtain them. This chapter also discussed several popular device-emulators developed by some of the world's major wireless device manufacturers. You learned where to find these products free of charge on the Internet.

This chapter concluded with instructions on setting up your PC computer to use and recognize WAP files. From here, you're now ready to begin building applications. In Chapter 3 you'll begin using WML to create your first WAP applications.

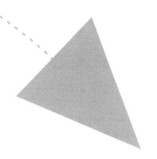

The Wireless Markup Language (WML)

In the last chapter, you looked at the tools needed to create WAP applications. In this chapter, you'll use these tools to begin developing WAP applications. In the process, you'll become familiar with the Wireless Markup Language (WML), which is the language you'll use in all your WAP development efforts.

If you're familiar with other markup languages, you'll find WML incorporates many of the features of these other languages. However, if you're new to markup languages, working through the next couple of chapters will get you up to speed quickly.

By the end of this chapter, you'll be familiar with the following:

- Where WML came from, what it's about, and how you'll use it within your WAP applications

- What WML can and can't do, and some of the similarities and differences between WML and other markup languages, such as HTML

- The WML structure and syntax, which help you produce efficient code

- The essential WML elements and attributes used with all WAP applications

What Is a Markup Language?

The goal of markup languages is to present information across many different systems. Most Web development languages today use markup languages in some fashion. With markup languages, text, tables, images, and user navigation display in a consistent manner. The type of platform that receives the information does not matter.

WML is a markup language and, like other markup languages, it works on several platforms. WML is also compact, working quickly and efficiently. These attributes make WML a perfect language for WAP development.

The WAP Forum (www.wapforum.org) originally developed the WML language. Chapter 1, "What Is WAP Development?" discussed the WAP Forum and their contributions to WAP technology and wireless development.

If you're familiar with other areas of Web development, you might find several similarities between HTML (the markup language used through Web development) and WML (the markup language used throughout WAP development). Table 3.1 details some of the similarities and differences between HTML and WML.

If you've never looked at HTML or WML before, don't worry about this table. By the time you're finished with this book, you'll have a thorough understanding of the information in Table 3.1.

Table 3.1 Similarities Between HTML and WML

Feature	HTML	WML	Example
Opening and closing tags	√	√	`<wml>...</wml>`
Self-closing tags	√	√	` `
Attributes	√	√	`<card id="Card1">`

Nesting elements	√	√	`<wml>`
			    `<card>`
			    `</card>`
			`</wml>`

White space	√	√	`<wml>` `<card>`

Images	√	√ (WBMP format only)	`<wml>`
			    `<card>`
			        `<img>`
			        `</img>`
			    `</card>`
			`</wml>`

Table 3.1   continued

Feature	HTML	WML	Example
Nested tables	√		```<table> <tr> <td> <table> <tr> <td> </td> </tr> </table> </td> </tr> </table>```
Heading levels	√		```<html> <body> <h1>Heading 1</h1> </body> </html>```
Nested scripting languages	√		```<html> <body> <language = "vbscript"> </body> </html>```

WML Terminology

Software applications typically consist of several screens. In the world of WAP development, a screen is known as a *card*. A collection of cards is known as a *deck*.

WML Decks

The purpose of the WML deck is to deliver more than one card to a WAP device at one time. Users can then navigate small portions of the WML-enabled application without waiting for each individual navigation action.

WML Cards

WML cards provide the structure of a WAP application. WML cards define how information displays on a device and how the user can navigate through an application.

Because of this responsibility, a WML card can never be empty. WML cards must contain at least one WML element. You'll look at using cards later in this chapter. Figure 3.1 displays the WML deck/card relationship.

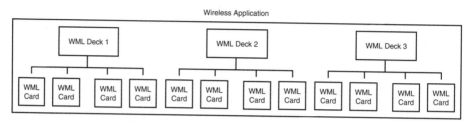

Figure 3.1 *The WML deck/card relationship.*

WML Syntax

All programming languages contain syntax rules. These rules must be followed to produce valid code. WML is no exception. However, you can rest easy; markup languages contain less syntax rules than other programming languages. The following are three important areas in regard to WML syntax:

- WML document prologue
- WML character sets
- WML case sensitivity

WML Document Prologue

Every WML deck you write must contain a document prologue. Compilers on the device, WAP gateways, and remote servers all use document prologues to interpret your code. Developers must include the XML document prologue at the top of every WML deck:

```
1 <?xml version="1.0">
2 <!DOCTYPE wml PUBLIC "-//WAPFORUM//DTD WML 1.1//EN"
3 "http://www.wapforum.org/DTD/wml_1.1.xml">
```

CAUTION

When reading any of the sample code in this book, you'll notice line numbers designated to the left of the prologue. When you start writing code (in a couple of pages), do not type these numbers into your text editor. The line numbers act as a reference for the explanation areas of this book. Including these line numbers in your written code will result in errors.

Be especially aware of the use of spaces in the document prologue. A WML deck produces errors if the document prologue does not include correct use of spacing and punctuation.

The following is a line-by-line explanation of the document prologue:

- The first line of the prologue designates the XML version of the WAP server and WML compiler. WAP servers and WML compilers use XML to interpret your code. These servers and compilers then transform this information back into WML, so that a WAP device can display the information.

- The second line of the prologue defines the version of WML used. This line of code states that you'll use WML version 1.1 within your applications.

NOTE

In the document protocol, you might notice that the XML and WML versions are not the most current. The reason for this is that not all WAP-enabled devices support the latest versions of these languages. Unless you're writing an application for a specific device, use the language versions specified in this prologue. These versions are usable by the widest range of devices.

- The third line specifies the location of the WML document type definition (DTD). In this prologue, you'll reference the WAP Forum's site. Any additional extensions or information for the WAP server or compiler are available from this site.

You're probably thinking all this sounds kind of complicated, huh? For our purposes, this prologue will never change. Only the server and compiler really use this information.

Character Sets

Character sets are the built-in methods for handling text characters. Character sets represent letters and symbols specific to several languages. WML supports the character set of ISO-10646 (Unicode 2.0). This term is a fancy name for the computer industry's basic international characters. Figure 3.2 shows some of the more commonly used English characters within this character set.

Because this character set is the default for WML, you won't need to declare it within your WML decks.

20	21 !	22 "	23 #	24 $	25 %	26 &	27 ,	28 (	29)	2A *	2B +	2C ,	2D -	2E .	2F /
30 0	31 1	32 2	33 3	34 4	35 5	36 6	37 7	38 8	39 9	3A :	3B ;	3C <	3D =	3E >	3F ?
40 @	41 A	42 B	43 C	44 D	45 E	46 F	47 G	48 H	49 I	4A J	4B K	4C L	4D M	4E N	4F O
50 P	51 Q	52 R	53 S	54 T	55 U	56 V	57 W	58 X	59 Y	5A Z	5B [	5C \	5D]	5E ^	5F _
60 `	61 a	62 b	63 c	64 d	65 e	66 f	67 g	68 h	69 i	6A j	6B k	6C l	6D m	6E n	6F o
70 p	71 q	72 r	73 s	74 t	75 u	76 v	77 w	78 x	79 y	7A z	7B {	7C		7D }	7E ~	

Figure 3.2   *The ISO/IEC-10646 (Unicode 2.0) character set (sample of English set).*

Case Sensitivity

Case sensitivity refers to recognition of character case. WML is a precise language when it comes to case sensitivity. In other words, character case does matter in WML.

The basic rule of WML case sensitivity is that all tags and attributes (you'll get into these in the next couple of pages) must be lowercase. For example, name1, Name1, and NAME1 are all different values because of character case.

TIP

Most programming errors tend to deal with problems with character case. No one writes bug-free code, but knowing where most errors occur will help you find errors quickly. As a rule of thumb, if your code doesn't work, check it for the correct use of character case.

WAP Design Considerations

When developing any type of WAP applications, keep in mind that WAP devices contain limited network bandwidth capabilities and memory compared to a PC. As a result, WAP developers must strive to create applications that are compact and efficient, but that do not lack the functionality users desire.

Part of the reason WML is such a great language for WAP development is that it is compact by design. WML doesn't take up much space within a WAP device. By using WML, you're halfway to creating compact and efficient code.

Of course, just because you're using WML doesn't guarantee you'll develop efficient applications. WAP developers must also remember that the devices they're developing for differ greatly from one another.

Some devices have display screens that support sub-VGA graphics, whereas others can't display any more than four lines of 32 characters at a time. As a developer, you must strive to create applications that work with the widest range of devices possible.

The following are a couple of tips to keep in mind when creating WAP applications:

- **Keep WML decks and images to less than 1.5KB**—To see the size of a file or graphic, find the icon for that file on your PC. Then, right-click the icon with your mouse, and select Properties from the drop-down list.

- **Avoid overuse of images**—Using a couple of images within an application is acceptable. However, several graphics will slow down a WAP application. In addition, many devices do not support images at the time of this writing.

- **Use simple and brief text within your applications**—You should avoid having users scroll within the applications if possible.

Programming Considerations

Good application development means writing readable code. In fact, most developers consider writing readable code a professional responsibility. One of the ways to best improve the readability of your code is with white space.

White Space

The term *white space* refers to how text displays in contrast to the surrounding white space. For example, in reading this book, the text displays in a readable manner due to the use of indents, spaces, and paragraphs.

Using white space in programming provides the same results as it does for this book: It provides easier readability. Consider the following two WML code samples.

The first example does not use white space, but the second example does. Which would you, as a developer, rather interpret if trying to understand this code?

An example of WML code without white space:

```
<wml><card><p>Sample text</p></card><wml>
```

An example of WML code with white space:

```
<wml>
  <card>
    <p>Sample text</p>
  </card>
</wml>
```

Notice the difference in appearance. Although not required, it's usually good practice to incorporate white space into your code. Readable code not only aids you in reducing and debugging errors quickly, but it also aids others who might need to read and understand your application's code at a later date.

NOTE

WML ignores white space when actually compiling the code. To control the way text displays on a device, you must use text-formatting tags (you'll learn more about this in Chapter 4, "Text Formatting for WML").

Comments

Another way for developers to produce readable code is to incorporate comments. Developers often use comments to leave notes about their application logic. This practice is especially useful when needing to update a portion of code or when another individual needs to edit your code.

To add comments within WML, you must use the `<!--` symbol before the comment. The `-->` symbol is then used to end the comment. Comments are solely for the use of developers—they never display on the application.

The following example displays the use of comments within a WML file. WAP device compilers do not interpret or read comments:

```
<wml>
<!-- This is a comment line -->
  <card>
    <p>Sample text</p>
  </card>
</wml>
```

In this example, the comment displays across only one line. You can, however, extend a comment across multiple lines. Until you end the comment with the `-->` symbol, the device compiler assumes that all information after the starting `<!--` tag is a comment. The following is an example of code using a comment that extends across multiple lines:

```
<wml>
<!-- This is also
a comment line -->
```

```
<card>
  <p>Sample text</p>
</card>
</wml>
```

CAUTION

Be sure you do not include any space within the starting and ending comment tags. For example, the following starting comment tag would produce an error when trying to run your code:

```
< ! --
```

The reason this tag is incorrect is because it contains spaces. The same is true for the ending comment tag. The following ending comment tag is also incorrect:

```
-- >
```

The most common error with comment tags occurs when developers place a space somewhere within a comment tag.

WML Elements: The Building Blocks of WAP Applications

In the world of WAP development, applications use things called *elements*. In the following pages, you begin your development efforts using the WML elements required for all WAP applications within this book.

Elements are the heart of markup languages, including WML. They designate functional and structural information used within a WML deck. All WML elements have one of the following structures:

- A start tag, some content, and an end tag. Here's an example:

  ```
  <tag>content</tag>
  ```

- A tag that contains no content is called an *empty-element* tag. These tags contain neither a start nor ending tag, such as

  ```
  <tag/>
  ```

In this chapter, you'll learn most of the WML that makes up WML decks and cards (you'll look at the TEMPLATE element, another WML deck-level element, in Chapter 5, "Navigation Using WML"). Table 3.2 summarizes the WML elements discussed in this chapter.

Table 3.2 The WML Deck/Card Elements

Element	Description	Syntax
WML	Starts and ends a deck and encloses all cards.	`<wml>content</wml>`

Table 3.2   continued

Element	Description	Syntax
CARD	A single WML unit, which can contain information such as text to present to the user, instructions for gathering user input, and so on. WML cards are to a WAP application as pages are to a Web site, or screens are to PC applications.	`<card>`*content*`</card>`
TEMPLATE	Specifies deck-level actions that apply to all cards in the deck.	`<template>`*content*`</template>`
HEAD	Contains information relating to the deck as a whole, including metadata and access control elements.	`<head>`*content*`</head>`

There are a few factors to remember when working with WML elements. First, all WML tags must be lowercase. Looking at Table 3.2, a WAP application would not recognize the `<CARD>` tag because it is uppercase. However, a WAP application would recognize the `<card>` tag because it is all lowercase.

NOTE

Just because WML tags must be lowercase does not mean that the content within the tags must be lowercase. For example, consider the P element, which defines text within a WAP application (the P element is discussed in the next chapter). Although the `<p>` tags must be lowercase, the content between the tags can contain both upper- and lowercase characters:

```
<p>EXAPLE of CAPITALIZATION in CONTENT</p>
```

WML tags must also be enclosed in angle brackets (< >). WML elements also must have a starting tag (such as `<card>`) and an ending tag (such as `</card>`). Ending tags contain a slash character to identify them as end tags.

WML Attributes

Some WML elements use settings (called *attributes*) to further define an element. For example, some attributes identify pointers that refer to areas outside a WML card; other attributes might label information that has to be communicated back to a Web server. Still, other attributes might label the code that specifies how to display an onscreen object.

Some attributes are mandatory, whereas others are optional. You'll look at the attributes available with each WML element as we come to them.

Creating the WML Deck

Every WAP application uses a required set of WML elements. Pay particular attention to the concepts within the rest of this chapter. The following elements are used to some degree with every WAP application you create.

NOTE

Besides simply reading the following examples, type these code examples on the text editor of your choice. Then, try running them from a device-emulator. Understanding and writing the WML elements will play an important part in learning WAP development.

Save your WML files in an easily retrievable directory, such as C:\My Documents.

THE WML ELEMENT

Every WML deck must contain three things: the document prologue, an element that designates the WML deck, and at least one card. You've already looked at the document prologue previously in this chapter. Now let's focus on the elements that designate the WML deck, specifically the WML elements.

The WML element is a simple, but powerful element. The WML element consists of no attributes, always follows directly after the document prologue, and is always the last tag element of a WML file. The following is a quick example of the WML element in action. Pay particular attention to the areas of code in boldface.

This example creates a WML deck with one card. Save this file as deck.wml. Figure 3.3 shows this code on a device screen:

```
1 <?xml version="1.0"?>
2 <!DOCTYPE wml PUBLIC "-//WAPFORUM//DTD WML 1.1//EN"
3 "http://www.wapforum.org/DTD/wml_1.1.xml">
4 <wml>
5     <card id="card1">
6         <p>This is the only card within this WML deck.</p>
7     </card>
8 </wml>
```

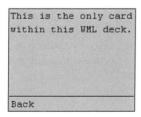

Figure 3.3 *The deck.wml file on a device screen.*

N O T E

When you click the Accept button (this button has the Back label above it), you are returned to the default main menu of the device-emulator. This main menu displays as your default page until you add navigational functionality to your applications (you'll do this in the Chapter 5).

The following is an explanation of this example:

- The first line specifies the XML version number.

- The second line specifies the public document identifier.

- The third line specifies the location of the WML document type definition.

- The fourth line uses the WML element to begin the WML deck. All WML decks must begin with a `<wml>` tag and end with a `</wml>` tag.

- The fifth line uses the `<card>` tag to start a card.

- The sixth line uses the `P` element to start a paragraph.

- The seventh line uses the `</card>` tag to end the card.

- The last line uses the `</wml>` tag to end the WML deck.

THE CARD ELEMENT

All WML decks require at least one card. The `CARD` element is one of the most widely used WML elements in WAP development. Think of cards as the screens of an application, and you can see the importance of the `CARD` element.

Cards have a lot of functionality, much more than the `WML` element. Table 3.3 lists the attributes available for the `CARD` element. Although there are a lot of them, the main attributes to concern yourself with are `id` and `title`.

*Table 3.3   The Attributes of the **CARD** Element*

Attribute	Required	Description
id	No	Specifies a name for the card. For easier programming, avoid using an `id` longer than eight characters.
newcontext	No	A true or false (Boolean) value that specifies whether the device should initialize the context whenever the card is loaded. The default value is `false`.
onenterbackward	No	Specifies the URL to open if the user navigates to this card through a `PREV` task (discussed in Chapter 5).
onenterforward	No	Specifies the URL to open if the user navigates to this card through a `GO` task (discussed in Chapter 5).

Table 3.3   *continued*

Attribute	Required	Description
ontimer	No	Specifies the URL to open if a specified TIMER element expires.
ordered	No	A true or false (Boolean) value that specifies the organization of the card content. The default is true.
title	No	Specifies a brief text label for the card.

The id attribute provides the card with an identifier. Identifiers are something of major importance, especially in navigating from one card to another. The id attribute also allows cards to access other cards in other, external decks.

The title attribute is the name of the card presented to the user. This attribute can also provide more advanced functionality such as creating pop-ups or bookmarks. Not all WAP devices use a browser that present title attributes.

NOTE

Don't worry if a WML element you're using isn't supported by all WML browsers. If a device does not support a WML element, the device browser ignores the element.

Most device manufacturers supply documentation regarding the WML elements their products do and do not support. For the most part, most WAP devices support all elements discussed in this book.

The syntax for using attributes is to start the element, and then set the attributes equal to a value. All this information is then set within brackets.

For example, in the case of the CARD element that uses the id and title attributes, the syntax would be something similar to this:

```
<card id="card1" title="Card 1">
```

When incorporating more than one card into a WML deck, you must include a unique id attribute for each card. The following example displays a WML deck with multiple cards and creates an application that allows users to navigate between the two cards within a deck. Save this file as card.wml. Figure 3.4 displays the card.wml file on a device screen.

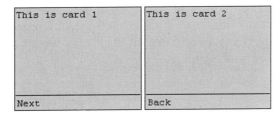

Figure 3.4 *The* card.wml *file on a device screen.*

```
1 <?xml version="1.0"?>
2 <!DOCTYPE wml PUBLIC "-//WAPFORUM//DTD WML 1.1//EN"
3 "http://www.wapforum.org/DTD/wml_1.1.xml">
4 <wml>

5 <!-- This is card 1 -->
6    <card id="card1" title="Card 1">
7      <do type="accept" label="Next">
8      <go href="#card2"/>
9      </do>
10       <p>This is card 1</p>
11     </card>

12 <!-- This is card 2 -->
13    <card id="card2" title="Card 2">
14      <do type="accept" label="Back">
15      <go href="#card1"/>
16      </do>
17        <p>This is card 2</p>
18     </card>
19 </wml>
```

NOTE

This example uses the DO element, which is discussed in more detail in Chapter 5 when you look at creating navigation within your applications.

The overall functionality created in this application is that by clicking the Accept button, the application navigates to one of the two cards in this deck.

The following is a line-by-line explanation of this example:

- The sixth line uses the <card> tag to start a card. In addition, the id and title attributes are used.

  The id attribute sets the reference name of the card to card1. This name is useful as your applications become more advanced and you begin to incorporate navigational functionality.

  The title of the card is Card 1. If the WAP device you're using supports the title attribute of the CARD element, the text Card 1 displays when accessed. Otherwise, if the device does not support this attribute, the title does not display. This isn't a big deal, but you should be aware of such factors.

- The seventh line uses the DO element to assign functionality to a user interface on the device. This line of code specifies that the device's Accept button be used for some sort of functionality. The label that displays above this Accept button is Next.

- The eighth line uses the GO element (which is one of WML's task elements). This line of code assigns a link to the user interface defined in the previous line of code. In this example, whenever the Accept button is clicked, users are taken to the card2 card.

- The ninth line uses the </do> tag to end the DO element.

- The tenth line uses the <p> tag to start a paragraph.

- The eleventh line uses the </card> tag to end the card.

- Lines 13–18 contain functionality similar to that found in lines 6–11. The only difference is that these lines create a second card named card2. This card also uses a DO element. In this second card, the DO element specifies the Accept button to return users to card1 when clicked.

The HEAD Element

Before concluding this chapter, we should discuss the HEAD element. The HEAD element provides the capability to specify information about the WML deck as a whole. Although you won't use this element within the applications in this book, the HEAD element is useful, especially for creating security within your WAP applications.

The HEAD element does not contain any attributes. Rather, it must contain one of these two elements:

- ACCESS

- META

The following sections examine these two elements and the functionality they provide within a deck-level header.

THE ACCESS ELEMENT

The ACCESS element provides the functionality that restricts unauthorized users from accessing content-sensitive information. You won't use the ACCESS element in the examples in this book, though.

The ACCESS element contains two attributes, summarized in Table 3.4.

Table 3.4   The ***ACCESS*** *Element Attributes*

Attribute	Required	Description
domain	Yes	The URL domain of other WML decks that can access the cards within the current deck. The default value is the domain of the current deck.
path	Yes	The URL root of other WML decks that can access the cards in the current WML deck.

The META Element

The META element provides information to the browser about meta-information. Meta-information tells a device to treat the data in a specific way.

Not all WAP devices support every meta-information type. The device browser ignores any meta-information it does not support. Refer to the device manufacturer's documentation if you have questions about whether a particular type of meta-information is supported by a WAP device. Table 3.5 lists the attributes included with the META element.

Table 3.5   *The **META** Element Attributes*

Attribute	Required	Description
content	Yes	Specifies the metadata value to assign to the property.
forua	Yes	A true or false value that specifies whether the content is intended for the device's browser (rather than, say, a proxy server or some other program).
name	Yes*	The property name that represents the meta-information.
property	Yes*	Used in place of the name attribute to specify information the browser should interpret as an HTTP header.
schema	No	Form or structure used to interpret the property value.

* Define either the *name* or the *property* attribute when using the *META* element.

In the world of WAP development, a common example of meta-information is the cache duration of a WAP device. *Cache* refers to previously downloaded material.

Caching is a WAP device's attempt at remembering the history of the data accessed. You can set a time limit within the META element that specifies how long the device will save cached cards.

Let's look at a quick example of how you could use the META element to change the memory cache.

The default cache for most devices is 30 days, or until the memory has exhausted. A developer does not need to define the cache, unless you want to lengthen, shorten, or disable the cache.

NOTE

For the most part, you should use a device's cache. Doing so improves the performance of a WAP application. Cache memory also enables cards to reload quickly because they're already stored within the device. Cards load more quickly from the cache than they do if accessed from a remote server.

However, some WAP developers like to disable the cache when working with cards that use user-inputted information. Disabling the cache ensures that the correct information is always used with a card.

The following example disables the memory cache. Save this file as `head.wml`. Figure 3.5 shows this example on a device screen:

```
1  <?xml version="1.0"?>
2  <!DOCTYPE wml PUBLIC "-//WAPFORUM//DTD WML 1.1//EN"
3  "http://www.wapforum.org/DTD/wml_1.1.xml">
4  <wml>
5      <head>
6      <meta http-equiv="Cache-Control" content="max-age=0" forua="true"/>
7      </head>
8      <card>

9          <p>The memory cache has now been disabled.</p>
10     </card>
11 </wml>
```

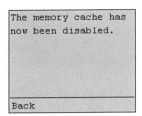

Figure 3.5 *The* `head.wml` *file on a device screen.*

The following is a line-by-line explanation of this example:

- The fifth line is the start tag of the HEAD element.

- The sixth and seventh lines instruct the device to drop the deck from the cache immediately by setting the `max-age` to 0. To length or shorten the time interval of the cache, the time interval must be written in seconds. For example, to set the cache equal to one hour, set the `max-age` equal to 3600 (the number of seconds in an hour).

NOTE

The META element is a little peculiar in that it does not require an ending tag. Instead, the META tag uses the following structure:

```
<meta/>
```

You won't use the HEAD and META elements very much throughout this book. However, they are important elements, especially when developing wireless applications where security and access are necessary.

Summary

This chapter looked at where the Wireless Markup Language (WML) came from and some of the main features it uses. You also learned some programming practices to keep in mind when developing WAP applications, such as the use of images, the style and structure of a good WAP application, and the use of white space and comments within your code.

This chapter then introduced you to the necessary components, syntax, and structure required of WML files. Specifically, you looked at the concept of WML decks and cards and how they play into the foundation of all wireless applications.

This chapter concluded with examples in the areas of WML you'll use with every WAP applications. Congratulations, you can now consider yourself a WAP developer. The next chapter expands further on the skills learned in this chapter.

Chapter 4 expands on the skills you've learned. In that chapter, you learn about controlling the look and feel of your applications by formatting text with WML elements. By then end of the next chapter, you'll have created an aesthetically pleasing WAP application. From there, you'll be ready incorporate more advanced functionality into your development efforts.

Text Formatting for WML

Chapter 3, "The Wireless Markup Language (WML)," introduced you to the WML used to create the structure of a WAP application. In this chapter, you jump further into WAP development by looking at using WML to format text within your applications.

Most WAP devices display applications from a two-inch screen, with data traveling over networks at average speeds of 9.6Kbps. With this type of speed, WAP applications must be efficient. However, this does not mean that your WAP applications can't be slick and exciting.

This chapter examines the WML that provides the capability to control the look and feel of how text displays for users. In other words, this chapter introduces you to the elements needed to give your WAP applications a little zing!

This chapter looks at the following:

- How to incorporate line breaks and paragraphs into a WAP application.

- Setting up line wrapping and breaking lines to control the display of text.

- Incorporating text styles into WAP applications.

- The use of reserved characters in your applications. Reserved characters are not available from the WML character set (see Chapter 3 for more information on character sets).

- How to create and use tables within WAP applications.

Creating Paragraphs with the P Element

All written communication uses paragraphs of some type or another. Paragraphs enable you to break information into separate entities for easier understanding. WML is no different. When creating any kind of text within your applications, you use the P element.

The P element is an important aspect of WAP development because it controls how all text displays on a WAP device's screen.

TIP

Although all WAP applications require some amount of text, you must use caution. Large amounts of text result in a lot of scrolling (and frustration) for your users.

The P element uses two attributes that enable you to define the alignment of the text, as well as its line-wrapping properties. Table 4.1 summarizes these attributes.

*Table 4.1   The Attributes of the **P** Element*

Attribute	Required	Description
align	No	Specifies the line alignment relative to the display area. If no value is specified, the align attribute defaults the line to left alignment. This attribute can be equal to left, right, or center.
mode	No	Specifies whether the display should automatically wrap or split text so that it is always viewable from the display. The nowrap value uses another mechanism, such as horizontal scrolling, to display long lines of text. If no value is specified, the default value is wrap.

NOTE

The following is a further definition of the line-wrapping options available through WML:

- **Wrapping**—Means the device spills extra text onto subsequent lines in the display. Scrolling the line from left to right is not necessary.

- **Horizontal scrolling**—Also referred to as times square scrolling, it means the device displays the entire text line on one line and then scrolls the line from left to right.

Let's look at the P element in action. Write the following code on a text editor, and then save it as par.wml. Then, run this file from a device-emulator. You might recognize the P element from the last chapter, which touched on it briefly. Figure 4.1 shows this file on a device screen:

```
1 <?xml version="1.0"?>
2 <!DOCTYPE wml PUBLIC "-//WAPFORUM//DTD WML 1.1//EN"
```

```
3  "http://www.wapforum.org/DTD/wml_1.1.xml">
4  <wml>
5     <card id="para" title="para">
6        <p>Welcome to the yourcompany.com system.</p>
7     </card>
8  </wml>
```

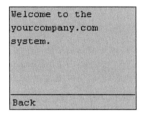

Figure 4.1   *The* para.wml *file on a device screen.*

The following is an explanation of this example:

- The sixth line uses the P element to begin the paragraph of text. Because you have not included any attributes with this element, the P element uses all default attributes with the text. In other words, even though you haven't set any attributes, the text aligns left and wraps by default.

SETTING LINE WRAP MODE

The WML code written previously used only the defaults of the P element. Let's look at how using the P element's attributes further enable you to control the look of your text. In these next examples, you add some line-wrapping functionality to the WML card. Line-wrapping specifies whether text should automatically wrap lines when it gets to the end of a device's screen.

NOTE

After you specify a line-wrapping mode, it applies to all subsequent lines until you specify a different mode. If you set the mode to horizontal scrolling and want to change back to text wrapping, you must explicitly specify this within your code.

Type the following code, and then save it as wrap.wml:

```
1  <?xml version="1.0"?>
2  <!DOCTYPE wml PUBLIC "-//WAPFORUM//DTD WML 1.1//EN"
3  "http://www.wapforum.org/DTD/wml_1.1.xml">
4  <wml>
5     <card id="wrap" title="Wrap">
6        <p mode="wrap">Welcome to the yourcompany.com system.</p>
7     </card>
8  </wml>
```

This example displays exactly the same result as the para.wml file (refer to Figure 4.1). This is because in line six, the mode attribute is set equal to wrap. Recall from Table 4.1 that the mode attribute's default value is wrap. Thus, because you didn't assign the mode attribute a value in the para.wml file, the device wrapped all text.

So, what happens if you decide not to wrap your lines of text? Let's take a look at this next example and see how WML handles the non-wrapping of lines of text.

Type the following code and save it as nowrap.wml. Then, run this code from a device-emulator. Figure 4.2 shows this code on a device screen:

```
1 <?xml version="1.0"?>
2 <!DOCTYPE wml PUBLIC "-//WAPFORUM//DTD WML 1.1//EN"
3 "http://www.wapforum.org/DTD/wml_1.1.xml">
4 <wml>
5    <card id="nowrap" title="Nowrap">
6      <p mode="nowrap">Welcome to the yourcompany.com system.</p>
7    </card>
8 </wml>
```

TIP

When running code on a device-emulator, you might need to clear the cache. Doing so removes any previous versions of your code. To clear the cache on the Openwave device-emulator, press the F12 key. You also can select Edit, Clear Cache from the toolbar of the device-emulator.

Other emulators have similar methods for clearing the cache. Check the product's documentation if you have any questions on clearing the cache of a device-emulator.

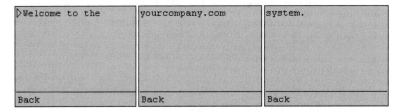

Figure 4.2 *The nowrap.wml file on a device screen.*

The following is an explanation of this example:

- The sixth line uses the P element to begin a paragraph. You've added the mode attribute to this element, as well. The value of this mode attribute is set to nowrap. Thus, your lines of text will not wrap. Rather, the device automatically scrolls horizontally to display your entire line of text. This is called horizontal scrolling, and it is enabled by setting the mode attribute equal to nowrap.

SETTING UP TEXT ALIGNMENT

You've looked at what the `mode` attribute of the P element does; now, let's take a look at the `align` attribute. The `align` attribute enables you to set your text alignment to either `left`, `center`, or `right`. The default text alignment is to the left.

To get a better understanding of how text alignment works, copy or type and paste the following code into your text editor. Save your work as `align.wml`, and then run it through a device-emulator. Figure 4.3 shows this file on a device screen:

```
1  <?xml version="1.0"?>
2  <!DOCTYPE wml PUBLIC "-//WAPFORUM//DTD WML 1.1//EN"
3  "http://www.wapforum.org/DTD/wml_1.1.xml">
4  <wml>
5     <card id="align" title="Align">
6        <p align="left">Line 1 uses left alignment</p>
7        <p align="center">Line 2 uses center alignment</p>
8        <p align="right">Line 3 uses right alignment</p>
9     </card>
10 </wml>
```

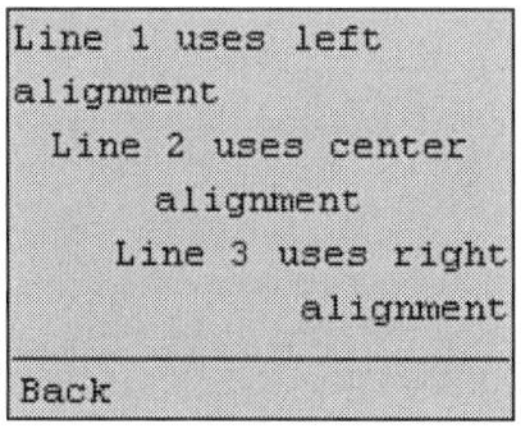

Figure 4.3   The `align.wml` file on a device screen.

The following is an explanation of this example:

- The sixth line uses the P element to begin a line of text. You've also added the `align` attribute, giving it a value of `left`. The text in this paragraph will align to the left.

- The seventh line uses the P element to begin another line of text. An `align` attribute has been added to this element. The value of this attribute is `center`. The text in this paragraph will align to the center.

- The eighth line uses yet another P element to begin a line of text. The `align` attribute is also present in this element. The value given to this attribute is `right`. The text in this paragraph therefore will align to the right.

Incorporating Line Breaks with the BR Element

Another WML element that allows you to define the look of text is the BR element. This element forces the insertion of a line break into the text.

Unlike most WML elements, the BR element contains no starting or ending tag. The BR element is an empty-element tag. In other words, a line break is created by simply inserting `<br/>` into the text whenever you want a new line of text to start.

The BR element is easy to use and contains no attributes. To see how the BR element works, type the following code into a text editor. Then, save it as break.wml, and run it from a device-emulator. Figure 4.4 shows this file on a device screen:

```
1   <?xml version="1.0"?>
2   <!DOCTYPE wml PUBLIC "-//WAPFORUM//DTD WML 1.1//EN"
3   "http://www.wapforum.org/DTD/wml_1.1.xml">
4   <wml>
5     <card id="break" title="Break">
6       <p align="center">Welcome to the<br/>
7       yourcompany.com<br/>
8       system.</p>
9     </card>
10 </wml>
```

Figure 4.4   The break.wml *file on a device screen.*

The following is an explanation of this example:

- The sixth line uses the P element to begin a line of text. Notice that the align attribute has also been used and is set to a value of center. As a result, every line of text that occurs between the starting `<p>` tag and ending `</p>` tag is centered within the device's display screen.

  In this line of code, you've also used a BR element after the text. It specifies that a new line will start.

- The seventh line continues some text, still contained within the P element. Again, a BR element begins a new line after your text.

- The eighth line contains a `</p>` tag that ends the CARD element.

NOTE

In the `break.wml` example, lines 6–8 could have also been written as follows:

```
<p align="center">Welcome to the<br/>yourcompany.com<br/>system.</p>
```

Writing lines 6–8 in this manner would have produced the same result because the only way to force text to separate into lines is through the BR element. If you do not use BR to designate where lines should break, the text wraps as defined by the confines of the device screen.

Defining Styles for Your Text

Up to this point, you've only explored the possibilities of how to modify the display of text lines within your applications. Let's now focus on how WML offers a number elements that enable you to define the font style of your text. Examples of font styles include bold, italic, and underline effects.

The following font style elements must be used within the P element. We'll look at incorporating font styles in a moment. First, let's take a look at the different WML elements that provide font styles for your WAP applications. Table 4.2 shows the WML elements that control font styles.

Table 4.2   The WML Font Style Elements

Element	Description	Syntax
B	Creates a bold font	`<b>content</b>`
BIG	Creates a big font	`<big>content</big>`
EM	Creates emphasis on the font	`<em>content</em>`
I	Creates an italicized font	`<i>content</i>`
SMALL	Creates a small font	`<small>content</small>`
STRONG	Creates a strong emphasis on the font	`<strong>content</strong>`
U	Creates an underlined font	`<u>content</u>`

None of these elements contain attributes. However, you can combine several of these elements to create combinations of styles (which is similar to the purpose of an attribute). For example, you can nest the `<small>` tag within the `<b>` tag to create a small, bold font.

The following code shows some of these elements in action. Type the following code into a text editor, and save it as `style.wml`. Then, run this file from a device-emulator. Figure 4.5 shows this code on a device screen:

```
1  <?xml version="1.0"?>
2  <!DOCTYPE wml PUBLIC "-//WAPFORUM//DTD WML 1.1//EN"
3  "http://www.wapforum.org/DTD/wml_1.1.xml">
4  <wml>
5    <card id="style" title="Style">
6      <p>Regular Font Style<br/>
```

```
7          <b>Bold Font Style</b>
8          <big>Big Font Style</big>
9          <em>Emphasis Font Style</em>
10         <i>Italics Font Style</i><br/>
11          <small>Small Font Style</small>
12          <strong>Strong Font Style</strong>
13          <u>Underlined Font Style</u>
14          <b><small>Bolded Small Font Style</small></b>
15      </p>
16    </card>
17 </wml>
```

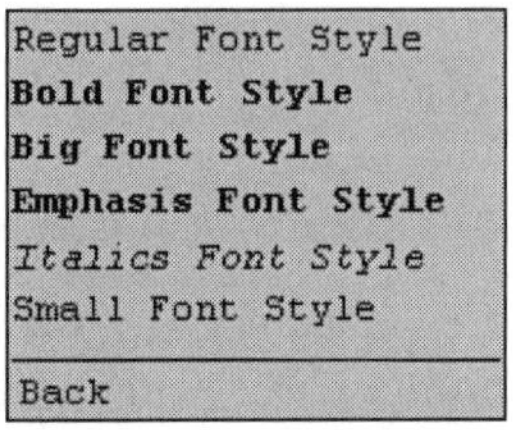

```
Regular Font Style
Bold Font Style
Big Font Style
Emphasis Font Style
Italics Font Style
Small Font Style

Back
```

Figure 4.5   *The* style.wml *file on a device screen.*

NOTE

Not all WAP devices support styles. A good rule of thumb is to use styles to enhance the look of your applications only. Avoid using styles to convey information (for example, creating bold links that represent areas for authorized users).

If a device does not recognize a style, it usually ignores the unrecognizable style and uses a default style in its place.

For the most part, WAP devices contain at least regular, bold, and italic font styles.

The following is an explanation of this example:

- Lines 7–14 designate the use of the font style elements within a P element. Notice that each line also contains a BR element, so that each reserved character begins on a new line on the display screen.

Displaying Named Character Entities

The last chapter mentioned that WML uses a default character set. Some characters are not included within this character set, however. WML reserves certain characters for coding purposes (these special characters are covered more in the chapters to come). These special characters are known as *named character entities*. Table 4.3 summarizes these.

Table 4.3   WML's Named Character Entities

Character	Character Name
<	Less than
>	Greater than
'	Apostrophe
"	Quote
&	Ampersand
$	Dollar sign
-	Soft hyphen

To use one of these characters within a card, you must use a special syntax where you want the character to display in your text. Table 4.4 shows the syntax required for reserved characters to display within a WML card.

Table 4.4   Syntax for WML's Named Character Entities

Character	Character Name	WML Syntax
<	Less than	<
>	Greater than	>
'	Apostrophe	'
"	Quote	"
&	Ampersand	&
$	Dollar sign	$$;
-	Soft hyphen	­

To use named character entities within your code, the reserved character must begin with the ampersand sign, except when dealing with the dollar sign character.

Notice that instead of the ampersand sign, the dollar sign special character uses two dollar signs with the semicolon ($$;). This is to avoid confusion with variable names, as you'll see in the following chapters.

The following code displays a card that uses all these characters. Type the code into a text editor, and save it as reserve.wml. Then, run the file from a device-emulator. Figure 4.6 shows this file on a device screen:

```
1   <?xml version="1.0"?>
2   <!DOCTYPE wml PUBLIC "-//WAPFORUM//DTD WML 1.1//EN"
3   "http://www.wapforum.org/DTD/wml_1.1.xml">
4   <wml>
5     <card id="reserve" title="Reserve">
6       <p>This is the ampersand &amp;<br/>
7       This is the apostrophe &apos;<br/>
8       This is the dollar sign $$;<br/>
9       This is the greater than &gt;<br/>
10      This is the less than &lt;<br/>
```

```
11      This is the quote &quot;<br/>
12      This is the soft hyphen &shy;</p>
13   </card>
14   </wml>
```

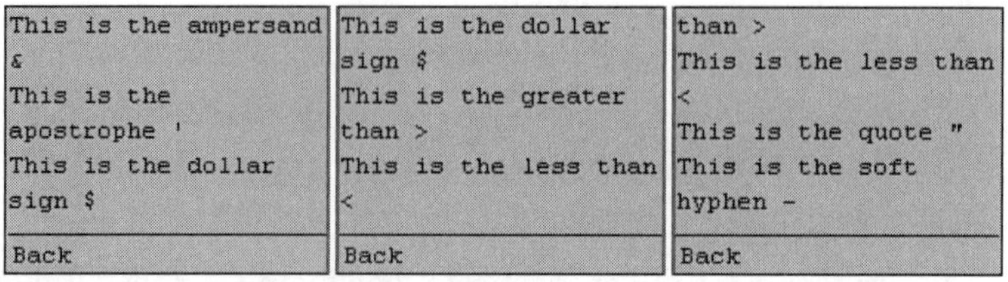

This is the ampersand & This is the apostrophe ' This is the dollar sign $ ... Back	This is the dollar sign $ This is the greater than > This is the less than < ... Back	than > This is the less than < This is the quote " This is the soft hyphen – ... Back

Figure 4.6   *The* reserve.wml *file on a device screen.*

The following is an explanation of this example:

- Lines 6–12 designate the use of reserved characters within a P element. Like the style.wml file, each line also contains a BR element, so that each reserved character begins on a new line on the display screen.

CAUTION

In working with reserved characters, realize that the semicolon(;) is part of the character element and must be included. If you omit it, you'll receive an error.

NONBREAKING SPACES

One additional stylistic consideration are nonbreaking spaces. Nonbreaking spaces enable you to force a WAP device to keep two words together, creating a group of words that must stay combined. A nonbreaking space between words replaces a regular space.

Nonbreaking spaces use the ampersand sign at the beginning of the syntax, and a semicolon immediately after the syntax (just as the named character entities). The syntax for a nonbreaking space is as follows:

```
 
```

The following code displays a WML card that uses nonbreaking spaces. Again, similar to special characters, nonbreaking spaces are tags that must exist within a P element.

Type the following code, and save it as nbsp.wml. Then, run this code from a device-emulator. Figure 4.7 shows this file on a device screen:

```
1   <?xml version="1.0"?>
2   <!DOCTYPE wml PUBLIC "-//WAPFORUM//DTD WML 1.1//EN"
```

```
3   "http://www.wapforum.org/DTD/wml_1.1.xml">
4   <wml>
5     <card id="nbsp" title="Nbsp">
6       <p align="center">Welcome to the yourcompany.com system.</p>
7     </card>
8   </wml>
```

Figure 4.7 *The nbsp.wml file on a device screen.*

The following is an explanation of this example:

- The sixth line uses the P element to create a paragraph with the non-breaking character. Notice how the nonbreaking character is typed directly into the space where we want to omit space and force the words to stay together. Now, if only relationships were this easy!

Creating Tables

As you progress through this book, you'll see that wireless applications are great for receiving information from a larger application or database server. However, receiving this information means having it presented to the user in a manner that is both intuitive and readable. Tables have proven to be extremely useful in the display of information to users in such a manner.

At the time of this writing, WML handles tables in only the simplest formats. To that end, many WML browsers do not even support tables, and some often produce errors or ignore the display of data altogether. However, table functionality within WML is important, and will undoubtedly improve with each specification of the WML language.

When creating tables for display on a WAP device, you'll use elements that might be familiar if you've worked with other markup languages. Specifically, you'll use

- TABLE—This element specifies a columnar table.
- TR—This element defines the number of rows within a table.
- TD—This element displays the content within the cells created by the table.

When working with tables in WML, think of these three elements as a group. All three elements must work together.

The TABLE Element

The TABLE element enables you to display information in a columnar form. This element must have a beginning tag and an ending tag.

When defining a table, you must define the number of columns that are present. You can also include empty rows or columns when defining the content that displays within your tables. Table 4.5 is a synopsis of the TABLE element's attributes.

Table 4.5   The **TABLE** Element's Attributes

Attribute	Required	Description
align	No	Specifies the text alignment relative to the column. If you do not specify an align attribute, the text is automatically left aligned. It must be equal to left, right, or center.
title	No	Specifies a label for the table.
columns	No	Specifies the number of columns for the row set. Specifying a zero value for this attribute is not allowed.

The TR Element

The TR element creates rows within a table. This element must be specified between the beginning and ending tags of the TABLE element. The TR element contains no attributes.

The TD Element

The TD element creates the content within the table rows. This element is specified between the beginning and ending tags of the TD element. The TD element contains no attributes.

This all makes much more sense when you actually jump in, write the code, and see how it fits together. Type the following code into a text editor. Then, save your work as table.wml, and run it through a device-emulator. Figure 4.8 shows this code on a device screen:

```
1   <?xml version="1.0"?>
2   <!DOCTYPE wml PUBLIC "-//WAPFORUM//DTD WML 1.1//EN"
3   "http://www.wapforum.org/DTD/wml_1.1.xml">
4   <wml>
5     <card id="table" title="Table">
6       <p>
7         <table columns="2">
8           <tr>
9             <td>Option 1:</td>
```

```
10              <td><anchor title="Go"><go href="#login"/>Login</anchor><br/>
                ➥</td>
11            </tr>
12            <tr>
13              <td>Option 2:</td>
14              <td><anchor title="Go"><go href="#help"/>Help</anchor><br/>
                ➥</td>
15            </tr>
16          </table>
17      </p>
18    </card>
19 </wml>
```

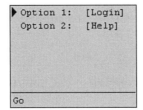

Figure 4.8 *The* `table.wml` *file on a device screen.*

N O T E

This example does not contain any navigational links yet. The links you created in this example (Option 1 and Option 2) will not work. You'll add functionality to these links in Chapter 5, "Navigation Using WML," when you learn more about creating navigational functionality to your applications.

The following is an explanation of this example:

- The seventh line uses the TABLE element to start the table. In this example, the column attribute is set equal to 2. This value specifies that there are two columns within this table.

- The eighth line uses the TR element to start a row. The TR element stands for table row.

- The ninth line uses the TD element to define the information contained within the first column of this row. WML tables can hold text, images, or anchors (which are a type of navigational link). In this column, the text Option 1: has been included.

- The tenth line uses the TD element to define the information contained within the second column of this row. In this example, an ANCHOR element is used. Don't worry too much about how these anchors work for now; you'll delve into them in greater detail in Chapter 5.

ANCHOR elements provide links to areas within your applications. They are similar to the DO element. The difference is that in addition to creating a label over a user interface of the device, the ANCHOR element also displays a text link on the device screen. You'll see what anchors look like in a moment, but they're similar to hyperlinks found on Web pages.

- The eleventh line uses the <tr> tag of the first row.
- The twelfth line uses the TR element to begin a new row.
- The thirteenth line uses the TD element to include the text Option 2:.
- The fourteenth line uses the TD element to define the information contained within the second column within this row. In this example, another ANCHOR element has been used.
- The fifteenth line uses the </tr> tag to end the second row.
- The sixteenth line uses the </table> tag to end the table.

With tables, you can also incorporate any of the styles or reserved characters into these table cells.

CAUTION

Tables don't tend to work very well with devices with small screens. Be sure you're keeping your tables no bigger than two to three columns.

Summary

In this chapter, you've begun to develop WAP applications. The lessons learned within this chapter are applicable to all WAP development applications in the future and provide a foundation for you to expand on in subsequent chapters.

You've looked at several aspects of text formatting and how to present text within your applications using the attributes of the P element. You've used these attributes to specify line alignment and horizontal scrolling of our text.

You've also looked at several WML style elements used to enhance the look of our text. You then learned about named character entities and how to work around them with shortcut forms provided within the WML language.

This chapter concluded with a discussion of incorporating simple tables into your WAP applications. In the coming chapters, you'll build on the knowledge you've gained, gradually developing a real-world WAP application.

As you'll see, the world of WAP development is limited only by your imagination.

This chapter concluded with a discussion of incorporating simple tables into our wireless applications. In the coming chapters, you'll build on the knowledge you've gained from this chapter, working your way into developing a WAP application that is applicable within the corporate world today.

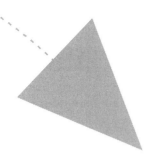

Navigation Using WML

WAP applications are a lot like conventional Web sites. WAP applications consist of a set of navigation functionality used to link WML cards, just as Web sites use navigational functionality to link the pages of that site together.

Typically, a WAP application should require as little user scrolling as possible. One way to reduce scrolling is to break information into multiple cards. To do this, however, developers must create mechanisms that allow users to navigate between these components quickly.

This chapter looks at the navigational functionality provided by WML and how to incorporate this functionality into your applications. Specifically, this chapter addresses the following issues:

- The differences between absolute and relative URLs

- How to define actions for multiple cards within decks

- How to override deck-level action

A WAP developer's most important goal must be to create applications that allow users to enter information as effortlessly as possible. This chapter discusses creating the navigational functionality to meet these goals. With that said, let's look at what WAP navigation is all about.

Specifying URLs

In WAP applications, uniform resource locators (URLs) provide the path to which cards navigate. URLs provide a network path for cards to connect to other cards and files, whether they are both contained within the same deck or on different networks and servers.

You'll use two types of URLs within your WAP applications: relative and absolute. The following pages discuss the definitions and differences between relative and absolute URLs and how they both can play a part in WAP development.

Relative URLs

A relative URL creates a link to a card that exists within the same WML deck. In other words, the card being linked to must be in the same directory (be it on a device or on a remote server) as the card that contains the link.

Relative URLs use a hash mark (#) at the beginning of the link to signify the beginning of the main directory. Relative links have the following syntax:

```
<go href="#card1">
```

Absolute URLs

Absolute URLs navigate between servers and access another file (be it a WML deck or some other file type) located within another directory. Absolute URLs must be used when your applications need to access files that reside on a remote server.

To create an absolute URL, a link must contain the entire address of the server location. In the following, the area in bold is the address of your WAP site:

```
<go href="http://wap.yourcompanysite.com/#card1">
```

Defining Links

WML contains two elements for navigation. These navigational elements are

- **Anchors**—Provided by the ANCHOR element in WML. Anchors place links around text or images to enable users to select and navigate throughout a WAP application. Anchors were discussed in Chapter 4, "Text Formatting for WML."

- **Events**—Provided by the DO and ONEVENT elements in WML. These enable you to set navigational functionality to a WAP device's user interface (such as the WAP device's Option or Accept button). Chapter 4 introduced you briefly to the DO element.

Let's look at a more in-depth explanation of both of these navigational methods and how to use them within a WAP application.

The ANCHOR Element

When creating links within the cards of your WAP application, you'll find the ANCHOR element useful. Anchors can link either text or images.

A WAP device usually displays linked text or images using underlining or by containing the text or image within brackets. Users can move from link to link using the device arrows. To accept a navigational link through a link, users click the Accept button.

NOTE

The Accept button is either the right or left button on a WAP device, and it resides beside the navigational arrows. The size of the Accept button depends on the vendor implementation.

Look for text above either the left or right button on a device to determine which is the Accept button.

When using the ANCHOR element, the Accept button provides the functionality to execute a user's choice. Table 5.1 summarizes the attributes of the ANCHOR element.

Table 5.1   The Attributes of the ***ANCHOR*** *Element*

Attribute	Required	Description
accesskey	No	Specifies a number (0–9) that is displayed to the left of the link. Users can press that keypad number, hash mark (#), or asterisk (*) to make a selection.
href	Yes	Specifies the designation URL.
title	No	Specifies a label for the card. This label can be used for bookmarked text, pop-ups, or other uses.

Chapter 4 discussed the table.wml file that contained anchors. Figure 5.1 shows this file on a device screen. However, in this chapter, two cards are added so that the links in the ANCHORS work correctly. Save this new code as table2.wml and run it through a device emulator:

```
1  <?xml version="1.0"?>
2  <!DOCTYPE wml PUBLIC "-//WAPFORUM//DTD WML 1.1//EN"
3  "http://www.wapforum.org/DTD/wml_1.1.xml">
4  <wml>
```

```
5 <!-- Card -->
6    <card id="table" title="Table">
7      <p>
8        <table columns="2">
9          <tr>
10           <td>Option 1:</td>
11           <td><anchor title="Go"><go href="#login"/>Login</anchor><br/>
               ➡</td>
12         </tr>
13         <tr>
14           <td>Option 2:</td>
15           <td><anchor title="Go"><go href="#help"/>Help</anchor><br/>
               ➡</td>
16         </tr>
17       </table>
18     </p>
19   </card>

20 <!-- Card 2 -->
21   <card id="login" title="Login">
22     <p>Login card</p>
23   </card>

24 <!-- Card 3 -->
25   <card id="help" title="Help">
26     <p>Please contact your system administrator at 800.555.1212</p>
27   </card>
28 </wml>
```

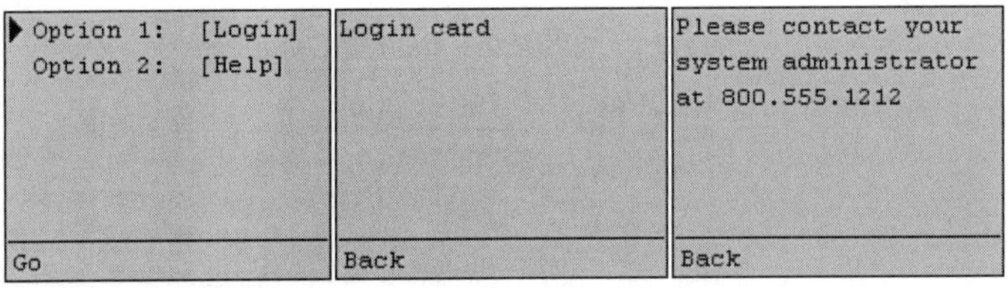

Figure 5.1 The `table2.wml` file on a device emulator.

The following is an explanation of this code:

- The eleventh line contains the first ANCHOR element. In this line, the title attribute is set equal to the text Go. If you do not specify a title, the default label that displays above the Accept button is the text Link.

  After the ANCHOR element, the GO element is used, set equal to #login. This is a relative link and states that whenever the Accept button is clicked, the device links to the login card.

The text (or image) that displays as a anchored link is written after the closing bracket of the GO element. In this example, the text written is Login. Thus, the text Login displays as an anchored link.

- The fifteenth line contains the same functionality as the tenth line. The only difference is that this anchor link is set to access the help card. The text Help is defined to display as an anchored link.

TIP

Some developers like to abbreviate the ANCHOR element by using the A element.

The A element is an abbreviation of an ANCHOR element that uses the GO element only. For example, in the table.wml code, line 11 could have been shorted by using the A element, like so:

```
. . . <a href="#login" title="Go">Login</a> . . .
```

This element contains the same attributes as the ANCHOR element (summarized in Table 5.1).

Assigning Events to Device Buttons

Up to this point, you've looked at creating hypertext links within applications. However, WAP devices also contain the capability to incorporate other navigational functionality into your applications. Two WML elements are available for creating navigational events besides the ANCHOR element. They are as follows:

- **The DO element**—Provides the capability to incorporate functionality into your WAP applications through a WAP device's user interface (such as the device buttons).

- **The ONEVENT element**—Provides the capability to incorporate functionality into your WAP application through intrinsic events (such as internal processing events).

Although button locations can differ on various WAP devices, most contain a left button that functions as the Accept button and a right button that functions as the Options button. Keep this in mind as you're working through the examples within this book.

The DO Element

Programming events with a device's buttons requires associating a URL with a button type. The DO element makes this possible.

The DO element enables developers to associate actions with a user interface mechanism. Similar to the ANCHOR element, the DO event must be associated with a task.

NOTE

Four WML elements provide task functionality—GO, NOOP, PREV, and REFRESH.

So far, you've associated links with the GO element. You'll look at the rest of the available WML task elements in a couple of pages. However, you'll find that the GO element is the most widely used task element.

The DO event contains several attributes, defined in Table 5.2.

*Table 5.2   The Attributes of the **DO** Event*

Attribute	Required	Description
label	No	Specifies a textual string used as a display label.
name	No	Specifies an element name that enables card-level binding to override deck-level binding.
optional	No	Specifies that the device should ignore this element if set to true. The available values are true and false; the default is false.
type	Yes	Specifies the device mechanism associated with this attribute. Several type attributes are available that can define the type of action the DO event executes. These are as follows:

    • accept—Affirms acknowledgement

    • prev—Backward history navigation

    • help—Request for help

    • reset—Clears and resets the current state

    • options—Request for options or additional operations

    • delete—Deletes item or choice

    • unknown—Generic type

USING THE DO ELEMENT WITH TEMPLATES

The DO element is most widely used with WML's TEMPLATE element. Templates provide a means to type code once and use it throughout all cards within a deck.

No one likes to do any more work than necessary, especially when it comes to repetitive work. This is especially true for developers and the typing of repetitive code.

Typing the same code repeatedly guarantees you a host of problems (not to mention headaches). Repetitive code means having to change your code in several places if you decide to make a change. Repetitive code also increases the chance of typing errors, and therefore bugs, in the code.

As you'll see in this next example, WML's TEMPLATE element provides the functionality to reduce repetitive code within your applications.

To see how the TEMPLATE element works, consider the following WML deck. This deck contains three cards, with each card using a couple of DO elements. The DO element can provide functionality to various user interfaces. The most common device interfaces used with the DO element are the Accept and Option buttons of a WAP device.

Look at this typing nightmare. Notice that each card contains a different label for the Accept button. However, each card contains the same label for the Option button:

```
<?xml version="1.0"?>
<!DOCTYPE wml PUBLIC "-//WAPFORUM//DTD WML 1.1//EN"
"http://www.wapforum.org/DTD/wml_1.1.xml">
<wml>

<!-- Card 1 -->
   <card id="home" title="Home">
     <do type="option" label="Help">
     <go href="#help"/>
     </do>
     <do type="accept" label="Go">
     <go href="#menu"/>
     </do>
        <p>Home card</p>
   </card>

<!-- Card 2 -->
   <card id="menu" title="Menu">
     <do type="option" label="Help">
     <go href="#help"/>
     </do>
     <do type="accept" label="Go">
     <go href="#home"/>
     </do>
        <p>Menu card</p>
   </card>
<!-- Card 3 -->
   <card id="help" title="Help">
     <do type="option" label="Help">
     <go href="#help"/>
     </do>
     <do type="accept" label="Go">
     <go href="#home"/>
     </do>
        <p>Please contact your system administrator at 800.555.1212.</p>
   </card>
</wml>
```

Look at all the repetitive information marked in bold—that's just a couple of cards. What if you had five cards with repetitive information? Or, for that matter, ten cards with the same information? That's a lot of typing, not to mention the creation of a bigger file size.

Use the TEMPLATE element within your WML applications to eliminate unnecessary code. The TEMPLATE element enables you to describe tasks that apply to a number of cards. Use this element at the start of a WML deck, directly following the starting WML element.

The TEMPLATE element does include a couple of attributes, but don't worry too much about these for now. Table 5.3 shows the attributes included with the TEMPLATE element.

*Table 5.3   The Attributes of the **TEMPLATE** Element*

Attribute	Required	Description
onenterbackward	No	Specifies the URL to open if the user navigates to this card through a PREV task
onenterforward	No	Specifies the URL to open if the user navigates to this card through a GO task
ontimer	No	Specifies the URL to open if a specified TIMER element expires

Let's modify this nightmare code, using the TEMPLATE element. In the following example, you use the TEMPLATE element to create labels for the Option buttons of all cards in this deck. Again, the TEMPLATE and DO elements always work together.

Type the following code, and then save this file as template.wml. Figure 5.2 shows this code on a device screen:

```
1 <?xml version="1.0"?>
2 <!DOCTYPE wml PUBLIC "-//WAPFORUM//DTD WML 1.1//EN"
3 "http://www.wapforum.org/DTD/wml_1.1.xml">
4 <wml>

5    <template>
6      <do type="options" label="Help">
7      <go href="#help"/>
8      </do>

9      <do type="accept" label="Home">
10     <go href="#home"/>
11     </do>
12   </template>

13 <!-- Card 1 -->
```

```
14    <card id="home" title="Home">
15      <p>Home card</p>
16 </card>

17 <!-- Card 2 -->
18    <card id="menu" title="Menu">
19      <p>Menu card</p>
20 </card>
21 <!-- Card 3 -->
22    <card id="help" title="Help">
23      <p>Please contact your system administrator at 800.555.1212.</p>
24 </card>
25 </wml>
```

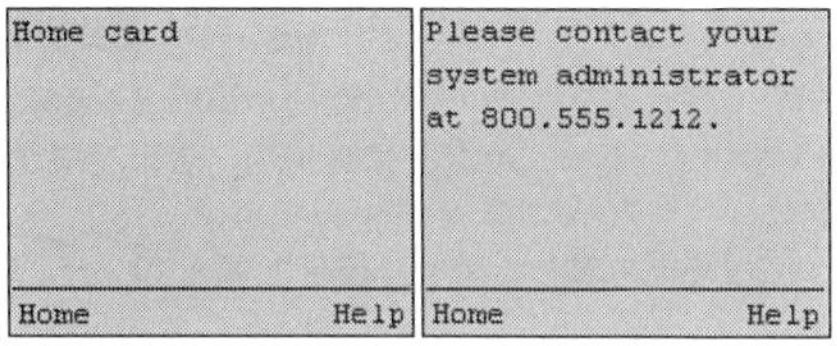

Figure 5.2   *The* template.wml *file on a device screen.*

Here's an explanation of the code:

- Lines 5–12 define the template used within this deck. This TEMPLATE element uses the DO element to create functionality for the WAP device.

- In the sixth line, the first DO element, the type attribute is set to options. The type attribute identifies the user interface mechanism that triggers a task. It being set to options means that this DO element contains functionality for the WAP device's Option button.

  The label attribute displays the text that appears over the user interface mechanism. In this case, the label attribute is set to the text Help. Thus, the text Help displays over the Option button.

- The seventh line contains the GO element, which is a task element.

  As you've seen, both the ANCHOR and DO elements require a task element. Although there are four possible WML task elements, the GO element is the most widely used. You'll look at the other possible task elements at the end of this chapter.

  In this example, the GO element equals #help (which is a relative URL). This means that whenever the Option button is clicked, the application displays the help card.

- The eighth line contains the </do> tag, which closes this first DO element.

- Lines 9–12 contain a similar DO element functionality as lines 6–8. The difference is that this second DO element sets the type attribute to accept. Thus, this second DO element contains functionality for the device's Accept button.

  This second DO element also contains a GO element, which equals #home. Thus, whenever the Accept button is clicked, the application displays the home card.

NOTE

When you run this code, you'll notice a slight problem (which we'll correct on the following pages). In this example, the TEMPLATE element is used to create constant links for the Option and Accept buttons. In all cards, the Option button accesses the help card, and the Accept button accesses the home card. Looking back at the template.wml code, notice that using the template does not allow users any way to navigate to the menu card (the second card in this example). You'll learn how to resolve this in a moment.

OVERRIDING THE TEMPLATE ELEMENT

The capability to override templates is a useful aspect of the TEMPLATE element. Templates can be overridden at the card level. In other words, say you were to define two tasks to the same user interface (such as the Option button). Say you defined one of these tasks in the TEMPLATE element and the other in the card. The task in the card always overrides the task in the TEMPLATE element.

Here's a WML deck that contains a card that overrides the template. Save this file as template2.wml. Figure 5.3 shows this code on a device screen:

```
1 <?xml version="1.0"?>
2 <!DOCTYPE wml PUBLIC "-//WAPFORUM//DTD WML 1.1//EN"
3 "http://www.wapforum.org/DTD/wml_1.1.xml">
4 <wml>

5   <template>
6     <do type="options" label="Help">
7     <go href="#help"/>
8     </do>

9     <do type="accept" label="Home">
10    <go href="#home"/>
11    </do>
12  </template>

13 <!-- Card 1 -->
```

```
14    <card id="home" title="Home">
15    <do type="accept" label="Go">
16     <go href="#menu"/>
17     </do>

18        <p>Home card</p>
19 </card>
20 <!-- Card 2 -->
21    <card id="menu" title="Menu">
22        <p>Menu card</p>
23 </card>
24 <!-- Card 3 -->
25    <card id="help" title="Help">
26        <p>Please contact your system administrator at 800.555.1212.</p>
27    </card>
28 </wml>
```

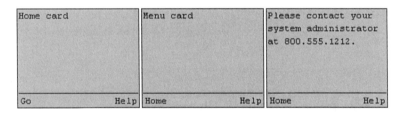

Figure 5.3   *The* `template2.wml` *file on a device screen.*

Notice the first card in this example contains a DO element that specifies functionality for the Accept button. The DO element in the first card speci-fies a different functionality for the Accept button from the DO element specified in the template. The first card's Accept button now links users to the menu card.

Because the elements in the card always take precedence over elements in the template, the DO element in the first card performs a task different from the template.

The ONEVENT Element

This chapter has looked at creating events using the DO element. The DO element has been useful in creating navigational tasks assigned to buttons.

Another useful WML element you can use to create intrinsic navigational events; in other words, events that are not triggered by the user but by an internal processing event from the device. The WML element that provides this ability is the ONEVENT element.

One of the most common uses of the ONEVENT element is with the use of timers. Chapter 8, "Incorporating Timers into WAP Applications," covers using the ONEVENT element and timers. However, for now, let's look at the one attribute of the ONEVENT—the type attribute. Thus, you'll be familiar with this element when it's discussed in greater detail in Chapter 8. Table 5.4 explains the ONEVENT element's attribute.

*Table 5.4   The Attribute of the **ONEVENT** Element*

Attribute	Required	Description
type	Yes	Specifies the device mechanism associated with this attribute. Several type attributes are available that can define the type of action the ONEVENT event executes. These are as follows:
		• onenterbackward—Specifies the URL to load when a card is entered by backward navigation
		• onenterforward—Specifies the URL to load when a card is entered by forward navigation, a bookmark, or direct entry
		• ontimer—Specifies the URL to load when a card's timer expires
		• onpick—Clears and resets the current state

The WML Task Elements

You might have noticed when working with anchors and events that these elements are always associated with some type of task (such as "go to another link," "refresh the screen," and so on). WML contains several task elements you can use in conjunction with your anchors or events.

Most of the time, you use the GO element, which is by far the most widely used task element. However, three other possible tasks are available with which anchors and events can be associated. Table 5.5 summarizes all available task elements within WML.

Table 5.5   The WML Task Elements

Element	Description	Syntax
GO	Specifies forward navigation to a URL. This element also can be used with the POSTFIELD element when posting data to a remote server. This element is the most widely used task element. You'll learn more about the POSTFIELD element in Chapter 15, when you begin posting user-inputted data to a remote database.	<go href=*URL*/>content</go>

Table 5.5   continued

Element	Description	Syntax
NOOP	Specifies that nothing is performed, and it is used to shadow deck-level tasks provided from the TEMPLATE element. This element is useful for overriding deck-level DO elements. The DO element contains no attributes.	`<noop/>`
PREV	Declares a previous task, indicating navigation to the previous URL recorded in the device's history. This task contains no attributes. Most devices incorporate an automatic back action (you might have noticed the text Back displaying above your Accept button).	`<prev>content</prev>`
REFRESH	Refreshes the specified variables to their initial or updated values. It contains no attributes.	`<refresh>content</refresh>`

Summary

This chapter examined the navigational functionality made available by WML. You began this chapter by looking at the difference between absolute and relative URLs and how both can be used in WAP applications. You then examined the WML hypertext and event elements, both providing the capability to link various tasks to a WAP application. This chapter also covered setting navigational links both at the deck and card levels.

You then examined the use of the DO element, and how its use with the TEMPLATE element enables users to create deck-level navigational settings.

This chapter concluded with a brief discussion of the topic of intrinsic navigation and gave you a good foundation for using this type of navigation when it's explored later in this book. You also looked at the other available WML task elements available for use within your applications.

Part I Example

As a final exercise to show just how far you've come, the following code incorporates all the information you've accumulated up to this point in the book. Type this code, and save it as home.wml. This file contains several cards, which you'll expand on in the coming chapters. Save this file within your C:\My Documents directory.

If you have any questions about any portion of this code, refer to the chapters in Part I. Figure I.1 shows how this file looks on a device screen:

```
<?xml version="1.0"?>
<!DOCTYPE wml PUBLIC "-//WAPFORUM//DTD WML 1.1//EN"
"http://www.wapforum.org/DTD/wml_1.1.xml">
<wml>
    <template>
      <do type="options" label="Help">
      <go href="#help"/>
      </do>

      <do type="accept" label="Home">
      <go href="#home"/>
      </do>
    </template>


<!-- Card 1 -->
    <card id="home" title="Home">
      <p align="center"><b>Welcome to the yourcompany.com system.</b>
        <table columns="2">
          <tr>
            <td>Option 1:</td>
              <td><anchor title="Go"><go
href="#login"/>Login</anchor><br/></td>
          </tr>
          <tr>
            <td>Option 2:</td>
            <td><anchor title="Go"><go href="#help"/>Help</anchor><br/></td>
          </tr>
        </table>
      </p>
    </card>

<!-- Card 2 -->
    <card id="login" title="Login">
      <p>Login card</p>
    </card>
```

```
<!-- Card 3 -->
  <card id="help" title="Help">
    <p>Please contact your system administrator at 800.555.1212</p>
  </card>
</wml>
```

| Welcome to
the yourcompany.com
system.
▶ Option 1: [Login]
   Option 2: [Help]

Go   Help | Login card

Home   Help | Please contact your
system administrator
at 800.555.1212

Home   Help |

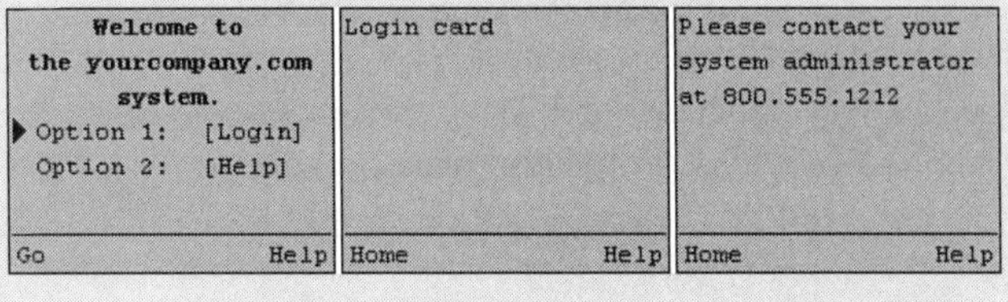

Figure I.1   *The* home.wml *file on a device emulator.*

Part II

Static WAP Development

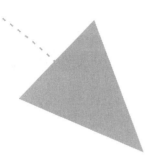

User Input with Variables

Up to this point, you've only looked at the formatting and navigation aspects of WAP development. Although these factors are important, what users really want is the ability to interact with an application. In this chapter, you begin incorporating user functionality into your WAP development efforts. You also learn how to create software that enables users to input data.

This chapter also introduces you to the concept of variables. *Variables* are temporary storage areas of applications and enable developers to use and manipulate user-inputted data. This book approaches the subject of variables by first discussing what variables are and then examining incorporating variables into WAP applications.

By the end of this chapter, you'll be familiar with the following:

- How to create applications that enable users to enter data

- How to create controls that force inputted data to follow a defined format

- What variables are and how to use them in WAP applications

- How to create selection lists as an alternative method of user input

Free-Form Input with the INPUT Element

Let's face it—no one likes being bossed around by some electronic device. People would much rather tell the device what to do. Keep this in mind as you develop your WAP applications because your users are people, too.

Users want the ability to input and interact with an application. They want control. Chapter 5, "Navigation Using WML," explored how to allow users to move from one area of an application to another. Although navigation is a necessity, what users really want is the ability to input data and have an application use this information to provide some type of task.

In WML, the ability of users to input information is provided through the INPUT element. This element enables you to create a place in your application for users to enter data. In the world of WML, data can consist of only one value—a string value. String values can be numbers, letters, or symbols, ranging in a series of zero or more characters.

The INPUT element is a useful tool in extending user-input possibilities.

Before getting too far into it with the INPUT element, you should probably get a feel for how the INPUT element works. Type the following code, and then save this code as input.wml. When you're ready, run this file through a device-emulator. Figure 6.1 shows this file on a device screen:

```
1   <?xml version="1.0"?>
2   <!DOCTYPE wml PUBLIC "-//WAPFORUM//DTD WML 1.1//EN"
3   "http://www.wapforum.org/DTD/wml_1.1.xml">
4   <wml>

5<!-- Card 1 -->
6     <card id="username" title="Username">
7       <do type="accept" label="Go">
8       <go href="#menu" />
9       </do>
10        <p>Enter username:
11        <input name="username" />
12        </p>
13    </card>

14<!-- Card 2 -->
15    <card id="menu" title="Menu">
16      <p>Welcome, $(username)</p>
17    </card>
18 </wml>
```

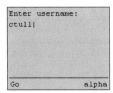 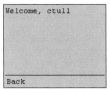

Figure 6.1 *The* input.wml *file on a device screen.*

The following is an explanation of the bold areas in this code (if you have any questions about other areas of this code, refer to the previous chapters for more detailed explanations):

- The eleventh line creates an input prompt. Later, you'll see that this line creates the variable username, a temporary storage area for the user's inputted data.

  As you can see, creating an input field in WML is easy. You only need to use the INPUT element and give it a name using its name attribute.

- The sixteenth line contains a welcome statement that references data entered by the user. The user's data is held by a variable (you'll learn more about variables in a couple of pages).

  In WML, to retrieve the user's inputted data, you just need to refer to the variable that holds the user's inputted data.

NOTE

In the figures in this example, you might notice an abbreviation located above the Option button (on the lower-right side of the screen). In the figures in this example, the abbreviation is alpha.

This abbreviation is called an *input format* and is provided on WAP devices by several device manufacturers. Input formats provide a shortcut for users to enter a variety of characters through their devices. Take a couple of minutes to play with your device's input formats to get a better understanding of how your users will enter information.

Although input formats make inputting data easier, don't get carried away and start creating applications that require users to enter a novel. Remember, brevity is the key in the world of WAP development.

Specifying Formatted Input

The previous example presented a user-input application. However, that example used only one of the INPUT element's attributes: the name attribute. The INPUT element contains several other attributes that enable you to expand user-input requirements. Table 6.1 lists the attributes available with the INPUT element.

Table 6.1   *The Attributes of the **INPUT** Element*

Attribute	Required	Description
accesskey	No	Specifies a number (0–9), a hash mark (#), or an asterisk (*) that displays to the left of a link. Users can click one of these buttons.
emptyok	No	Specifies whether this field can be left blank. The only values available for this attribute are true and false. The default value is false.
format	No	This attribute enables developers to specify the format of characters that can be inputted. For example, with format masks, you can specify whether the user can input upper- or lowercase characters, the number of characters allowed for input, and so on. Formatting masks are covered in the next example of code.
maxlength	No	Specifies the maximum field length available for user input. The default value is unlimited characters allowed.
name	Yes	Specifies the name of the variable (remember, variables are the placeholders that contain the users' inputted data).
size	No	Specifies the width of the input field (in characters).
tabindex	No	Specifies the tabbing position in a card.
title	No	Specifies a title that can be displayed by the browser (depending on the WAP device being used).
type	No	Specifies whether the input field is a text or password input field. The default value is text.
value	No	The initial value of the field. This attribute is used only if the variable specified in the name attribute has no value.

The input.wml example used only the name attribute. Let's look at some of the other optional attributes of the INPUT element.

DISPLAYING AND HIDING ENTRIES WITH THE type ATTRIBUTE

The type attribute enables developers to select an input field that either displays or hides the characters a user types into the field. Only two values are available for the type attribute: text and password. If a user sets the type attribute to text, the data displays directly on the screen. If a user sets the type attribute to password, the data is replaced with asterisks (*) or some other type of shrouding character onscreen. Depending on the device, the shrouding character might differ; however, most devices use the asterisk.

The following example demonstrates both type attributes in action. Type the following information into a text editor. Save the file as input2.wml, and then open this file in a device-emulator. Figure 6.2 shows this file on a device screen:

```
1   <?xml version="1.0"?>
2   <!DOCTYPE wml PUBLIC "-//WAPFORUM//DTD WML 1.1//EN"
3   "http://www.wapforum.org/DTD/wml_1.1.xml">
4   <wml>

5   <!-- Card 1 -->
6     <card id="username" title="Username">
7       <do type="accept" label="Go">
8       <go href="#password" />
9       </do>
10        <p>Enter username:
11          <input name="username" type="text"/>
12          </p>
13    </card>

14  <!-- Card 2 -->
15    <card id="password" title="Password">
16      <do type="accept" label="Go">
17      <go href="#menu" />
18      </do>
19        <p>Enter password:
20        <input name="password" type="password"/>
21          </p>
22    </card>

23  <!-- Card 3 -->
24    <card id="menu" title="Menu">
25      <p>Welcome, $(username)</p>
26    </card>
27  </wml>
```

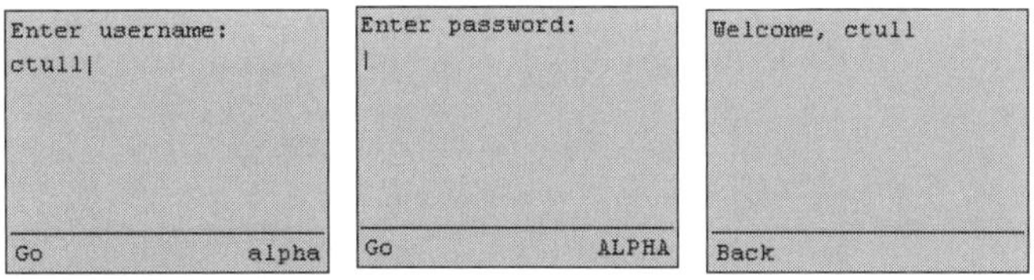

Enter username:	Enter password:	Welcome, ctull
ctull|			
Go alpha	Go ALPHA	Back

Figure 6.2   *The input2.wml file on a device screen.*

The following is an explanation of this code:

- The eighth line changes the link of the Accept button to access a new card named password.

- The eleventh line identifies the input prompt for the username, creating the variable username. This line designates that the username input field displays text.

- Lines 14–19 use tags that create a second card named password. This card contains many similar features as that of the first card. The main difference is in the seventeenth line, where the Accept button now links to the menu card.

- The twentieth line identifies the input prompt for the username, creating the variable username. This line designates that the username input field displays shrouded text.

INCORPORATING RESTRICTED INPUT USING THE FORMAT ATTRIBUTE

In the previous examples, the applications created provided simple input fields. Let's expand the code you've written to also include a certain format for the username and password fields. In the next example, you'll create input fields that require a certain combination of alphabetic and mixed-case input only. Specifically, you'll use the format attribute to add this additional functionality.

The format attribute contains a number of legal codes (also known as *format control characters*) you can use to define the restriction characters of an input field. Table 6.2 describes the various format control characters for the format attribute. When creating a format for an input field, any combination of these characters can be used.

*Table 6.2   The Format Control Characters for the **format** Attribute*

Character	Description
A	Defines the entry of any uppercase letter, symbol, or punctuation character. Numeric characters are excluded.
a	Defines the entry of any lowercase letter, symbol, or punctuation character. Numeric characters are excluded.
M	Defines the entry of any character valid in the current languages, including any letter, numeric, symbol, or punctuation character. If the language supports case and the hardware supports both upper- and lowercase entry, the user agent can choose to default to uppercase entry mode but must allow entry of any character.
m	Defines the entry of any character valid in the current languages, including any letter, numeric, symbol, or punctuation character. If the language supports case and the hardware supports both upper- and lowercase entry, the user agent can choose to default to lowercase entry mode but must allow entry of any character.
N	Defines the entry of any numeric character. Symbols, punctuation, and alphabetic characters are excluded.

To get a feel for how these format control characters play a part in WAP development, type the following code. Save your work as input3.wml, and run the code from a device-emulator. Figure 6.3 shows this file on a device screen:

```
1  <?xml version="1.0"?>
2  <!DOCTYPE wml PUBLIC "-//WAPFORUM//DTD WML 1.1//EN"
3  "http://www.wapforum.org/DTD/wml_1.1.xml">
4  <wml>

5<!-- Card 1 -->
6    <card id="username" title="Username">
7      <do type="accept" label="Go">
8      <go href="#password" />
9      </do>
10       <p>Enter username:
11       <input name="username" format="5a" type="text"/>
12       </p>
13   </card>

14<!-- Card 2 -->
15   <card id="password" title="Password">
16     <do type="accept" label="Go">
17     <go href="#menu" />
18     </do>
19       <p>Enter password:
20       <input name="password" format="NAAA" type="password"/>
21       </p>
22   </card>

23<!-- Card 3 -->
24   <card id="menu" title="Menu">
25       <p>Welcome, $(username)</p>
26   </card>
27 </wml>
```

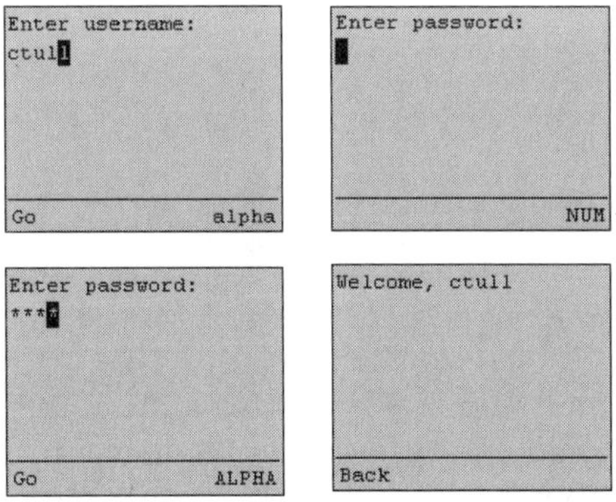

Figure 6.3   *The* input3.wml *file on a device screen.*

N O T E

Notice that the Accept button does not become functional until the user has entered the correct format for the input field.

The following is an explanation of the bold areas in this code:

- The eleventh line identifies the input prompt for the username, creating the variable username. The format attribute is equal to 5a, meaning the username input field allows for the input of only five lowercase characters. This input field is a text field, as designated by the type attribute set equal to the value text.

- The twelfth line identifies the input prompt for the password, creating the variable password. The format attribute is equal to NAAA, so the password input field allows the input of only a number followed by three uppercase characters. This input field is a password field, as designated by the type attribute of password. This input field thus shrouds the text with asterisks.

THE format ATTRIBUTE USING EMBEDDED HELPER CHARACTERS

You've learned about creating an input format that uses a specific form of characters. Let's expand on this slightly and discuss creating an input format that uses embedded helper characters.

Embedded helper characters are things such as the dashes needed for a credit card number or the parentheses used with phone numbers. These characters are useful in that they enable developers to insert uneditable characters into an input field, thus imposing a known format on user-entered data.

N O T E

When working with static characters, realize that this format becomes part of the actual value of the user's inputted data.

Using embedded helper characters is especially helpful when sending this data back to a database. Embedded helper characters also help ensure that the information written to a database keeps its data integrity. In other words, the information being sent from the WAP application matches the format of the data in the database.

Let's now tweak the input format you created a little. In the next example, you change the password input field format to enable the input of a password that contains a dash. Specifically, you create a card that specifies the user to input information in the format NN-NNNN. To do this, you use embedded helper characters.

To add embedded helper characters, you must insert each character in the desire position in the format attribute of your code. Then, you must precede each of these characters with a backslash (\). A WAP device inserts the character in the field as the user enters a value.

For example, the specifying format \(NNN\) instructs the WAP device to insert a left parenthesis before the user enters anything and a right parenthesis and dash after the user enters three numbers.

Here's another example that uses the format attribute. Type the following code, and save it as input4.wml. Then, run it through a device-emulator. Figure 6.4 shows this file on a device screen:

```
1   <?xml version="1.0"?>
2   <!DOCTYPE wml PUBLIC "-//WAPFORUM//DTD WML 1.1//EN"
3   "http://www.wapforum.org/DTD/wml_1.1.xml">
4   <wml>

5<!-- Card 1 -->
6     <card id="username" title="Username">
7       <do type="accept" label="Go">
8       <go href="#password" />
9       </do>
10        <p>Enter username:
11        <input name="username" format="5a" type="text"/>
12        </p>
13    </card>

14<!-- Card 2 -->
15    <card id="password" title="Password">
16      <do type="accept" label="Go">
17      <go href="#menu" />
18      </do>
19        <p>Enter password:
20        <input name="password" format="NN\-NNNN" type="password"/>
21        </p>
22    </card>

23<!-- Card 3 -->
24    <card id="menu" title="Menu">
25      <p>Welcome, $(username)</p>
26    </card>
27 </wml>
```

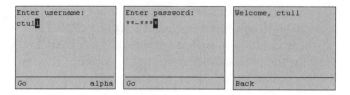

Figure 6.4 *The `input4.wml` file on a device screen.*

The following is an explanation of the bold areas of this code:

- The twelfth line identifies the input prompt for the password, creating the variable `password`. The `format` attribute is equal to `NN\-NNNN`.

With all this talk about user input, you might not have realized that you've been using variables. Variables are a necessity in the world of programming. Let's take a moment to examine what variables are and how they can aid you in your WAP development efforts.

What Are Variables?

Variables are, simply stated, the contents of a temporary storage area in an application. This storage area holds information, usually inputted into the program by a user. In the previous examples, the values of the `name` attributes were variables.

For example, in a previous line of code you wrote, you defined an input field with the `name` attribute equal to `username`:

```
<input name="username" type="text" />
```

When users access this line of code in the application, they can input information. The application then saves this input information in a temporary storage area, using the `name` attribute as the name of the temporary storage area. In other words, a temporary storage area (a variable) called `username` holds the user's inputted information.

Later in the application, the application refers to the variable `username` to display the inputted information:

```
<p>Welcome, $(username)</p>
```

In more robust programming languages, the type of information that can be stored may be numbers, a true or false value, a date, or text. However, WML makes it easy on developers—the only type of data is text data (better known as *string values*).

NOTE

As you get into WMLScript later in this book, you'll see the possibilities of variables increase. With the introduction of WMLScript, you'll be able to create different types of data to use as variables. However, for now, you'll concentrate only on the possibilities of WML—thus, all variables you create in this chapter will be strings.

Variables can store only one piece of data at a time. So, when you store a different value in a variable, the original value is replaced. Variables will make a lot more sense after you actually delve into them in our coding examples. For now, just realize that variables are storage areas in your applications that can be used to hold data and that they can be used to hold data inputted by users. You then can use this inputted data in your application for several purposes.

Before jumping into any more examples using variables, you first must understand how to name variables in WML. The next section discusses some of the pitfalls to avoid when naming variables for use in WAP applications.

Naming Variables

When naming WML variables, the general rule is that they can be any combination of letters, digits, and underscores. The following are some examples of valid variable names:

- `variable`
- `1variable`
- `variable_1`
- `VARIABLE`

WML doesn't have a character limit on the length of variable names. However, these names should be kept as short as possible. A longer variable name means that more information needs to be transmitted, possibly over a low-bandwidth link. Longer variable names also take up more room when stored in a device's limited memory.

TIP

Try to stick to a single naming convention (such as naming all variables in lowercase). Sometimes developers find that errors within applications are often the result of variables not referencing correctly.

Allowing User Input Through a List

The rest of this chapter discusses creating a list of choices from which users can select. A list of information provides an even more restricted way to get input from a user—enabling the developer greater control of the form of data presented. Also, creating lists from which users can select choices provides an easier method of data entry from the user's perspective.

The SELECT Element

The SELECT element enables you to create a list of options for user selections. As you'll see, the OPTION and OPTGROUP elements are used in conjunction with the SELECT element. The OPTION element provides choices available in a list. The OPTGROUP element must also be included and is used to group your list of options hierarchically. Essentially, the SELECT element creates the framework in which you create an options list for user selection.

Let's take a look at the attributes available from the SELECT element (see Table 6.3).

*Table 6.3   The Attributes of the **SELECT** Element*

Attribute	Required	Description
iname	No	Specifies the index number of the default option.
ivalue	No	Specifies the default index number value.
multiple	No	Specifies whether multiple selections can be made. The available values are true and false. The default value is false.
name	Yes	Specifies the name of the variable to contain the value of the selected <option>.
tabindex	No	Specifies the tabbing position in a card.
title	No	Specifies the field value.
value	No	Specifies the default value for the variable.

Before you write an application using the SELECT element, you should familiarize yourself with the OPTION and OPTGROUP elements. Whereas the SELECT element creates the framework in which you create an options list for user selection, the OPTION and OPTGROUP elements are used to add and group the information in these lists. Only the OPTION element is required with the SELECT element; however, the OPTGROUP element provides a means to create subgroups in a selection list, if necessary.

The OPTGROUP Element

The OPTGROUP element enables you to group options. The purpose of doing this is to enable the browser to optimize the display appropriately.

The OPTGROUP element provides a method for grouping options in a list neatly when you need to create lists that use a couple levels. Table 6.4 explains the single attribute of the OPTGROUP element.

*Table 6.4   The Attribute of the **OPTGROUP** Element*

Attribute	Required	Description
title	No	Title for the group. If this attribute is used, it should be unique in a card to avoid confusion.

THE OPTION ELEMENT

The OPTION element creates the options that exist within a selection list. To use these elements correctly, the OPTION element must follow the SELECT element. You'll see more on this when you begin writing the WML code for your selection list.

The OPTION element contains a few attributes that can enhance the options list (see Table 6.5).

*Table 6.5   The Attributes of the **OPTION** Element*

Attribute	Required	Description
onpick	No	Specifies the URL to navigate to upon option selection
title	No	Specifies an optional title
value	No	Specifies the value to be returned if the option is selected

Now that you've looked at the elements necessary to create selection lists, let's see how these elements are used in action. Type the following code into a text editor. Save the file as select.wml, and run it from a device-emulator. Figure 6.5 shows this code on a device screen:

```
1  <?xml version="1.0"?>
2  <!DOCTYPE wml PUBLIC "-//WAPFORUM//DTD WML 1.1//EN"
3  "http://www.wapforum.org/DTD/wml_1.1.xml">
4  <wml>
5     <card id="menu" title="Menu">
6<!-- Card 1 -->
7       <do type="accept" label="Go">
8       <go href="#deptinfo"/>
9       </do>
10        <p>Select a dept.:
11          <select name="dept" value="5" multiple="false">
12            <optgroup>
13              <option onpick="#deptinfo" value="Sales">Sales</option>
14              <option onpick="#deptinfo" value="Mrkt">Mrkt</option>
15              <option onpick="#deptinfo" value="Acct">Acct</option>
16              <option onpick="#deptinfo" value="Plant">Plant</option>
```

```
17                  <option onpick="#deptinfo" value="IT">IT</option>
18              </optgroup>
19            </select>
20          </p>
21        </card>

22<!-- Card 2 -->
23        <card id="deptinfo" title="Dept Info">
24          <p>This is the $(dept) dept.</>
25        </card>
26 </wml>
```

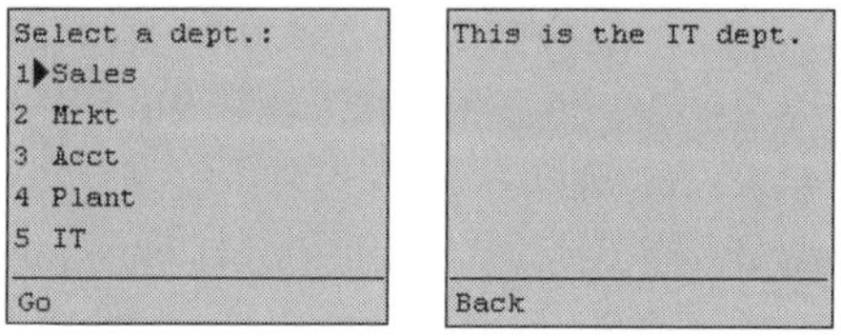

Figure 6.5 *The* select.wml *file on a device screen.*

The following is an explanation of the bold areas in this code:

- The eleventh line begins the SELECT element and specifies the beginning of a selection list. The name that's assigned here (dept) acts as a variable and stores the value of the option the user selects.

- Lines 12–18 are the options available from the selection list. Two attributes are used with the OPTION elements: the onpick attribute and the value attribute. The onpick attribute specifies the URL to navigate when the option is selected. In this case, when a user picks an option, the WML specifies navigation to the deptinfo card located in this same deck. (It's a relative URL.)

  The other attribute is the value attribute, which equals the value to be returned if the option is selected. This value is what returns when the variable is retrieved.

- The nineteenth line is the end tag of the SELECT element.

Summary

This chapter covered quite a bit of WML. It began by examining the INPUT element and how it creates user-input functionality within a WAP application. Many of the attributes of this element, which provide more flexibility to create a variety of input field types and formats, were also discussed.

Then, the concepts of variables and how they're essentially storage areas for user-inputted information were covered. Variables are important—they provide the ability to create applications that are responsive to user input. The chapter then looked at some guidelines to naming and referencing variables in code to lessen the need for debugging efforts.

This chapter concluded with an example of creating user input via the SELECT element. This element provides the ability to create a selection list in which users can input data. Selection lists are the easiest method for user input and are the method of choice when creating user-interactive applications.

The next chapter discusses improving the look of your application even further by first converting images into a format that WAP devices can use. You'll then learn about incorporating these images into your application. Because of the limitations placed on text, you'll find images a useful tool in conveying meaning to users.

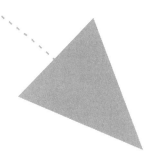

Working with Images

In previous chapters, you've learned about defining the look and feel of WAP applications. By now, you're probably hungry for more. In fact, you're probably asking, "So, does WAP allow me to incorporate images into my applications?"

The answer to that question is, "Yes, WAP applications can use images." You picked a good time to ask that question because in this chapter you'll learn just that—mainly, how to include images into your WAP development efforts.

Everyone loves images in their software programs. Images provide several advantages, for both users and developers of an application. Images provide symbolic meanings to application functionality, making software easier and more fun to use. They convey meanings, often better than lines of text ever could.

Because text space is limited with WAP devices, images are a useful means to communicate ideas in the smallest space possible. The old idiom "a picture is worth a thousand words" rings especially true in the world of WAP development. In fact, many WAP applications use images solely for their user interfaces.

However, before planning to color your WAP applications with flowering, colored images and spectacular graphical effects, remember that WAP devices do have limited storage capacities. This doesn't have to be a problem, though. In this chapter, you'll learn how to work around such factors. By the end of this chapter, you'll be incorporating images into your applications, all without sacrificing efficiency.

Specifically, this chapter addresses the following:

- The WBMP graphic format, the image format that WAP applications must use

- Converting several graphic formats into the WBMP format

- The use of local icons present in some WAP device browsers

- Some examples of using images in WAP applications

Before you begin incorporating images into applications, it's important to remember the possibilities of the devices for which you are developing.

In application development, the first law of using images is *use images only to enhance an application*. If an image looks great but ends up limiting the application in some way, you shouldn't use the image.

Developmental Limitations of WAP Devices

When developing for any type of device—be it a mobile phone, personal digital assistant (PDA), or PC—that device's limitations dictate the functionality that can be developed. In the case of WAP devices, two main limitations must be taken into considerations. These limitations are bandwidth and screen size.

Bandwidth

Chapter 1, "What Is WAP Development?" first presented the topic of bandwidth. If you recall, *bandwidth* refers to wavelengths provided by telecommunication networks. These wavelengths determine the amount of data transmitted in a fixed amount of time.

WAP device bandwidth is expressed in bits per second (bps). Currently in the United States, the average bandwidth for wireless devices is around 9600KBps (or 9,600 kilobits per second)—not the most blazing speed when you consider DSL and T1 lines that transfer data to PCs at much faster rates of around 2MBps–4MBps.

NOTE

One Kbps is 1,000 bits per second, whereas one KB (kilobyte) is 1,024 bytes. We're talking in terms of KBps.

What all this bandwidth talk comes down to is that transferring data to WAP devices is slower than transferring data to PCs. Because of this, data transferred to wireless devices should be small—text data being the smallest and easiest type of data to transfer.

But what about images? Does this mean that WAP applications shouldn't use images? The answer is of course not. However, at the time of this writing, most devices can't store images. Applications that use images must retrieve them over a wireless network. Keep this in mind as you use images. Again, use images to enhance applications. If images slow an application down to the point of user frustration, you're better off not using them.

If you do decide that images are right for your application and you've determined that they won't affect application efficiency, it's time to consider the second factor of images and WAP applications: screen size.

Screen Size

At the time of this writing, most WAP devices allow only 4–10 lines of text to display without scrolling. Ideally, users should need to scroll as little as possible. Scrolling (although it seems simple enough) actually makes an application more difficult to use in the eyes of your users.

Because you're developing applications for WAP phones, your applications should be no larger than 96×14 pixels (a size capable of supporting images on most WAP phones). Wireless applications and WML do not yet provide the functionality to set image sizes, although the specifications have been set in the language. Therefore, setting image sizes within the WML language will be available in the future.

If your image is larger than the display screen, users will need to scroll to view the entire image. This is a bad design practice; your users should never need to scroll to view an entire image. Figure 7.1 displays the right and wrong ways to use images within a wireless application.

TIP

A good rule of thumb for your images is 96×14 metrics on a WAP phone. However, if you are developing WAP applications for other types of WAP devices, the size and shape of your images might differ.

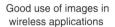

Good use of images in   Bad use of images in
wireless applications   wireless applications

Figure 7.1   *The correct and incorrect ways to use images in your wireless applications.*

The Wireless Bitmap Format

Currently, the wireless bitmap format (also known as WBMP) is the only graphical format supported by wireless devices. The WAP Forum has provided support for this type of format within the WML specification. The WAE stack specifies the WBMP format (discussed in Chapter 1).

Although WAP 2.0 includes support for color images, you might want to stick with WBMPs that consists of only black-and-white pixels. The reason is twofold. For one, most WAP devices today contain display screens that support only black-and-white images. The other reason is that the scaled-down properties of black-and-white pixels work well with the limited memory and processing power of today's devices.

The type of images that work best in WAP applications are simple logos and symbol-like pictures. Detailed graphics (such as a picture of an individual or an image in which the detail is very fine) do not translate well into the WBMP format. When using images for a WAP application, remember: Keep it simple.

Most (although not all) WAP browsers support images. If a browser does not support images, it won't display the image. In other words, the browser will ignore the image.

To create (or convert) an image into the WBMP format, an image conversion tool is required. The next couple of pages are dedicated to the variety of image conversion tools available for WAP developers.

Image Conversion Options

The conversion of any graphical format is made possible by a process called *dithering*. Essentially, dithering changes the way a user device interprets monochrome colors. Several tools are available for converting existing graphics into the WBMP format, ranging from desktop software, to plug-ins available for popular graphic software programs, to online sites that provide the necessary tools.

All these tools essentially provide the same results. Deciding which tool works best really comes down to user preference. In this book, you'll use freeware desktop software to convert images into the WBMP format.

Image Conversion Desktop Tools

With image conversion desktop tools, you must first download the software from the Internet. Several desktop shareware programs are available for graphic conversion. This book uses WAPPictus for the examples in this book. WAPPictus is an excellent product produced by Check It.

WAPPictus is an excellent freeware program that enables users to convert existing standard graphics into a WBMP format. WAPPictus contains several new features, such as the capability to convert .png files (this is in addition to .jpeg, .gif, and .bmp files), a conversion preview to enable users to view what their results will look like, and a number of resizing options.

To download WAPPictus, click the WAPPictus desktop button from the menu on the right side of the page. You must first enter your name and e-mail address. An executable then downloads to your PC. To install WAPPictus, double-click the executable and accept all defaults. WAPPictus installs onto your desktop. Figure 7.2 shows the WAPPictus main menu.

NOTE

Using image conversion desktop software requires downloading software onto your desktop. If you prefer not to download software, you can use the online image converters described in the next section.

Figure 7.2 *WAPPictus main menu with image.*

WAPPictus enables users to develop WBMP images within the program using its editing functionality. Users can also convert existing graphics into a WBMP format, either accessing them from their desktop computers or pulling them from the Internet.

However, this product is by no means the only one available to developers. Table 7.1 lists other desktop image conversion programs and the URLs where they are available for download.

Table 7.1   Other Desktop Image Conversion Programs

Image Editing Tool	Company	Available From	Cost
Image Magick	ImageMagick Studio LLC	http://www.imagemagick.org	Freeware.
Pic2wbmp	Ginco New Media	http://www.ginco.de/wap	Freeware.
WAPDraw	Jarno Kyh	http://www.phnet.fi/public/jiikoo	Around $20. Also available as shareware from the Web site.
WAPPictus	CheckIT	http://www.checkit.cz/	Free (first must fill out contact information).
Wap Tiger BMP Converter	WAPTiger	http://wap.infotiger.de/download/html	Freeware.

Online Image Converters

Online converters are another means for converting images into the WBMP format. *Online converters* are Web pages that enable you to select an image from your computer. The Web page then converts the image into a WBMP format, allowing you to save this new format wherever you want.

As with the desktop image conversion programs, several online image converters are available from which to choose. The advantage of using online image converters is that software isn't required for installation onto your PC. The disadvantage, though, is that you must be online to use these tools. Table 7.2 lists some of the most popular online image converters available.

Table 7.2   Other Online Image Converters

Online Converter	Company	Available From	Cost
Applepie Online Image Converter	Applepie Solutions	http://www.applepiesolutions.com	Free
Dwbmp	Morpheme	http://www.morpheme.co.uk	Free (for non-commercial use)
WAPuSeek Online Converter	wapuseek	http://wapuseek.com	Free
WAP Tiger Online Converter	Wap Tiger	http://wap.infotiger.de/download/html	Free

Image Conversion Plug-Ins

Image plug-ins are additional pieces of software added to a larger software product. Plug-ins provide additional features for a larger software program.

In the case of these plug-ins, they add image conversion functionality for the WBMP format. Table 7.3 lists a couple available plug-ins for WMBP image conversion.

Table 7.3   WBMP Image Conversion Plug-Ins

Online Converter	Company	Available From	Cost
Photoshop and/or Paintshop plug-ins (for Windows)	RCP	http://www.rcp.co.uk	Free (must have Photoshop 5.x or Paintshop Pro already installed)
Photoshop plug-ins (for Macintosh)	Creation Flux	http://www.creationflux.com	Free (must have Photoshop 5.x already installed)

NOTE

Image conversion plug-ins require a base commercial software program (such as Photoshop) installed on your computer.

The IMG Element

To display images within your WAP applications, you must use the IMG element, which contains several attributes used to enhance the way images display on a WAP device.

You'll notice that in Table 7.4, not all device browsers support these. These attributes exist in the WML specification for use in the future. As devices improve with time, you can expect to see and use images increasingly within your applications. Thus, it's a good idea to begin familiarizing yourself with these IMG attributes, even if they're not all available at the time of this writing.

Table 7.4   The Attributes of the **IMG** Element

Attribute	Required?	Description
align	No	Represents where the image is aligned relative to the current line of text. The available entries for this attribute are top, middle, and bottom.
alt	Yes	Specifies the text that displays if the device has a problem displaying the image (for example, if images are not supported on the device or the device can't find the image).
height	No	Represents a height setting for the image. Several devices do not support this attribute.

Table 7.4   continued

Attribute	Required?	Description
hspace	No	Represents the amount of empty space to the left or right of the image. The default setting for this attribute is 0.
localsrc	No	Represents the name of a known icon that exists within the device's browser. Even if a localsrc icon is used, users must include the localsrc attribute in their code.
src	Yes	Specifies the URL of the image displayed.
vspace	No	Represents the amount of empty space above or below the image. Several devices do not support this attribute.
width	No	Represents a width setting for the image. Several devices do not support this attribute.

TIP

When using images or icons, you should test their appearance on a variety of devices. Different devices display both icons and images differently.

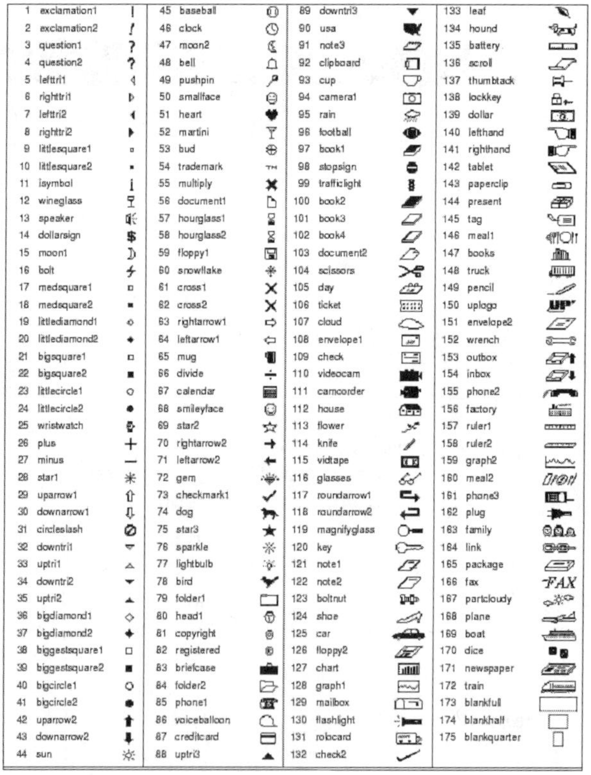

Figure 7.3   *The local icons of the UP.Browser.*

NOTE

The Openwave emulators include this figure in their documentation. In addition, this figure is available online at http://developer.phone.com/htmldoc/41/wmlref/ (refer to Figure 2.6 in Chapter 2, "Tools of the Trade").

Creating an Application with a WBMP Logo

To get an idea of how to incorporate images into your WAP applications, let's create a title page (also known in the development world as a *splash page*). Eventually, you'll add a timer function to this image that shows the picture for a period of time and then moves onto the main menu (this functionality is discussed in Chapter 8, "Incorporating Timers into WAP Applications").

To begin, type the following code. Save your work as title.wml. Before you test this application on a device emulator, you first need to create a simple logo to use within this application:

```
1  <?xml version="1.0"?>
2  <!DOCTYPE wml PUBLIC "-//WAPFORUM//DTD WML 1.1//EN"
3  "http://www.wapforum.org/DTD/wml_1.1.xml">
4  <wml>
5    <card id="title" title="title">
6      <p align="center">Yourcompany.com
7      <img src="logo.wbmp" alt="Yourcompany.com"/>
8      </p>
9    </card>
10 </wml>
```

The following is an explanation of the previous bolded code:

- The fifth line begins a card that acts as the application's title page. You'll create the logo image this page uses in a moment.

- The sixth line begins a paragraph that holds the logo image and additional text included within this splash page.

- The seventh line uses the IMG element to include a logo image within this card. Remember, only the WMBP format is available for images within a WAP application. The IMG element uses the src attribute, set equal to a file named logo.wbmp. You'll create this logo in a moment. This image is to be included within the same location as our wml file.

  The IMG element also includes the required alt attribute. This attribute must be text, and it displays if the device can't display the image.

CREATING A LOGO IMAGE

You can perform the following steps to create and convert a logo into the WBMP format:

1. Go to your Start menu, and select Start, Programs, Accessories, Paint. The Microsoft Paint program executes.

NOTE

The path to select the Microsoft Paint program can differ depending on the operating system on which you are working. Microsoft Paint is included with all Microsoft operating systems.

---

2. After Microsoft Paint is open, create the following logo (or another if you want). This logo represents the mythical company that uses this application (The mythical company's name is *yourcompany.com.*) Figure 7.4 displays this logo created in Microsoft Paint.

NOTE

Remember that simple images work best in WAP applications. Detailed images do not translate well into the WBMP format.

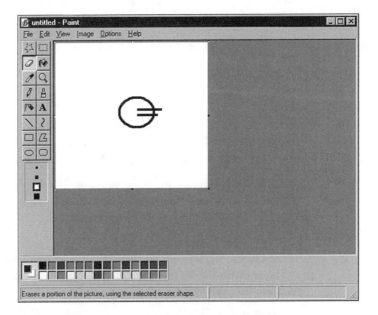

Figure 7.4 *The yourcompany.com logo created in Microsoft Paint.*

3. To save the image, select File, Save As. Be sure the image file type is set to some sort of BMP format. Typically, the best WBMP conversions result from BMPs with good resolution. Thus, you should try to save your BMP as a 16-color bitmap, a 256-color bitmap, or a 24-bit bitmap.

CONVERTING THE IMAGE INTO A WBMP FORMAT

Several options and tools are available to convert images into WBMP formats. See the section "Image Conversion Options," earlier in this chapter, for a review of the options. The example in this chapter uses the WAPPictus product to convert a logo into a WBMP format. Refer to the beginning of this chapter for information about downloading this product:

1. Be sure you have downloaded the WAPPictus program onto your computer.

2. From the Start menu, select Start, Programs, WAPPictus. The WAPPictus program executes.

3. Select the Open option from the menu bar. Then, select your image from the location where you saved it on your computer. The image displays in the WAPPictus window (see Figure 7.5).

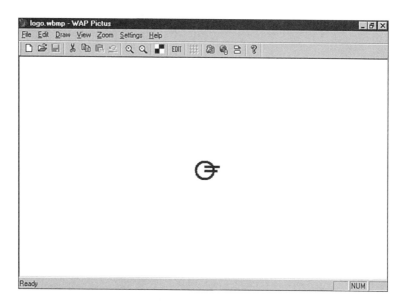

Figure 7.5   *The logo image open in the WAPPictus program.*

4. Select the Settings option on the menu bar, and select Advanced Settings to control the type of dithering and position of the image. You can also select the File, Save As to save it.

5. Name your file `logo`. Be sure the file type is WBMP. You should save this file in the same location as your wml files.

Now that you've created a logo and converted it into a WBMP format, let's try running the `title.wml` file. Figure 7.6 shows the results of the code from a device emulator.

Figure 7.6 *The `title.wml` file on a device screen.*

Creating an Application with Icons

Many browsers now include several embedded icons developers can use within their applications. In this example, you'll incorporate some of these icons into an application menu list.

They say that a picture is worth a thousand words. This is especially true in the case of WAP applications, where space for text is limited.

To use local icons of a browser, you use the `IMG` element. However, you also need to use the `localsrc` attribute.

NOTE

When using local icons within a WAP application, the `src` and `alt` attributes are still required.

To see local icons in action, let's modify the `select.wml` file first created in Chapter 6, "User Input with Variables." In this example, you'll add icons to the menu options.

Type the following changes, and resave this file as `menu.wml`. The bolded areas represent additional code added to this file. After you have made and saved your changes, run this code through a device emulator:

```
1 <?xml version="1.0"?>
2 <!DOCTYPE wml PUBLIC "-//PHONE.COM//DTD WML 1.1//EN"
3 "http://www.phone.com/DTD/wml_1.1.xml">

4 <wml>
5 <!-- Card 1 -->
```

```
6    <card id="menu" title="Menu">
7     <do type="accept" label="Go">
8     <go href="#deptinfo"/>
9     </do>
10      <p>Select a dept.:
11        <select name="dept" value="5" multiple="false">
12          <optgroup>
13            <option onpick="#deptinfo" value="Sales">
14              <img localsrc="briefcase" alt="Sales" src=""/>Sales</option>
15            <option onpick="#deptinfo" value="Mrkt">
16              <img localsrc="chart" alt="Mrkt" src=""/>Mrkt</option>
17            <option onpick="#deptinfo" value="Acct">
18              <img localsrc="dollar" alt="Acct" src=""/>Acct</option>
19            <option onpick="#deptinfo" value="Plant">
20              <img localsrc="factory" alt="Plant" src=""/>Plant</option>
21            <option onpick="#deptinfo" value="IT">
22              <img localsrc="floppy1" alt="IT" src=""/>IT</option>
23          </optgroup>
24        </select>
25      </p>
26    </card>

27 <!-- Card 2 -->
28    <card id="deptinfo" title="Dept Info">
29      <p>This is the $(dept) dept.</p>
30    </card>
31 </wml>
```

In this code, you've modified the options to contain local icons in addition to text. The modified options are bolded in this example and exist on lines 13–22. Although the options contain different local icons, the syntax used is the same for each.

The following is an explanation of the bolded areas of this code:

- Lines 1–3 require the use of the Openwave document prologue to use the icons included in their browser.

- Line 13 defines the option that displays in the main menu options list. If you recall from the last chapter, the OPTION element defines option lists.

  In this example, the OPTION element uses the onpick and value attributes. The onpick attribute specifies the URL to navigate after users select the option, whereas the value attribute defines a variable to the option.

Thus, if users select the option, the value is stored and displayed to them in the card deptinfo (which begins at line 28).

- Line 14 defines the local icon used with the option. In this example, the localsrc attributes define the icons. This example uses icons associated with the UP.Browser (refer to Figure 7.3).

To use icons associated with a browser, the localsrc attribute is set equal to the name of the icon. Developers must also include the alt and src attributes.

The alt attribute defines text used if the device is incapable of finding or displaying the image. Because the localsrc attribute already defines the source of the image, the src attribute is set equal to a blank value.

The rest of the options follow this same syntax. The only difference is that the localsrc attribute is set equal to different icons. Figure 7.7 displays this example on a device emulator.

NOTE

Remember, the localsrc attribute defines icons included with a browser. The src attribute, on the other hand, defines WBMP images that exist outside the browser.

Figure 7.7 *The application using local icons on a device emulator.*

Summary

In this chapter, you've learned to create and convert images for use with WAP applications. You're now ready to unleash the artist within. Who knows, maybe you'll become the Van Gogh or Rembrandt of the WAP world!

As you've learned in this chapter, images are important for several reasons: They enhance the look of applications, and they provide shortcuts and improve an application's usability.

In this chapter, you've learned about WBMP, the only type of image format supported by WML. You learned the limitations of this format and looked at the types of images that work as WBMPs. You also examined some of the software tools available for converting existing images into the WBMP format.

This chapter then introduced you to the IMG element and discussed how it enables WAP developers to incorporate WMBP images into their applications. Local icons (present in browsers) were also discussed, as was how to incorporate these icons into your WAP applications.

The next chapter covers incorporating functionality into the images and icons used in this chapter, by using timers to add animation to your images. You'll learn about the security aspects of timers, as well. In addition, at the end of the next chapter (which concludes Part II), you'll be ready to tackle some section exercises. These exercises allow you to practice some of the skills learned in the last couple of chapters.

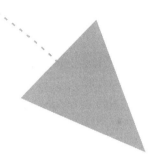

Incorporating Timers into WAP Applications

Chapter 7, "Working with Images," examined converting and incorporating images into WAP applications. This chapter takes images one step further by adding timer functionality. Timers are a useful tool in creating dynamic and animated applications that result in a better user experience.

Timers provide a means for applications to measure time intervals. Developers use timers to incorporate a variety of capabilities into an application. Timers provide the ability to incorporate functionality such as a flashing logo at the beginning of an application, interstitial banner ads, or a page that updates data on a real-time basis.

By the end of this chapter, you'll be familiar with the following concepts:

- The TIMER element, its attributes, and the various ways WAP applications use this element

- Incorporating timers to set time intervals for an application

- Using variables in timers so users can set time intervals

- Using timers to create animation effects within a WAP application

What Are Timers?

Without realizing it, you've probably used hundreds of software programs that contain timers. For example, one of the more widely used areas of timers is in title pages (better known as splash pages). Splash pages display a type of logo or title for a defined period of time. Splash pages then display the next screen after the time interval expires, all without any direct user involvement.

Another popular use for timers is applications that contain flashing messages. Advertisement blurbs also sometimes use timers. These applications display a text message or advertisement blurb for a moment and then change without any direct user involvement.

Real-time applications also use timer functionality. Applications that provide information such as weather forecasts, stock prices, currency rates, or movie times all use timers to update information at a regular interval.

Timers bring a variety of functions to applications. In the following pages, you'll look at incorporating some of the functionality described previously into your own WAP applications.

How Do Timers Work?

In the development world, timers provide some type of functionality after their time intervals expire.

For example, a developer might use a timer in an application that updates stock prices every 15 minutes. The application works in that it keeps track of time for 15 minutes. After a time interval of 15 minutes expires, the functionality of updating stock prices occurs.

The TIMER Element

The WML element that makes all this functionality possible is the TIMER element. You'll use the TIMER element throughout this chapter. Thus, it's important that you familiarize yourself with this element early.

The TIMER element is actually quite simple to use. This element contains only two attributes, both of which are required. Table 8.1 lists the attributes of this element.

*Table 8.1   The Attributes of the **TIMER** Element*

Attribute	Required	Description
name	No	Specifies the name of the variable to be set with the value of the timer. The variable named by the name attribute is set with the current timer value when the card is exited or the timer expires.
value	No	Specifies the default value of the variable named in the name attribute. This attribute sets the timeout period upon timer initialization.

Setting Time Intervals

When using the TIMER element, time units are 1/10 of a second. So, if the value attribute equals 100, the timer value signifies 10 seconds. Table 8.2 summarizes some of the most commonly used time intervals.

Table 8.2   Time Interval Conversion Table

Value	Time Interval
100	10 seconds
300	30 seconds
600	1 minute
900	1 minute and 30 seconds
1200	2 minutes
3000	5 minutes
6000	10 minutes
8200	15 minutes

NOTE

When using time intervals, you should avoid having long waits for pages to change. If you're creating a splash page or timed message, avoid making timers last longer than a 10-second interval.

One time interval value not listed above is 0. The value 0 is actually special in its use. Declaring a TIMER value equal to 0 specifies the time interval equals 0 seconds. When a time interval has a value of 0, the TIMER is disabled.

Adding Timer Functionality to a Splash Page

To get an idea of how the TIMER element works, type the following code, and save it as timer.wml. Then, run the code from a device-emulator. Figure 8.1 shows the results of this example on a device screen.

> **NOTE**
>
> This deck links to the `home.wml` file (created at the end of Chapter 5, "Navigation Using WML"). Be sure you save both of these files in the same directory (such as `C:\ My Documents`) so that the relative URL used in this example works.

```
1  <?xml version="1.0"?>
2  <!DOCTYPE wml PUBLIC "-//WAPFORUM//DTD WML 1.1//EN"
3  "http://www.wapforum.org/DTD/wml_1.1.xml">
4  <wml>
5    <card id="splash" title="Splash" ontimer="home.wml">
6      <timer name="splashlogo" value="50"/>
7        <p align="center">Yourcompany.com
8        <img src="logo.wbmp" alt="Yourcompany.com"/>
9        </p>
10   </card>
11 </wml>
```

Figure 8.1   *The `timer.wml` file on a device screen.*

The following is an explanation of this example:

- The fifth line begins the splash card. Notice that the `ontimer` attribute has been added to this CARD element. The `ontimer` attribute designates a link to follow after the time interval has expired. In this example, after the splash page expires, the application displays the `home.wml` file (created in Chapter 5).

> **NOTE**
>
> In the `timer.wml` example, an abbreviated form of the `ontimer` attribute was used. You could have also written the fifth line of code as follows:
>
> ```
> <card id="splash" title="Splash">
>    <onevent type="onevent">
>      <go href="#username">
>    </onevent>
> ```
>
> Both versions work the same—they both produce the same results. However, the first version is much more efficient. You can bind a GO task to an event using either syntax.

- The sixth line defines the TIMER element. In this example, the timer's name is `splashlogo`. You've defined this by setting the timer's name attribute equal to `splashlogo`.

In this line of code, the value attribute is set equal to 50. This means the splash page's timer expires after 5 seconds (or 50/10 of a second).

- The seventh line differs slightly from previous examples. We've added the align attribute to the P element and added text before the IMG code. This centers a text title above the image. In addition, the image is centered because it is part of the P element now.

NOTE

For the logo100.wbmp image to display, be sure this file is in the same location as the timer.wml and home.wml files.

Adding Timer Functionality to the Username Input

In addition to using timers to create splash pages, timers are also useful for creating additional content-sensitive areas of an application.

For example, in Chapter 6, "User Input with Variables," you created some WML decks that allowed users to input a username and password. In your code, you added some security to the password input page. If you recall, you used the following line of code to shroud the password input field:

```
<input name="password" type="password"/>
```

In this line of code, the password input uses a type attribute set to "password". Setting the type attribute to "password" shrouds all entered text with the asterisk character.

So, some security is in place for our password input. However, what about security for the username input? In Chapter 6, you did not add any type of security for the username input.

Let's look at adding security to the username input using timers. In this next example, you add functionality that allows the username card to display for only a limited time interval. If the username card exceeds the defined time interval, a message displays.

To begin, add the following changes to the username card of the input2.wml file (in Chapter 6). Then, save your changes as timer2.wml, and run it from a device-emulator. You incorporate this file into a larger application at the end of this chapter.

Figure 8.2 shows this file on a device screen.

NOTE

When running this application, try not entering any information in the username card. When you get to the username card, wait for a moment and see what happens.

```
1  <?xml version="1.0"?>
2  <!DOCTYPE wml PUBLIC "-//WAPFORUM//DTD WML 1.1//EN"
3  "http://www.wapforum.org/DTD/wml_1.1.xml">
4  <wml>

5  <!-- Card 1 -->
6    <card id="username" title="Username" ontimer="#message">
7      <timer name="nametime" value="50"/>
8        <do type="accept" label="Go">
9        <go href="#password"/>
10       </do>
11         <p>Enter username:
12         <input name="username" format="5a" type="text"/>
13         </p>
14     </card>

15 <!-- Card 2 -->
16   <card id="password" title="Password">
17     <do type="accept" label="Go">
18     <go href="#menu" />
19     </do>
20       <p>Enter password:
21       <input name="password" format="NN\-NNNN" type="password"/>
22       </p>
23     </card>

24 <!-- Card 3 -->
25   <card id="menu" title="Menu">
26     <p>Welcome, $(username)</p>
27     </card>

28 <!-- Card 4 -->
29   <card id="message" title="Message">
30     <do type="accept" label="Go">
31     <go href="home.wml"/>
32     </do>
33       <p>Expired input time limit. Login again?</p>
34     </card>
35 </wml>
```

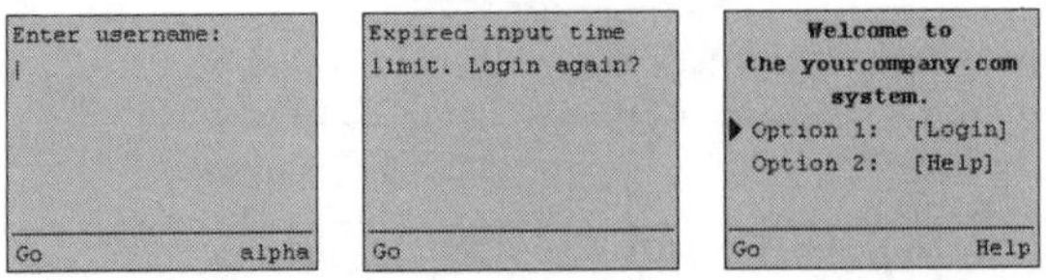

Figure 8.2 *The* timer2.wml *file on a device screen.*

The following is an explanation of this example:

- The sixth line begins the username card. Like the first example in this chapter, you've added the ontimer attribute to the CARD element. The ontimer attribute specifies the URL to link to after the TIMER value has expired. This line of code creates a timer that links to the message card. The message card is new and is added later in this code.

- The seventh line defines the TIMER element. The timer's name attribute is nametime.

  In this line of code, the timer has been set to a value of 50. Therefore, the username's timer expires after 5 seconds (or 50/10 of a second). After the timer expires, the application takes users to the message card.

- Lines 28–34 define the message card that displays if the timer in the username card expires. In this card, the following message displays:

  Expired input time limit. Login again?

Users can click the Accept button to return to the home.wml file.

On the username card, if users do not click the Accept button within five seconds, the application displays a message page.

Allowing Users to Set the Time Interval

One of the nice things about the TIMER element is that both the name and value attributes can use variables. This is especially useful in adding functionality where users determine the time interval for a timer.

Let's look at creating a card that uses variables that allow users to set the timer interval for a card. Type the following code into a text editor, and save the file as timer3.wml. You should read the explanations of the code on the following page before running this file through a WAP emulator. Figure 8.3 shows this file on a device screen:

```
1   <?xml version="1.0"?>
2   <!DOCTYPE wml PUBLIC "-//WAPFORUM//DTD WML 1.1//EN"
3   "http://www.wapforum.org/DTD/wml_1.1.xml">
4   <wml>
5   <!-- Card 1 -->
6      <card id="username" title="Username" ontimer="#message">
7        <timer name="nametime" value="$nametime"/>
8          <do type="accept" label="Go">
9          <go href="#password"/>
10         </do>
11           <p>
12           <anchor title="Go"><go href="#set"/>Settings</anchor><br/>
13           Enter username:
14           <input name="username" format="5a" type="text"/>
15           </p>
16       </card>

17   <!-- Card 2 -->
18       <card id="password" title="Password">
19         <do type="accept" label="Go">
20         <go href="#menu" />
21         </do>
22           <p>Enter password:
23           <input name="password" format="NN\-NNNN" type="password"/>
24           </p>
25         </card>

26   <!-- Card 3 -->
27       <card id="menu" title="Menu">
28         <p>Welcome, $(username)</p>
29       </card>

30   <!-- Card 4 -->
31       <card id="message" title="Message">
32         <do type="accept" label="Go">
33         <go href="home.wml"/>
34         </do>

35         <do type="option" label="Settings">
36         <go href="#set"/>
37         </do>
```

```
38        <p>Expired input time limit. Login again?</p>
39     </card>

40 <!-- Card 5 -->
41   <card id="set" title="Settings">
42     <do type="accept" label="Go">
43     <go href="#username"/>
44     </do>
45       <p>Set input time:
46       <input name="nametime" format="*N"/>
47       </p>
48   </card>

49 </wml>
```

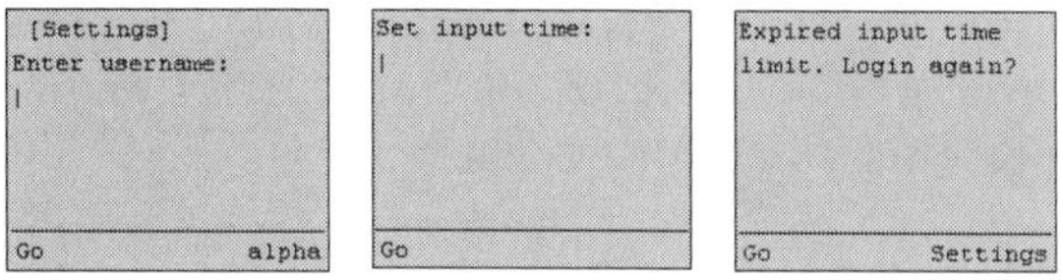

Figure 8.3   *The* timer3.wml *file on a device screen.*

The following is an explanation of this example:

- The seventh line adds a TIMER element to the username card. Notice that the value of this timer is set to $nametime. If you recall from Chapter 6, a dollar sign is used to reference variables.

  The variable nametime stores a user's inputted time interval. The data in the set card holds the value of the timer in the username card.

- The twelfth line uses the ANCHOR element to create a link (named Settings on the display). This text links to the set card. Thus, whenever users select the Settings link on their device screens, the application goes to the set card.

  As you'll see in a moment, this card enables users to define the amount of time allowed by the timer before it expires.

- Lines 35–37 use the DO element to create a link associated with the Option button in the message card. The Option button within this card now links users to the set card.

- Lines 40–47 define the set card. Notice in line 43 that the GO element returns users to the username card. Thus, after users input a time interval variable, they return to the username card. The time interval is defined using the INPUT element in line 46. Here the name attribute is set to nametime (the name of your variable). The format attribute is also included, forcing the user to enter any number.

NOTE

When running this application, try entering a number of different time intervals. Notice the difference in time of one second (a value of 10) in comparison with ten seconds (a value of 100).

Animation Using the TIMER Element

This chapter has discussed a number of ways timers create time intervals within applications. As you've seen, timers are useful in providing several functionalities to applications.

This chapter concludes with a look at using WMLScript in conjunction with timers to create simple animation effects.

The way animation works in this example is that images fire quickly one after another, giving the illusion of movement. This example creates some simple animation that you'll incorporate into a splash page.

Before you can begin, you first must create some additional images to use with this animation example. In this example, you'll create animation that causes the logo image created in the last chapter to grow and shrink.

Resizing an Image

This book uses the WAPPictus application (introduced in Chapter 7) in this example. However, you can use any graphic application that allows you to resize graphics. WAPPictus is a good application to use because you can use it to resize images and then convert them into the WBMP format. Although you can use other graphic programs, most do not directly support the WBMP format. With most other graphic programs, you must resize the images in a known graphical format, save all these images as separate graphics, and then convert each of the images.

The following example shows how to resize images using the WAPPictus program. To begin the resizing effort, do the following:

1. Start the WAPPictus program.

2. Open the logo.wbmp file created in Chapter 7.

3. From the toolbar, select Zoom, Resize, Percentage. A display box appears, asking you to Enter resize factor. Figure 8.4 shows an example of accessing the resizing tool from the WAPPictus application.

4. Create the following sizes, and save each one separately: 25%, 50%, 75%, and 125%. For each size, you'll need to reopen the original image and then save with as a new size.

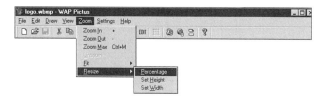

Figure 8.4 *The WAPPictus resizing functionality.*

NOTE

Be sure that each file has a different name. Name your files using the percentage in the name. For example, name your 25% image `logo25.wbmp`. Your filenames should be `logo25.wbmp`, `logo50.wbmp`, `logo75.wbmp`, and `logo125.wbmp`. `Logo100.wbmp` already exists because it was created in the last chapter.

Now that you've created the images for the animation, let's write the code. Type the following code, and save it as `timer4.wml`. Then, run this file from a device-emulator. Figure 8.5 shows this file on a device screen:

```
1   <?xml version="1.0"?>
2   <!DOCTYPE wml PUBLIC "-//WAPFORUM//DTD WML 1.1//EN"
3   "http://www.wapforum.org/DTD/wml_1.1.xml">
4   <wml>
5   <!-- Card 1 -->
6      <card id="splash25" title="Splash" ontimer="#splash50">
7        <timer name="splashlogo25" value="5"/>
8          <p align="center">
9          <img src="logo25.wbmp" alt=""/>
10          </p>
11     </card>

12 <!-- Card 2 -->
13     <card id="splash50" title="Splash" ontimer="#splash75">
14       <timer name="splashlogo50" value="5"/>
15         <p align="center">
16         <img src="logo50.wbmp" alt=""/>
17         </p>
18     </card>

19 <!-- Card 3 -->

20     <card id="splash75" title="Splash" ontimer="#splash100">
21       <timer name="splashlogo75" value="5"/>
22       <p align="center">
23       <img src="logo75.wbmp" alt=""/>
24       </p>
25     </card>
```

```
26 <!-- Card 4 -->
27   <card id="splash100" title="Splash" ontimer="#splash125">
28     <timer name="splashlogo100" value="5"/>
29       <p align="center">
30       <img src="logo.wbmp" alt=""/>
31       </p>
32     </card>

33 <!-- Card 5 -->
34   <card id="splash125" title="Splash" ontimer="timer.wml">
35     <timer name="splashlogo125" value="5"/>
36       <p align="center">
37       <img src="logo125.wbmp" alt=""/>
38       </p>
39     </card>

40 </wml>
```

NOTE

This code links to the `timer.wml` file created at the beginning of this chapter. Be sure that the `timer.wml` and `timer4.wml` files are saved within the same folder. If these files are not saved in the same folder, the relative URL used in this example (in line 29 of this code) will not work correctly.

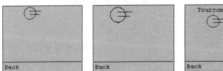

Figure 8.5 *The* `timer4.wml` *file on a device screen.*

The way this code works is that you've created five cards, each with a timer set to a value equal to 5 (which means 5/10 of a second, or one half second). Each timer contains an image, each one smaller than the previous image.

As each card's timer expires, the larger image displays, giving the animated illusion of the logo growing. Finally, in the last card of the `splash.wml` file, the `ontimer` attribute is set equal to the following location:

```
<card id="splash125" title="Splash" ontimer="timer">
```

This line of code states that after the timer expires, the next card to display is the `timer.wml` file (located in the same directory as the `timer4` file).

Summary

This chapter expanded on the use of images to see how incorporating timers enables developers to create dynamic splash pages. The various uses of timers within WAP applications were also covered, as was the fact that the concept of time is used widely throughout the development world.

This chapter examined several uses of timers, including the creation of splash pages and pages that display for only a limited time. This latter example is especially useful for pages that contain content-sensitive data.

This chapter concluded with a discussion of how to use timers to create simple animation effects within your applications. We have now covered all of the WML language, and you should feel comfortable and confident in your abilities.

In the coming chapters, you'll move on to more advanced areas of wireless development, first discussing incorporating WMLScript into applications. As you'll see, WMLScript is another programming language that will help improve the power and capabilities of your WAP applications greatly.

Part II Examples

The following code is a continuation of the application created at the end of Part I. In Part I, you created a file named home.wml. Here, you'll expand on that code, as well as additional files. All these new files incorporate information learned within Part II of this book.

As a final exercise to show just how far you've come, the following code incorporates all the information you've accumulated up to this point of this book. Remember to save all these files within the same directory (such as C:\My Documents). Then, run the splash.wml file first to start the application.

If you have any questions about any portion of this code, refer through Part II. Figure II.1 displays these files on a device screen.

splash.wml

This file acts as the first page of the application you're building. This file contains the same code as the timer4.wml file created at the end of Chapter 8:

```
<?xml version="1.0"?>
<!DOCTYPE wml PUBLIC "-//WAPFORUM//DTD WML 1.1//EN"
"http://www.wapforum.org/DTD/wml_1.1.xml">
<wml>

<!-- Card 1 -->
   <card id="splash25" title="Splash" ontimer="#splash50">
     <timer name="splashlogo25" value="5"/>
       <p align="center">
       <img src="logo25.wbmp" alt=""/>
       </p>
   </card>

<!-- Card 2 -->
   <card id="splash50" title="Splash" ontimer="#splash75">
     <timer name="splashlogo50" value="5"/>
       <p align="center">
       <img src="logo50.wbmp" alt=""/>
       </p>
   </card>

<!-- Card 3 -->

   <card id="splash75" title="Splash" ontimer="#splash100">
     <timer name="splashlogo75" value="5"/>
       <p align="center">
       <img src="logo75.wbmp" alt=""/>
       </p>
   </card>
```

```
<!-- Card 4 -->
  <card id="splash100" title="Splash" ontimer="#splash125">
    <timer name="splashlogo100" value="5"/>
      <p align="center">
      <img src="logo.wbmp" alt=""/>
      </p>
  </card>

<!-- Card 5 -->
  <card id="splash125" title="Splash" ontimer="timer.wml">
    <timer name="splashlogo125" value="5"/>
      <p align="center">
      <img src="logo125.wbmp" alt=""/>
      </p>
  </card>

</wml>
```

timer.wml

This file works with the splash.wml file and presents a title page for a couple of seconds before moving on to the home.wml file. This code was created at the beginning of Chapter 8:

```
<?xml version="1.0"?>
<!DOCTYPE wml PUBLIC "-//WAPFORUM//DTD WML 1.1//EN"
"http://www.wapforum.org/DTD/wml_1.1.xml">
<wml>
    <card id="splash" title="Splash" ontimer="home.wml">
      <timer name="splashlogo" value="50"/>
        <p align="center">Yourcompany.com
        <img src="logo.wbmp" alt="Yourcompany.com"/>
        </p>
    </card>
</wml>
```

home.wml

You first created this file at the end of Part I. This code is similar; however, you'll create a couple of changes. The changes are in the links—instead of linking to cards within the deck, you create links to decks that are outside the home.wml file. The changes are marked in bold:

```
<?xml version="1.0"?>
<!DOCTYPE wml PUBLIC "-//WAPFORUM//DTD WML 1.1//EN"
"http://www.wapforum.org/DTD/wml_1.1.xml">
<wml>
  <template>
    <do type="options" label="Help">
    <go href="#help"/>
```

```
        </do>

        <do type="accept" label="Home">
        <go href="#home"/>
        </do>
    </template>

<!-- Card 1 -->
    <card id="home" title="Home">
        <p align="center"><b>Welcome to the yourcompany.com system.</b>
        <table columns="2">
            <tr>
            <td>Option 1:</td>
                <td><anchor title="Go"><go href="login.wml"/>
                Login</anchor><br/></td>
            </tr>
            <tr>
            <td>Option 2:</td>
            <td><anchor title="Go"><go href="#help"/>Help</anchor><br/></td>
            </tr>
        </table>
        </p>
    </card>

<!-- Card 2 -->
    <card id="help" title="Help">
        <p>Please contact your system administrator at 800.555.1212</p>
    </card>
</wml>
```

login.wml

This file contains knowledge gained in Chapters 4, 5, 6, and 8. This file contains the same code as the `timer3.wml` file, created in Chapter 8. The only difference is that in the second card, you are setting the link to the `menu.wml` file:

```
<?xml version="1.0"?>
<!DOCTYPE wml PUBLIC "-//WAPFORUM//DTD WML 1.1//EN"
"http://www.wapforum.org/DTD/wml_1.1.xml">
<wml>
<!-- Card 1 -->
    <card id="username" title="Username" ontimer="#message">
        <timer name="nametime" value="$nametime"/>
        <do type="accept" label="Go">
        <go href="#password"/>
        </do>
            <p>
            <anchor title="Go"><go href="#set"/>Settings</anchor><br/>
            Enter username:
```

```
            <input name="username" format="5a" type="text"/>
            </p>
      </card>

<!-- Card 2 -->
      <card id="password" title="Password">
         <do type="accept" label="Go">
         <go href="menu.wml" />
         </do>
           <p>Enter password:
           <input name="password" format="NN\-NNNN" type="password"/>
           </p>
      </card>

<!-- Card 3 -->
      <card id="message" title="Message">
         <do type="accept" label="Go">
         <go href="home.wml"/>
         </do>

         <do type="option" label="Settings">
         <go href="#set"/>
         </do>

           <p>Expired input time limit. Login again?</p>
      </card>

<!-- Card 4 -->
      <card id="set" title="Settings">
         <do type="accept" label="Go">
         <go href="#username"/>
         </do>
           <p>Set input time:
           <input name="nametime" format="*N"/>
           </p>
        </card>

</wml>
```

menu.wml

This file contains the same code as the menu.wml file created at the end of Chapter 7. Remember, this file must use the Phone.com DTD to display the local icons correctly:

```
<?xml version="1.0"?>
<!DOCTYPE wml PUBLIC "-//PHONE.COM//DTD WML 1.1//EN"
"http://www.phone.com/DTD/wml_1.1.xml">
```

```wml
<wml>
<!-- Card 1 -->
  <card id="menu" title="Menu">
    <do type="accept" label="Go">
    <go href="#deptinfo"/>
    </do>
      <p>Select a dept.:
        <select name="dept" value="5" multiple="false">
          <optgroup>
            <option onpick="#deptinfo" value="Sales">
              <img localsrc="briefcase" alt="Sales" src=""/>Sales</option>
            <option onpick="#deptinfo" value="Mrkt">
              <img localsrc="chart" alt="Mrkt" src=""/>Mrkt</option>
            <option onpick="#deptinfo" value="Acct">
              <img localsrc="dollar" alt="Acct" src=""/>Acct</option>
            <option onpick="#deptinfo" value="Plant">
              <img localsrc="factory" alt="Plant" src=""/>Plant</option>
            <option onpick="#deptinfo" value="IT">
              <img localsrc="floppy1" alt="IT" src=""/>IT</option>
          </optgroup>
        </select>
      </p>
  </card>

<!-- Card 2 -->
  <card id="deptinfo" title="Dept Info">
    <p>This is the $(dept) dept.</p>
  </card>
</wml>
```

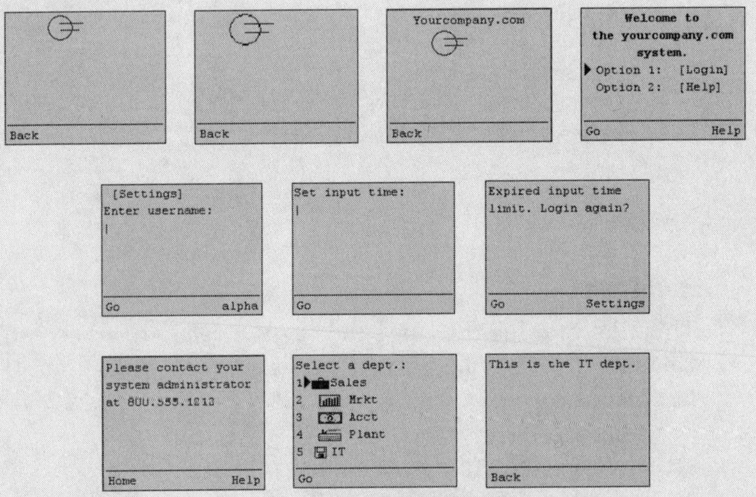

Figure II.1 *The Part II example on a device screen.*

Part III

Advanced WAP Development

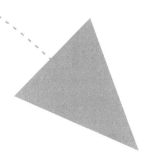

Introduction to WMLScript

In the previous chapters, you looked at the WML language and the functionality it provides developers. As you've seen, WML provides the capability to create static content and some simple user interaction. But what if you want to include some more dynamic functionality into your applications? The rest of this book looks at the choices WAP developers have for adding and manipulating data in their applications.

WML does not provide developers with the ability to manipulate data, such as to perform calculations. Except for the simplest of applications, WML alone does not provide the tools needed for incorporating dynamic functionality into your WAP development. To create the types of applications users want will probably require the use of another programming language in conjunction with WML.

Developers have two options when adding dynamic functionality to WAP application. They can add dynamic functionality on the *client side* (this is where the manipulation occurs on the device). Or, they can have the manipulation of data performed on the remote server—this known as *server-side* functionality. Server-side development is especially useful for applications that need to access data from a remote database (this topic is covered in Part IV, "Dynamic Wireless Development").

This chapter (as well as the other chapters in Part III, "Advanced WAP Development") covers using WMLScript to add dynamic functionality with client-side development. As you'll learn in this chapter, WMLScript is an object-oriented, procedural scripting language and is useful for complementing the functionality of WML.

Specifically, this chapter examines the following topics:

- What WMLScript is

- Why you should use WMLScript

- Referencing a WMLScript file

- Understanding WMLScript syntax for correct coding

- What WMLScript statements are and how they are used in a WMLScript file

Why Use WMLScript?

The introduction mentioned that WMLScript provides client-side functionality to WAP applications. Unlike other scripting languages, such as JavaScript, WMLScript is a language designed to specifically work on mobile devices.

WMLScript is a small, and somewhat limited, scripting language. The reasons for this are similar to WML—any language that works on a WAP device must be small to contend with the devices' low processing power and limited memories.

You might be wondering, "Why bother to do any data manipulation on the client then? Why not do all data manipulation at the server level, where more robust languages can be used, and where processing power and memory are not an issue?"

Obviously, server-side scripting cannot (and should not) be avoided—the real reward of WAP applications is to be able to access the same information that is available to a PC. The goal of any WAP development is to allow users to become truly mobile, accessing information anywhere and anytime, whether they're using a mobile device or a PC.

WAP applications do not have the luxury of seemingly unlimited bandwidth, like most PCs. Each time a WAP application requests information from a server, the user must contend with slow processing times and greater load on the device and battery life. Couple these factors with the inherent latency in mobile networks today (caused by the technical level of equipment, as well as frequency spectrum limitations), and you have a challenging development environment.

To deal with such a development environment, you'll find the use of WMLScript beneficial in eliminating unnecessary trips over networks. WMLScript offers a wonderful opportunity to remove some of the overload occurring in mobile networks.

What Is WMLScript?

WMLScript is a scripting language based on ECMAScript—also known as ECMA-262. ECMAScript was created by the European Computer Manufacturer's Association and uses many of the elements of JavaScript 1.1.

JavaScript is currently one of the most popular languages used in Internet technologies. Thus, by learning WMLScript, you'll also begin familiarizing yourself with many of the elements of JavaScript as well.

If you're familiar with JavaScript, you already know 90% of WMLScript. In fact, WMLScript is essentially a modified JavaScript whose purpose is to handle low-bandwidth communication and thin clients. Many of the programming concepts found in WMLScript, such as declaring variables and using operators and functions, are found in a number of other programming languages, including JavaScript. If you're familiar with programming languages, you might want to simply review this chapter. You also can read Appendix B, "WMLScript Reference," which summarizes the WMLScript information found in Part III.

NOTE

Before you look at how WMLScript works, your development environment must be set up to support WMLScript MIME types. See Chapter 2, "Tools of the Trade," to determine how to add WMLScript MIME types to your development environment.

How WMLScript Works

The first thing to keep in mind when dealing with WMLScript is that WMLScript files are not embedded within the WML deck. They are always located in a file separate from the parent WML document.

To understand this concept, let's look at the model of the wired Internet and how an HTML page that uses JavaScript looks. In an HTML page that uses JavaScript, the JavaScript code is embedded within the document. Figure 9.1 shows the structure of an HTML page (a Web page) with some additional functionality (created with JavaScript). This type of file would have the following type of structure.

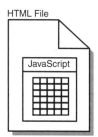

Figure 9.1   *The structure of an HTML page with JavaScript functionality.*

If you were creating an HTML page with JavaScript, you'd have a file with the .html extension only. This .html file would contain the JavaScript code inside the document.

In comparison, WMLScript is not embedded within WML. With an application that uses WML and WMLScript, two files are stored separately. The two files use the .wml and .wmls extensions; the .wml extension represents the WML file. The .wmls extension represents the WMLScript file.

The way WML and WMLScript work together is as follows: The WML file accesses the WMLScript file via a hyperlink. After accessed, the WMLScript file performs some sort of functionality and then sends the results to the device. Figure 9.2 shows the structure of a WAP application that uses a WML and WMLScript.

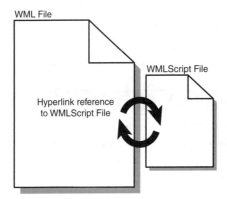

WML File

WMLScript File

Hyperlink reference
to WMLScript File

Figure 9.2 *The structure of a WML page with WMLScript functionality.*

Referencing a WMLScript File

WMLScript manipulates data through functions. Functions are discussed more in Chapter 10, "Variables and Functions." In addition, Chapter 12, "Working with WMLScript Libraries," contains a WMLScript library of pre-existing functions located within the language that you can use.

A *function* is a process or action. Say you wanted to create some kind of functionality that checked whether the user entered enough characters in a field. The steps required to do this are all considered a function.

As previously stated, a WML file references a WMLScript file using a hyperlink. This hyperlink must contain two pieces of information:

- The name of the WMLScript file.

- The name of the WMLScript function. This function must be preceded by the hash mark character (#).

To get an idea of how WML references a WMLScript file, let's look at an example. The following is the `login.wml` file, created at the end of Part II, "Static Wireless Development." There is a slight change in the code, which is marked in bold.

Type the changes to this code, and then save it again as `login.wml`:

```
1   <?xml version="1.0"?>
2   <!DOCTYPE wml PUBLIC "-//WAPFORUM//DTD WML 1.1//EN"
3   "http://www.wapforum.org/DTD/wml_1.1.xml">
4   <wml>
5   <!-- Card 1 -->
6       <card id="username" title="Username" ontimer="#message">
7         <timer name="nametime" value="$nametime"/>
8           <do type="accept" label="Go">
9           <go href="#password"/>
10          </do>
11            <p>
12            <anchor title="Go"><go href="#set"/>Settings</anchor><br/>
13            Enter username:
14            <input name="username" format="5a" type="text"/>
15            </p>
16      </card>

17  <!-- Card 2 -->
18      <card id="password" title="Password">
19        <do type="accept" label="Go">
20        <go href="validate.wmls#checkpass()" />
21        </do>
22          <p>Enter password:
23          <input name="password" type="password"/>
24          </p>
25      </card>
26  <!-- Card 3 -->
27      <card id="message" title="Message">
28        <do type="accept" label="Go">
29        <go href="home.wml"/>
30        </do>

31        <do type="option" label="Settings">
32        <go href="#set"/>
33        </do>

34          <p>Expired input time limit. Login again?</p>
35      </card>

36  <!-- Card 4 -->
37      <card id="set" title="Settings">
```

```
38        <do type="accept" label="Go">
39        <go href="#username"/>
40        </do>
41          <p>Set input time:
42          <input name="nametime" format="*N"/>
43          </p>
44      </card>

45 <!-- Card 5 -->
46      <card id="badpass" title="Error">
47        <do type="accept" label="Go">
48        <go href="home.wml"/>
49        </do>
50          <p>Your password must be 6 digits. Login again?</p>
51      </card>

52 </wml>
```

The following is an explanation of the bolded changes within this code:

- Notice that line 20 contains the following hyperlink:

```
<go href="validate.wmls#checkpass( )"/>
```

This hyperlink uses the WML GO task to reference a file named validate.wmls (which you'll create in a moment). This file represents a WMLScript file, specifically the WMLScript file that holds the additional functionality for this application. For this link to work, you must save the validate.wmls file in the same directory as this login.wml file.

- Line 23 removes the format attribute. The reason for this is that you'll create a check within the validate.wmls file to determine whether the user's input is in a correct format.

- Lines 45–51 create a new card, which essentially displays a message if the user's password is found (by the validate.wmls file) to be in an incorrect format. If the password is in an incorrect format, the user has the option to return to the home.wml file to log in again.

NOTE

The rules for using hyperlinks to reference a WMLScript function are the same as using hyperlinks to reference cards or images in a WML file. See Chapter 5, "Navigation Using WML," for more information.

The function referred to is named checkpass(). Notice the hash character before this function. The parentheses following this function are places where the function can hold arguments—don't worry about these for now; arguments of functions are covered in Chapter 10.

Now that you've gotten an idea of how to reference a WMLScript file, let's dig in further and write the code for the WMLScript file to which this WML is referring. Type the following code, and name this file `validate.wmls`. Again, be sure to save the file in the same location as the `login.wml` file.

TIP

If you find that your text editor (such as Notepad) is adding the extension .txt after your files, try using your Windows Explorer to access the file. Right-click the file, and select Rename from the drop-down list. Then, you can correctly rename the file with the correct extension.

```
1   extern function checkpass()
2   {
3       var password = WMLBrowser.getVar("password");

4       if (String.length(password) != 6)
5       {
6           WMLBrowser.go("login.wml#badpass");
7       }
8       else if (String.length(password) == 6)
9       {
10          WMLBrowser.go("menu.wml#menu");
11      }

12  };
```

Notice that the bold area of the code is the name of the function being calling from the WML file. Although this WMLScript file contains only one function, in actuality, a WMLScript file can contain several functions.

Figure 9.3 shows the results of these files on a device screen. At this point, don't worry too much about how the WMLScript code works—you'll learn about these elements in the next couple of chapters.

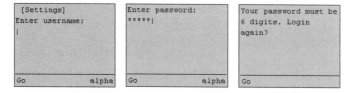

Figure 9.3   *WML file using WMLScript.*

This example has created an application that uses input fields that have a required format but do not force the user to enter that format. This type of functionality is good in that it prevents a user from sending an invalid format of data to the server for verification. Sending information to a server takes time; thus, you'll want to help your users ensure that the information is in a correct format when they send it remotely.

NOTE

Earlier versions of the Openwave emulator do not provide an easy means for debugging your WMLScript. You might want to try the Nokia SDK, which provides some useful messages for debugging WMLScript.

Also, if you are debugging your application, be sure to clear the cache before attempting to run any files again. Sometimes, emulators use files stored in their histories rather than calling a new file. Most emulators contain a Clear Cache option you can access from the device-emulator's title bar.

Familiarizing Yourself with WMLScript Syntax

Now that you've seen a preview of what WMLScript can do and how to reference WMLScript from a WML file, let's backtrack a moment and look at the syntax of the WMLScript language.

WMLSCRIPT SYNTAX

If you recall from Chapter 3, "The Wireless Markup Language (WML)," syntax is nothing more than the required structure of a programming language. For a programming language's code to work correctly, it must first be in a required format. All languages, whether they're spoken languages or programming languages, require structure.

Think about some of the syntax rules of the English language—a period or some other punctuation mark must always end a sentence, a capital letter must always begin a sentence, a sentence must contain a noun and a verb, and so on. Programming languages are no different. Languages require structure to convey information.

Case Sensitivity

WMLScript (similar to WML) is a case-sensitive language, meaning that it interprets upper- and lowercase characters as different characters. This is especially critical when declaring functions or variables, as you'll see in the next chapter. For example, in the WMLScript code previously presented in this chapter, the first line of code reads

```
extern function checkpass( )
```

The function name declared earlier in this chapter is checkpass. However, notice the following variations of the function's name. All these names differ because of case-sensitivity:

- CHECKPASS

- Checkpass

- checkpass

Case-sensitivity is important. Say that somewhere in your code you reference a variable. However, in your reference you've typed the variable's
name differently from the way the function was declared. The result is that
you'll receive an error message. The following example demonstrates this
scenario using the previous WML example and a modified version of the
WMLScript example:

```
extern function checkpass()
  {
  var password = WMLBrowser.getVar("password");

    if (String.length(Password) != 6)
  {
      WMLBrowser.go("login.wml#badpass");
  }
    else if (String.length(PASSWORD) == 6)
  {
      WMLBrowser.go("menu.wml#menu");
  }

};
```

Notice the bold areas of the code—they represent variables. The variables
`password`, `Password`, and `PASSWORD` differ because of case-sensitivity.

Along the same lines, when naming different variables, be sure that the
names differ by more than simply case. Differentiating variables by case
only is not a good design practice because it makes debugging efforts more
difficult.

Figure 9.4 shows the results of using this WMLScript file with the
`login.wml` file created earlier in this chapter.

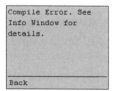

Figure 9.4 *Result of running the incorrect WMLScript.*

White Space

Similar to WML (as well as a number of other languages, such as HTML
and JavaScript), WMLScript ignores white space. The term *white space*
refers to things such as spaces, tabs, and new lines that appear within
code.

It's usually a good idea to incorporate white space into your applications. Doing so improves the readability of your code. For example, the following examples look very different; however, both produce the same results. Listing 9.1 does not use any white space, whereas Listing 9.2 does. Take a look at both—which would you rather read through if you were required to debug them?

Listing 9.1   WMLScript Without White Space

```
extern function checkpass(){var password = WMLBrowser.getVar("password");
➥if (String.length(password) != 6){WMLBrowser.go("login.wml#badpass");}
➥else if (String.length(password) == 6){WMLBrowser.go("menu.wml#menu");}};

};
```

Listing 9.2   WMLScript with White Space

```
extern function checkpass()
  {
  var password = WMLBrowser.getVar("password");

    if (String.length(password) != 6)
    {
        WMLBrowser.go("login.wml#badpass");
    }
    else if (String.length(password) == 6)
    {
        WMLBrowser.go("menu.wml#menu");
    }
};
```

Both Listing 9.1 and Listing 9.2 produce the same result. However, the second WMLScript code (the code that uses white space) is much easier to read. It's usually a good idea to include white space in programming code. Not only will the code be easier for you to read and debug if necessary, but it will also allow other developers to read and understand your code.

NOTE

Because of the rules of white spacing, statements can occur on a single line or be stretched across several lines before ending with a semicolon.

Adding Comments

WMLScript provides the capability to add comments to the code. *Comments* are additional text messages that developers can include within the WMLScript but that are ignored by the application when the code executes.

Comments are not part of the WMLScript syntax or an element of the code; they are a means for developers to provide notes within a code and are especially useful for explaining a code's functionality.

Two types of comments forms are available within WMLScript:

- Comments using /*
- Comments using //

THE /* CHARACTERS

The /*...*/ characters can be used to enter comments into a WMLScript. This comment syntax is similar to that found in the C programming language.

When using the /*...*/ characters, you must start the comment with the /* character. You then can type in your comments on as many lines as you want. When you're finished with your comments, the comment must end with the */ characters. Listings 9.3 and 9.4 contain examples of comments using the /* characters. These comments are acceptable within WMLScript code.

Listing 9.3 WMLScript with Comments on One Line (Using /*)

```
  extern function checkpass()


/*This code presents conditions on the password variable*/

    {
    var password = WMLBrowser.getVar("password");
      if (String.length(password) != 6)
    {
        WMLBrowser.go("login.wml#badpass");
    }
      else if (String.length(password) == 6)
    {
        WMLBrowser.go("menu.wml#menu");
    }

  };
```

Listing 9.4 WMLScript with Comments on Multiple Lines (Using */)

```
  extern function checkpass()


/*This code grabs the
variables from the
lgoin.wml file*/
```

```
     {
     var password = WMLBrowser.getVar("password");
       if (String.length(password) != 6)
     {
          WMLBrowser.go("login.wml#badpass");
     }
       else if (String.length(password) == 6)
     {
          WMLBrowser.go("menu.wml#menu");
     }

};
```

NOTE

Another beneficial aspect of comments is to using them when testing your code. If you don't want to delete a line of code but want to test a particular line, use the comment characters to remove the line temporarily. This is sometimes referred to as *commenting out* a line of code. To restore the code, simply remove the comment characters.

Semicolons

WMLScript, like JavaScript, requires the use of semicolons at the end of all statements. Statements are the lines of code that direct a computer to perform some specified action. You'll get more into what statements are in a moment. For now, think of them as sentences—instructional sentences. Using this metaphor, think of semicolons as the periods at the ends of these sentences.

Semicolons separate one statement from another statement. The WMLScript code we wrote previously in this chapter was all one large statement. Semicolons are required after each statement.

When reading WMLScript code, a good way to find the statements is to look for the semicolons and then backtrack from there. The following code presents some WMLScript code, with notes designating where the end of statements occur:

```
extern function checkpass()

     {
     var password = WMLBrowser.getVar("password");

/*The semicolon in the previous line ends one statement*/

       if (String.length(password) != 6)
     {
          WMLBrowser.go("login.wml#badpass");
```

```
/*The semicolon in the previous line ends another statement*/

  }
    else if (String.length(password) == 6)
  {
      WMLBrowser.go("menu.wml#menu");

/*The semicolon in the previous line ends yet another statement*/

  }

};
```

```
/*The semicolon at the end of this code ends the statement that contains
➥multiple statements*/
```

Using Statements Within Your WMLScript

Now that we've looked at the syntax necessary to write valid WMLScript code, let's focus on the language itself. The first concept to discuss is statements. Statements make up the set of commands executed in WMLScript, and these commands provide the functionality to an application.

A *statement* is a set of functions or variables that evaluates to a single value. This value can be a number, string, or logical value. You'll look at functions and variables in more detail in Chapter 10. For now, here's a quick summary:

- **Functions**—Some type of action the code provides. Functions can be procedure code written by a developer or a built-in library.

- **Variables**—A value provided either by the user or the developer. If the developer provides the variable, the value is coded into the WMLScript and is said to be a literal value.

A number of statements are often nested within a larger statement. Each statement is evaluated until one single value is provided. This value is then used by the application to perform some procedure.

WMLScript contains a few types of statements. The following sections summarize the available statements. You learn more about most of them as you progress through the next couple of chapters. The statements are

- Expression
- Block
- if

- while

- for

- break

- Variables

Expression

An expression is used in all WMLScript operations that perform some type of calculation. These statements are discussed in Chapter 11, "Using Standard Libraries":

```
var message = message + "The password must be 6 digits."
```

Block

Here's a block statement that is enclosed by curly brackets { }:

```
{WMLBrowser.go("login.wml#badpass");}
```

if

An if statement enables you to conditionally perform one of two operations. These statements use a Boolean (true or false) data type to determine the value of the condition:

```
if String.length(password == 6)
```

while

A while statement performs the action of a statement as long as an expression remains true:

```
while (x > 10)
{
some sort of action
}
```

for

This statement enables users to use up to three optional statements. In most cases, all three statements are used and work in the following manner:

- The first statement initializes a variable.

- The second statement executes the third statement as long as it is true.

- The third statement performs some type of operation.

```
for (var a = 0, a > 10)
{x +=1;
some sort of action
}
```

break

A break statement ends the while or for loop. This statement then executes statements following the ended loop:

```
while (x > 10)
{
some sort of action
if (10==x)
break;
}
```

Variables

These statements declare variables. All variables within WMLScript files must be declared before they can be used. Variables can be declared within or outside of a block statement:

```
var password =
WMLBrowser.getVar("password");
```

For example, let's look at the WMLScript written earlier in the chapter. You might not have realized it, but the WMLScript you wrote actually contains four statements:

```
extern function checkpass()

  {
  var password = WMLBrowser.getVar("password");
    if (String.length(password) != 6)
  {
      WMLBrowser.go("login.wml#badpass");
  }
    else if (String.length(password) == 6)
  {
      WMLBrowser.go("menu.wml#menu");
  }
};
```

An Explanation of Statement One

In the previous example, statement one is as follows:

```
var password = WMLBrowser.getVar("password");
```

This statement declares a variable named password and uses one of the WMLScript libraries (a built-in function). Built-in functions aren't covered until Chapter 12, but for clarity, let's summarize what this function states.

WMLBrowser.getVar is a function from the WMLBrowser library. This function tells the application to grab a variable from the WML file from which the WMLScript was called. The name of the variable to grab is considered an argument of the function—arguments are additional pieces of information used by a function. In this case, the variable is the password variable pulled from the login.wml file.

Thus, this variable equals a function. This function gets the value of the user's inputted password from the login.wml file, so you can use that information within this WMLScript file.

An Explanation of Statement Two

In the previous example, statement two is as follows:

```
{
        WMLBrowser.go("login.wml#badpass");
}
```

This statement also uses a function from the WMLBrowser library—specifically, the WMLBrowser.go function. This function tells the application to return to some other location. Again, this function uses an argument. In this statement, the location is the argument information used by the function. The badpass card of the login.wml file is the location used within this function's argument.

Notice that this statement ends with a semicolon and is contained within two curly brackets. A statement contained within curly brackets is considered a block statement.

An Explanation of Statement Three

In the previous example, statement three is as follows:

```
{
        WMLBrowser.go("menu.wml#menu");
}
```

This statement is similar to statement two. This statement uses the same built-in function as statement two—the WMLBrowser.go function. This function tells the application to return to some other location; the location is the function's argument. In statement three, the location is the menu card of the menu.wml file.

Again, because this statement is contained in parentheses, it is a block statement.

An Explanation of Statement Four

In the previous example, statement four is as follows:

```
{
var password = WMLBrowser.getVar("password");
  if (String.length(password) != 6)
{
    WMLBrowser.go("login.wml#badpass");
}
  else if (String.length(password) == 6)
{
    WMLBrowser.go("menu.wml#menu");
}
```

This statement encompasses statements one, two, and three.

You'll find in your development that statements are usually grouped together to work as a whole. To do this, you often must create an overall statement that contains smaller statements.

One type of statement frequently used to combine a number of statements is the if statement. In this example, statement four is an if statement that combines statements 1, 2, and 3. The if statement is actually made up of two clauses: the if clause and the else if clause. Because if statements are one of the more frequently used statements in all types of development, it's important to have an understanding of how they work. The following sections discuss in a little more detail the various clauses of the if statement.

THE IF CLAUSE

In the validate.wmls code, the if statement contains two clauses. A *clause* is a type of provision in a statement. The if clause in the validate.wmls file states

```
if (String.length(password) != 6)
```

It then is followed by statement one:

```
{
        WMLBrowser.go("login.wml#badpass");
}
```

The first if clause uses yet another built-in function—this one is called String.length. This function states the following:

The string (character) length of the password variable is != 6.

The != 6 characters represents an operator (see Chapter 11 for more information). Operators are used to perform some type of mathematical or comparative operation. The characters != stand for "not equal." Thus, this if clause states

> If the length of the password variable is "not equal" to 6 characters, then go to the badpass card of the login.wml file (statement two).

THE ELSE IF CLAUSE

An if statement also contains an else if clause, which performs a comparison. The else if clause in the validate.wmls files states

```
if (String.length(password) == 6)
```

It's then followed by statement three:

```
{
        WMLBrowser.go("menu#menu");
}
```

Like the if clause, this else if clause also uses the String.length function. This function states

> The string (character) length of the password variable is == 6.

The ==6 characters represent an operator that stands for equal. Thus, this else if clause says

> If the length of the password variable "is equal" to 6 characters, then go to the menu card of the menu.wml file (statement two).

Opening and Closing Brackets

Looking at all the code on the previous pages, you've probably noticed two types of brackets used: curly ({ }) and parentheses (( )). Let's take a moment to look at the different brackets used within WMLScript and their purposes.

CURLY BRACKETS

Curly brackets are used to contain WMLScript statements. Any statement enclosed by curly brackets is considered a block statement. A block statement can contain single statements (as is the case with the second and third statements in the previous example). A block statement can also contain multiple statements (as is the case with the fourth statement in the previous example). All statements, whether they are single or multiple, must use opening and closing brackets.

The following code represents a block statement. Notice how this code uses curly brackets:

```
{
        WMLBrowser.go("login.wml#badpass");
}
```

PARENTHESES

Parentheses are used to contain a function's arguments. Functions perform some sort of action and can be procedure code written by a developer or a built-in library. Here's an example:

```
if (String.length(password) == 6)
```

A function's arguments can also be left blank. For example, at the beginning of the WMLScript code, the following function is used:

```
extern function checkpass( )
```

In this function, there is no need to include any argument information; the function simply acts as a reference. This function is referenced from the WML file, and because it provides no actual functionality except as a reference, we can leave the arguments blank.

SQUARE BRACKETS

Although we haven't used any in the examples in this chapter, square brackets ([ ])are used with operators to create computational formulas. Here's an example of an operator that uses square brackets:

```
var calc = [3+2] + 7
```

Summary

In this chapter, you've begun to look at WMLScript as a means of adding client-side functionality to our WAP applications. The chapter began by examining WMLScript, where it came from, and the advantages of using this scripting language in wireless development. You then learned about some of the advantages of using WMLScript to provide additional functionality, such as performing validation checks on user input.

This chapter then looked at how you reference a WMLScript file from a WML file and how this methodology differs from other scripting languages. Next, we examined the WMLScript syntax and how to correctly produce accurate code in a valid format.

This chapter concluded with an introduction to the various statements available within WMLScript. In the next couple of chapters, you'll examine these more closely, learning to use WMLScript to further expand the possibilities of your WAP applications.

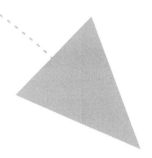

Variables and Functions

You should be proud of how far you've come in learning WAP development. By now, you've explored most of WML, incorporating such advanced functionality as variables and even animation into your applications. And as if all this wasn't enough, the last chapter saw you introducing a whole new level of flexibility to your efforts. You must be an overachiever!

In this chapter, you'll further expand on your knowledge, learning to incorporate functions and variables into your scripting code. After reading this chapter, you'll know how to control and use data that flows through both your WML and WMLScript files.

In this chapter, you'll learn about functions, which are the building blocks of a WAP application. Functions specify the tasks to perform within an application. As you'll learn, you can program your own functions or use built-in functions provided in the WMLScript specification.

In this chapter, you'll also look at pragmas, a new area of WMLScript that enables developers to control how content compiles. This area is unique to WMLScript and can give some indication of future specification for other scripting languages.

Specifically, this chapter discusses the following:

- The data values WMLScript recognizes

- Naming conventions necessary for declaring variables and functions

- What variables and functions are and how they work in WMLScript

- How to use variables, functions, and pragmas in WMLScript

Dissecting a WAP Application

In WAP development, you've learned that additional languages can add real power and excitement to your applications. Consider the possibilities of WMLScript, which you began looking at in Chapter 9, "Introduction to WMLScript."

The way WMLScript adds functionality is through the use of programming constructs, such as variables, functions, and pragmas. You'll learn about these constructs within this chapter. Figure 10.1 shows a graphical representation of the structure of a WAP application, coupled with the power of WMLScript.

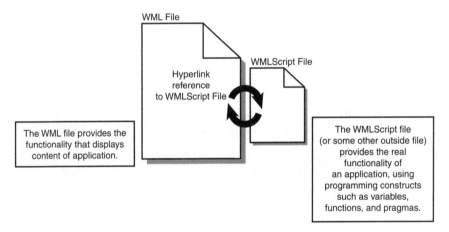

Figure 10.1 *The structure of a WAP application.*

You'll look at functions, variables, and pragmas in more detail later in this chapter. For now, here's a quick summary:

- **Functions**—Some sort of action the code provides. Functions can be procedure code written by a developer or a built-in library.

- **Variables**—Provide a temporary storage area in an application. This storage area holds information, usually information inputted into the program by a user.

- **Pragmas**—Provide functionality that controls how code is interpreted, as well as how WMLScript is handled by the content server.

Figure 10.2 shows the structure of a WAP application, with a detailed look at the parts of the WMLScript file.

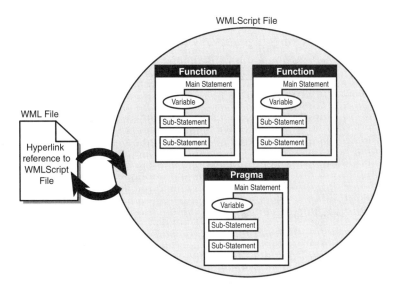

Figure 10.2 *The detail behind a WMLScript file.*

Before getting down and dirty with any of these programming constructs, you first need to know a couple of ground rules—mainly, how to name these constructs and the types of data these constructs can and can't use. With that said, let's look at some brief background information before exploring these programming constructs further.

Naming Conventions for Programming Constructs

When you're naming programming constructs (such as variables or functions), you must follow a couple of rules in the name structure:

- The variable or function identifier can't be a reserved word (see the section "Reserved Words," later in this chapter for more information).

- The identifier can't contain any blank spaces.

- The identifier's first character can only be a letter of the alphabet (either upper- or lowercase), a number, or an underscore.

These rules are similar to those found in Chapter 6, "User Input with Variables," in which you learned about naming variables in WML. These aren't difficult to learn, but they are important. Remember, an incorrect programming construct name will result in errors in your applications.

Reserved Words

Several keywords are used by the WMLScript language. These keywords are called *reserved words*. Reserved words can't be used when declaring programming constructs. The following list contains words that are reserved by WMLScript:

access	div=	header	private	use
agent	do	http	public	user
break	domain	if	return	var
case	else	import	sizeof	void
continue	enum	in	struct	while
catch	equiv	isvalid	super	with
class	export	lib	switch	
const	extends	meta	this	
debugger	extern	name	throw	
default	finally	new	try	
delete	for	null	typeof	
div	function	path	url	

NOTE

Some of these constructs are not yet functional in the current specifications of WMLScript, but they have been set aside as reserved words for possible future enhancements.

WMLScript Data

The topic of values and data was discussed briefly in Chapter 6. Let's return to this topic for a moment, as you look at how it comes into effect with WMLScript.

Data is simply information, such as a user's first and last names, address, phone number, stock quote, bank account number, and so on. Typically, the purpose of an application is to access and use this data for a particular purpose.

Data comes in many shapes and sizes. Some data is made up of numbers; other data is text. And then there's data that's a true or false value. In a sense, one could say that there are different data values.

If you recall from Chapter 6, WML recognizes only string values. Sure, a user can input numbers into a device, but WML will treat this as text. Everything that is a string is text. Thus, in WML, strings cannot perform numerical calculations.

In comparison, WMLScript offers a little more variety in the available data types. Table 10.1 shows the data types available in WMLScript.

Table 10.1   Data Types Available in WMLScript

Data Type	Description	Examples
Boolean	Values represented by either true or false. These values are case sensitive.	`true` `false`

Float	A number in the IEEE single-precision format in the range of 3.40282347E+38–1.17549435E-38. These numbers can contain a decimal point and an exponent part. Note, not all WMLScript interpreters support floating-point numbers.	`.32`
		`100e5`
		`.55E+15`

Integer	A whole number in the range of -2147483648–2147483647. Integers can include octal (numbers that start with 0), decimals (numbers that start with a nonzerodigit), or hexadecimal values (numbers that start with the sequence 0x).	`1992`
		`013422`
		`0x31e5`

Invalid	Represents values that aren't any of the previous data types. This value is usually used in error conditions.	5/0 (cannot divide by 0) 3/(2/0) (cannot divide 0)
String	Any combination of characters, including numbers, text, or symbols. Either single or double quotation marks can enclose strings.	`"This is an acceptable string."` `'This is also an acceptable string.'`

The list of data types in Table 10.1 might seem somewhat small, especially if you're coming from languages such as Visual Basic, Java, or C++. However, you'll find this small set of data types more than sufficient to meet the needs of your application development efforts.

Data Types in Action

To get an idea of how data types work within WMLScript, let's look at the WMLScript code you created in Chapter 9. You saved this code as `validate.wmls`:

```
extern function checkpass()

  {
  var password = WMLBrowser.getVar("password");

/*The semicolon in the previous line ends one statement*/

    if (String.length(password) != 6)
  {
      WMLBrowser.go("login.wml#badpass");

/*The semicolon in the previous line ends another statement*/

  }
    else if (String.length(password) == 6)
  {
      WMLBrowser.go("menu.wml#menu");

/*The semicolon in the previous line ends yet another statement*/

  }

};

/*The semicolon at the end of this code ends the statement that contains
➥multiple statements*/
```

This code has several statements, contained within two clauses (the `if` clause and `else if` clause). Both of these clauses evaluate to a single value (either `true` or `false`). This value determines what action the overall statement should perform (go to the `badpass` card or the `menu` deck). After the value is determined and an action performed, the value is discarded. The value only provides information in order for the application to provide functionality.

The data type these statements evaluate to are `true` or `false` values—better known as the Boolean data type. In addition to Boolean, WMLScript can use any of the data types in Table 10.1 to incorporate functionality into your applications.

Now that you have an idea of how data types guide the behavior of an application, let's move on to variables and functions—the real building blocks of a WAP application.

Using Variables in WMLScript

Chapter 6 discussed the concept of variables and how they are essentially areas within applications where you can store user-inputted data.

Variables are an important part of any type of programming because they enable developers to write flexible code. Variables represent data and provide a temporary storage area for data.

In other words, when an application is used, variables are replaced with real data. This enables the same application to process different sets of data. In WML, the only type of data a variable can hold is a string value. However, in WMLScript, variables can hold not only strings, but a variety of data types (refer to Table 10.1).

In WMLScript, variables are available only within a specific function.

Declaring Multiple Variables (Declared Separately)

The `validate.wmls` file created in Chapter 9 uses only one variable. However, as you'll see in this next example, WMLScript enables developers to declare multiple variables using either the same or separate var keywords.

The way this next example works is the application checks each user input to ensure that the format entered is correct. If the format is not correct, an error message displays (an error message defined within the WMLScript file). As you'll see, WMLScript is useful not only for validating user data, but also for holding user prompts and messages.

Let's first modify the WML page that will access these multiple variables. This WML code is similar to the `login.wml` file, created in the last chapter. However, there are a couple of changes. Type the following changes, and then save this file again as `login2.wml`. The changes to this code appear in bold:

```
1   <?xml version="1.0"?>
2   <!DOCTYPE wml PUBLIC "-//WAPFORUM//DTD WML 1.1//EN"
3   "http://www.wapforum.org/DTD/wml_1.1.xml">
4   <wml>
5   <!-- Card 1 -->
6     <card id="username" title="Username">
7       <do type="accept" label="Go">
8       <go href="#password"/>
9       </do>
10      <p>
11      Enter username:
```

```
12          <input name="username" type="text"/>
13        </p>
14    </card>

15 <!-- Card 2 -->
16    <card id="password" title="Password">
17       <do type="accept" label="Go">
18       <go href="validate2.wmls#checkpass()" />
19       </do>
20          <p>Enter password:
21          <input name="password" type="password"/>
22          </p>
23    </card>
24 </wml>
```

The following is an explanation of this code:

- The sixth line removes the format attribute included in the login.wml file. This is because you'll add functionality to a WMLScript file that checks the user's inputted username. The WMLScript functionality replaces the need for the format attribute.

- The eighteenth line changes the link of the WMLScript file to access. In this example, you'll access a WMLScript file named validate2.wmls.

- You've removed the badpass card that was included in the login.wml file created in Chapter 9. This card is not needed because you'll create the functionality of this card in the new WMLScript file.

NOTE

You might notice that we've also removed some of the timer functionality from this example. This is to avoid any problem with the linking of the different decks of your application. You'll add this functionality back into your application when you work through the example in Part III.

You've written the login2.wml file, so let's move on to the new WMLScript. Type the following WMLScript code; then, save it as validate2.wmls:

```
1  extern function checkpass()
2  {
3     var username = WMLBrowser.getVar("username");
4     var password = WMLBrowser.getVar("password");

5        if (String.length(username) != 5)
6     {
```

```
7              Dialogs.alert("You have entered an incorrect username format.");
8    }
9      else if (String.length(password) != 6)
10   {
11             Dialogs.alert("You have entered an incorrect password format.");
12   }
13     else if (String.length(password) == 6)
14   {
15             WMLBrowser.go("menu.wml#menu");
16   }

17 };
```

NOTE

It's usually good practice to place error messages and information prompts within the WMLScript file and place application instructional messages in the WML file (like this latest example does). Doing so improves the readability and organization of your code.

The following is an explanation of the bold areas in this WMLScript code:

- The third line declares a variable named username. This variable is set equal to the WMLBrowser library function (you'll learn more about functions in a moment). Essentially, this function grabs the username information entered by the user from the login2.wml file. This information is then made available throughout the WMLScript.

- The fourth line declares a variable named password. This variable is also set equal to the WMLBrowser library function. This function grabs the password information entered by the user from the login2.wml file. This information is then made available throughout the WMLScript.

- The seventh line uses a new library function not yet introduced. This line of code uses a Dialogs library function, which enables developers to send various types of messages back to the user. In this case, you've set up the following clause:

```
    if (String.length(username) != 5)
    {
        Dialogs.alert("You have entered an incorrect username format.");
    }
```

In this clause, the WMLScript checks whether the username is not equal to five characters. If it is not, the alert message displays. If the username is five characters, the else if clause executes (see line 11).

- The eleventh line also uses the `Dialogs` library function. Like the previous `Dialogs` function, this function allows developers to send a message back to the user. In this case, the clause is as follows:

```
else if (String.length(password) != 6)
{
    Dialogs.alert("You have entered an incorrect password format.");
}
```

In this clause, the WMLScript checks whether the password is not equal to six characters. This clause executes only if the first conditional statement (the one associated with the username [see line 7]) is false. In other words, the password clause executes only if the username equals to six characters.

Figures 10.3–10.5 show this code on a device screen. Figures 10.3 and 10.4 display the functionality that occurs when users enter an incorrect username or password format; Figure 10.5 displays how the application works if both the username and password are in a correct format.

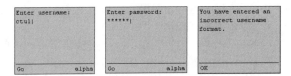

Figure 10.3 *WAP application with multiple variables (with an incorrect username format entered).*

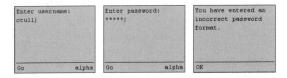

Figure 10.4 *WAP application with multiple variables (with an incorrect password format entered).*

Figure 10.5 *WAP application with multiple variables (with correct username and password formats entered).*

NOTE

Be sure to save these files within the same directory as the files created in the Part II exercise (such as C:\My Documents). Otherwise, some of the links within the examples in this chapter might not work correctly.

TIP

You can use the Back button on a WAP device to scroll backwards through cards. Try using this feature to scroll back to the username or password fields if you need to reenter an incorrect input.

Declaring Multiple Variables (Declared Together)

In the previous example, you declared multiple variables within two separate variable statements. However, WMLScript also allows developers to declare multiple variables using only one var keyword. So, developers have the choice of declaring multiple variables within separate var statements or all together in one var statement.

The following is an example of the validate2.wmls file with the two variables declared using one var keyword. When declaring multiple variables on one line, you must be sure to separate them with a comma:

```
1  extern function checkpass()
2  {
3     var username = WMLBrowser.getVar("username"),
4     password = WMLBrowser.getVar("password")

5        if (String.length(username) != 5)
6     {
7           Dialogs.alert("You have entered an incorrect username format.");
8     }
9        else if (String.length(password) != 6)
10    {
11          Dialogs.alert("You have entered an incorrect password format.");
12    }
13       else if (String.length(password) == 6)
14    {
15          WMLBrowser.go("menu.wml#menu");
16    }

17 };
```

This code provides the same results as the validate2.wmls file; the only difference is that using a single var statement provides a type of shorthand.

CAUTION

Using a single var statement to declare all variables is a useful shortcut. However, grouping too many variables together within a single statement can make your code difficult for others to interpret. Consider the readability of your code when deciding whether to use a single or multiple var statements for your WMLScript variables.

Using Functions in WMLScript

Functions are a named portion of a program that performs a specific task. In other words, functions are a type of procedure or routine.

Most programming languages come with a prewritten (or built-in) set of functions that are kept in libraries. WMLScript is no exception. You'll learn more about WMLScript's libraries and built-in functions in Chapter 12, "Working with WMLScript Libraries."

In addition, developers can write their own functions to perform specialized tasks.

You might not have realized it, but you used both built-in and user-created functions in your `validate2.wmls` file. Let's look at this code again. The bold areas of this code represent the different function names you used:

```
extern function checkpass()
{
    var username = WMLBrowser.getVar("username");
    var password = WMLBrowser.getVar("password");
      if (String.length(username) != 5)
    {
        Dialogs.alert("You have entered an incorrect username format.");
    }
      else if (String.length(password) != 6)
    {
        Dialogs.alert("You have entered an incorrect password format.");
    }
      else if (String.length(password) == 6)
    {
        WMLBrowser.go("menu.wml#menu");
    }

};
```

In this code, the checkpass function (created by you) gains its functionality from several built-in functions (provided within WMLScript).

Built-in functions enable you to use previously coded tasks rather than having to devise your own. For example, in the `validate2.wmls` file, you use a function in WMLScript's `String` library to check the length of the user input rather than having to write out lines of code that perform this same task.

The Structure of User-Created Functions

WMLScript functions—whether they are built-in or user-created—have essentially the same structure. The following is an example of the user-created function you created earlier in this chapter. This function has two areas regarding its structure—the name of the function, and its arguments:

```
extern function checkpass()
```

In this function, `checkpass` is the name of the function and the argument is contained within the parentheses.

DECLARING A USER-CREATED FUNCTION

In WMLScript, user-created functions require a declaration keyword. User-created functions can use two types of declarations.

The first type of declaration determines whether the user-created function is to be available only within the WMLScript file it is declared in. This type of function is known as an *internal* function and is preceded by the keyword `function`. You won't use internal functions within the examples in this book.

The other type of declaration available for user-created functions enables the function to become available for files other than just the one in which it's created. These types of functions are known as *external* functions and are preceded by the keywords `extern function`.

The `checkpass` function example is a user-created function that uses the `extern function` keywords. Therefore, the `checkpass` function is an external function. This function allows the application to use information (such as variables) from other files outside the `validate2.wmls` file. In this case, this function uses a variable from the `login2.wml` file.

The Structure of Built-In Functions

Built-in functions also require a name and arguments. Consider this example:

```
Dialogs.alert("You have entered an incorrect username format.")
```

Built-in functions must contain the WMLScript library to which the function belongs, a period separator, and the name of the function. Similar to the user-created functions, any arguments must be contained within the parentheses.

In the previous example, `Dialogs` represents the WMLScript library, and `alert` represents the name of the function found in this library. The two pieces are separated by a period.

Again, you'll learn more about how these built-in functions work in Chapter 12.

DECLARING A BUILT-IN FUNCTION

The difference between built-in functions and user-created functions is that built-in functions contain a preexisting name. User-created functions, on the other hand, can use any name decided by the developer (as long as the name follows the naming conventions outlined earlier in this chapter).

Built-in functions, in comparison, must use the name defined within the WMLScript specification. To declare a built-in function, you simply write the library and function together, separated by a period (for example, `Dialogs.alert`).

Declaration of Arguments in a Function

Arguments store data provided by the developer rather than the user. For example, in the following function, the developer has entered a text message. This message is considered an argument:

```
Dialogs.alert("You have entered an incorrect username format.")
```

Arguments are optional—a function can use no arguments if desired. Recall the `checkpass` function you created? This function contains an empty space contained within the parentheses, which designates that no argument value is present:

```
extern function checkpass()
```

NOTE

Think of arguments as variables that are of a value designated by the developer. Values designated by the developer are referred to as *literal values*. A literal is a value that's written exactly as it's meant to be interpreted.

Using Multiple User-Created Functions in WMLScript

Up until this point, you've created WMLScript files that have used only one user-created function. Let's expand on the `validate2.wmls` file and add multiple user-created functions. As your WAP applications become more involved, you'll find that your WMLScript files are nothing more than a running list of functions, one after the other.

To begin using multiple functions, let's modify the login2.wml file created earlier in this chapter. You'll change the code so that the WML file asks to perform a check after each username and password input. Type the following code. Then, save this code as login3.wml:

```
1   <?xml version="1.0"?>
2   <!DOCTYPE wml PUBLIC "-//WAPFORUM//DTD WML 1.1//EN"
3   "http://www.wapforum.org/DTD/wml_1.1.xml">
4   <wml>
5   <!-- Card 1 -->
6     <card id="username" title="Username">
7       <do type="accept" label="Go">
8       <go href="validate3.wmls#checkname()"/>
9       </do>
10        <p>
11        Enter username:
12        <input name="username" type="text"/>
13        </p>
14    </card>

15  <!-- Card 2 -->
16    <card id="password" title="Password">
17      <do type="accept" label="Go">
18      <go href="validate3.wmls#checkpass()" />
19      </do>
20        <p>Enter password:
21        <input name="password" type="password"/>
22        </p>
23    </card>
24  </wml>
```

Notice in lines 8 and 18 that the application is set to access two functions from the validate3.wmls file (which you'll create in a moment). These two functions enable the application to validate that the user's information has been entered correctly after every entry. This differs from the first application in this chapter, where the user was able to enter all the information and then got an error message if one of the entries was in an incorrect format.

After you've saved the login3.wml file, modify the validate.wmls file. Type the following code, and then save this file as validate3.wmls:

```
1   extern function checkname()
2   {
3       var username = WMLBrowser.getVar("username");
4         if (String.length(username) != 5)
5       {
6           Dialogs.alert("You have entered an incorrect username
            ➥format.");
7       }
```

```
 8          else if (String.length(username) == 5)
 9      {
10          WMLBrowser.go("login3.wml#password");
11      }
12  }

13  extern function checkpass()
14  {
15      var password = WMLBrowser.getVar("password");
16        if (String.length(password) != 6)
17      {
18          Dialogs.alert("You have entered an incorrect password format.");
19      }
20        else if (String.length(password) == 6)
21      {
22          WMLBrowser.go("menu.wml#menu");
23      }

24  };
```

All you've done with this code is add a new user-created function called checkname. This function works similarly to the checkpass function. The only difference is that the checkname function checks to ensure that the format of the user's input is equal to five characters. If the input is incorrect, users will not be able to move on to the password input card. Figures 10.6 and 10.7 show the results of this application on a WAP emulator.

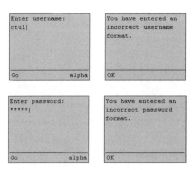

Figure 10.6 *WAP application that validates after every input (with incorrect username and password formats entered).*

Figure 10.7 *WAP application that validates after every input (with correct username and password formats entered).*

A Word on Pragmas

One last area to explore in this chapter is pragmas. Pragmas might be a new concept to you, especially if you're mostly familiar with JavaScript or other scripting languages where the concept of pragmas aren't present.

Pragmas enable developers to control how code is compiled. They are typically used for two purposes: to call external files and to control the access of information. All pragmas start with the keyword use and are then followed by pragma-specific attributes.

WMLScript supports three types of pragmas:

- access
- meta
- url

Table 10.2 summarizes these constructs.

Table 10.2   Pragmas Available in WMLScript

Pragma	Description	Example
access	Enables a user to protect a file's content. This pragma specifies which URLs can call the external function in an access-controlled compilation unit.	use access domain "yourcompany.com/apps/scripts";
meta	Specifies how the originating servers, connecting servers, and user agents use information.	use meta name "Submitted";
url	Specifies the location (URL) of an external WMLScript file. This pragma gives the external file a local name.	use url NameofScript "http://www.yourcompany.com/app/scripts"

Creating Access Control Using Pragmas

One common use of pragmas is the protection of a file's contents. An access control pragma can perform checks on an external file, checking to see whether the destination file allows access from the caller. By default, access control is disabled.

To get a better understanding of how access control works, consider the following pragma:

```
use access domain "yourcompany.com" path "/apps;
```

For a caller to access an external file, the external file must match the domain suffix (`yourcompany.com`) and the path prefix (`/apps`) defined by the access control pragma. In other words, the following URLS would be accessible to the caller, according to the pragma defined:

- `http://www.yourcompany.com/apps/scripts`

- `https://yourcompany.com/apps/scripts`

- `http://www.yourcompany.com/apps/scripts/demos.cgi`

In comparison, the following URLS are not accessible according to the pragma defined:

- `http://www.mycompany.com/apps/scripts`

- `http://www.yourcompany.com/internal/apps`

Don't worry about using access control pragmas—you won't be exploring this topic in the examples in this book. However, as you continue your WAP development efforts, you might find pragmas a useful tool, especially when you need to incorporate content-sensitive functionality into your applications.

Accessing External Information Using Pragmas

Another use for pragmas is accessing external WMLScript files that reside on remote servers.

To access an external WMLScript file, you can use the `url` pragma. Consider the following code:

```
use url NameofScript http://www.yourcompany.com/app/script.wmls;
```

```
extern function checkpass()
{
    return NameofScript#check()
};
```

Notice that the first line of code uses a pragma to call an external file. This code works as follows:

1. The pragma specifies the URL location of the WMLScript file (`http://www.yourcompany.com/app/script`).

2. The pragma specifies the external file according to the given URL (`NameofScript`).

3. The external file's content is then made available within your script (`return NameofScript#check`). In this example, the `check` function within the external file `NameofScript` is made available.

Specifying Metadata with Pragmas

In computer science, the prefix *meta* is often used. *Meta* means about. Thus, when you hear the term *metadata*, it means data that describes other data (data about data). A *metalanguage* is a language that describes other languages, and a *metafile* is a file that contains other files.

Pragmas control the capability to specify characteristics of metadata, such as how, when, and by whom a particular set of data was collected, or how the data is formatted.

Three types of metadata exist that pragmas can define within a WAP device. These are as follows:

- **Name**—Specifies the metadata used by remote servers
- **HTTP equiv**—Specifies the metadata that indicates the property that should be interpreted as an HTTP header
- **User agent**—Specifies metadata intended to be used by WAP devices

For example, say you wanted to ensure that metadata was not ignored by a WAP device. You could define the following pragma:

```
use meta name "Created" "07-January-2001";
```

In this pragma, the WAP device will not ignore any metadata named within it.

Summary

Congratulations! After finishing this chapter, you can consider yourself a budding WAP developer! You're now familiar with the various data types available in WMLScript and how they play an important part in determining how your application operates.

You also learned more about variables and functions and how the two together provide the real heart of a WAP application. Specifically, you learned how to create functions yourself but were also introduced to several built-in functions (better known as WMLScript libraries). WMLScript libraries are summarized in Chapter 12.

This chapter concluded with a look at the concept of pragmas, which control how code is compiled. Although pragmas aren't used much at the time of this writing, you can expect them to become more and more important in the future as devices and user needs become more involved.

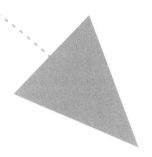

Operators in WMLScript

Chapter 10, "Variables and Functions," covered using variables and functions to create expressions. These expressions then allowed you to compare and manipulate data. Using expressions, you created the functionality to check the user's input to see whether it was in a correct format.

As you'll learn in this chapter, for expressions to work correctly, they must use something known as an *operator*. An operator performs some type of manipulative action on a value (such as addition, multiplication, comparisons, and so on). In essence, operators are the glue that holds an expression together. In this chapter, you'll learn about some of the most widely used operators available in WMLScript.

The following is a summary of the topics covered in this chapter:

- Using WMLScript operators to assign values
- Creating mathematical functionality with WMLScript operators
- Using operators to compare values
- Manipulating strings with the WMLScript operators

NOTE

This chapter looks at the most widely used operators. However, Appendix B, "WMLScript Reference," provides a reference of all WMLScript operators provided in the WMLScript 1.2 specification. This specification is also available from `www.wapforum.org`. See Appendix B for more information.

What Are Operators?

Operators are the tools that enable developers to perform actions on values to obtain a result. This result can then be used to fuel another action in code, and then to fuel another action.

Chapter 10 examined the creation of variables to store user-inputted information. As your applications become increasingly complex, you might find the need to perform additional operations on this data. This chapter looks at the operators available in WMLScript to provide additional functionality to your applications.

NOTE

If you're familiar with JavaScript or C, you will find many of these operators to be familiar to you. WMLScript derives much of its syntax and operators from these languages.

Assigning Values with the Assignment Operators

Assignment operators are useful for setting variables to some value. In fact, you've already used one of these operators in previous examples in Part III: the equal sign (=).

Of course, just because the assign operator might be familiar to you, the rest of the assignment operators might not be. Table 11.1 lists the assignment operators designated in WMLScript.

Table 11.1   The WMLScript Assignment Operators

Operation	WMLScript Operator
Assign.	=
Add (numbers)/concatenate (strings) and assign.	+=
Subtract and assign.	-=
Multiply and assign.	*=
Divide and assign.	/=
Divide (integer division) and align.	div=
Remainder or modulus and assign. The sign of the results equals the sign of the dividend.	%=

Table 11.1   *continued*

Operation	WMLScript Operator
Bitwise left-shift and assign.	<<=
Bitwise right-shift with sign and assign.	>>=
Bitwise right-shift zero file and assign.	>>>=
Bitwise AND and assign.	&=
Bitwise XOR and assign.	^=
Bitwise OR and assign.	|=

Simple assignment (through use of the equal sign) is probably the most widely used of WMLScript's assignment operators. Simple assignment assigns values to operands.

However, a close second is WMLScript's compound addition assignment operator. This operator uses the plus and equal signs (+=) to combine two operands (that are not numbers) together. Let's take a moment to look at both of these operators in closer detail.

Simple Assignment (=)

You've already used simple assignment in your code earlier in Part III. Recall the `validate.wmls` file created in Chapter 9, "Introduction to WMLScript":

```
1  extern function checkpass()

2  {
3      var password = WMLBrowser.getVar("password");

4      if (String.length(password) != 6)
5      {
6          WMLBrowser.go("login.wml#badpass");
7      }
8      else if (String.length(password) == 6)
9      {
10         WMLBrowser.go("menu.wml#menu");
11     }

12 };
```

In line 3 of this code, the expression sets the `username` variable (used throughout the WMLScript code in this example) equal to the `username` variable value entered by users from the WML file.

In this example, the value assigned by the equal sign is a string value. However, simple assignment also can assign numeric values to variables. For example, consider the following line of code:

```
pwrdLength = 6
```

In this example, the value of the variable `pwrdLength` is equal to the value 6.

NOTE

This previous line of code is not anything that you've included with any examples. The example expresses the concept that the equal sign can be used with numeric, as well as string, values.

Compound Addition Assignment (+=)

Apart from simple assignment, another useful assignment operation is known as *compound addition assignment*. Compound addition assignment provides a means for combining a couple of programming steps together. Compound addition assignment is useful in creating code that is tighter and more efficient.

For example, consider the following lines of code that add two variables together:

```
var username = WMLBrowser. getVar ("username")
var password = WMLBrowser. getVar ("password")
```

They then put the result back into one of these variables:

```
var username = WMLBrowser. getVar ("username") +
➥WMLBrowser.setVar("password")
```

This entire process could be shortened using compound addition assignment. To combine these two operators, you use the assignment with addition operator. This same code using the assignment with addition operator is as follows:

```
var username += WMLBrowser. getVar ("username") +
➥WMLBrowser.setVar("password")
```

NOTE

Referring to Table 11.1, you might find yourself scratching your head, wondering what exactly some of these bitwise things are at the bottom of the table. Let's take a moment to demystify bitwise operators.

You've probably heard about computers working with bits, which are nothing more than 0s and 1s. Bitwise operators enable developers to create calculations using bit flag operators.

For the most part, most developers do not frequently use bitwise operators. You won't need to worry about bitwise operations in the examples in this book.

Creating Mathematical Functionality with the Arithmetic Operators

When you think of the word "operator," the idea of mathematical functionality might first pop into your head. The reason for this isn't coincidence—most operations that occur in applications are of a mathematical nature. WAP applications are no exception.

To provide mathematical functionality, WMLScript provides several arithmetic operators. Arithmetic operators provide some capability to perform calculations, always take numerical values as their operands, and return a single numeric value.

Many of the arithmetic operators should be familiar to you (drudging up those terrible days of junior high math—sorry to have to do that to you). The most common arithmetic operators are addition (+), subtraction (-), multiplication (*), and division (/).

Arithmetic operators are especially important when you are creating formulas in your applications. The basic WMLScript arithmetic operators are the same as those equipped with JavaScript. Table 11.2 lists WMLScript basic arithmetic operators.

NOTE

Arithmetic operators perform both unary and binary calculations. Unary calculations involve calculations with only one values; binary calculations involve calculations with two or more values.

Table 11.2   The Basic Binary WMLScript Arithmetic Operators

Operation	WMLScript Operator	Description
Add (numbers)/ concatenate (strings)	+	Returns the sum of adding operands
Subtract	-	Returns the remainder of deducting one operand from another
Multiply	*	Returns the product of multiplying two operands together
Divide	/	Returns the quotient of dividing one operand by another (provides a remainder)
Integer division	div	Returns the quotient of dividing one operand by another when handling integers (does not provide a remainder)

In addition to these, a set of more complex binary operations is also available. These are summarized in Table 11.3.

Table 11.3   The Complex Binary WMLScript Arithmetic Operators

Operation	WMLScript Operator
Remainder	%
Bitwise left-shift	<<
Bitwise right-shift with sign	>>
Bitwise &	&
Bitwise OR	|

Unary operations—operations that are used with only one operand, as opposed to binary operations, which use two operands—are also supported by WMLScript arithmetic operators. WMLScript's unary arithmetic operators are summarized in Table 11.4.

Table 11.4   The Unary WMLScript Arithmetic Operators

Operation	WMLScript Operator
Plus	+
Minus	-
Pre- or post-decrement	- -
Pre- or post-increment	++
Bitwise NOT	~

Let's try a couple of examples with the arithmetic operators. First, type the following WML and save the file as arith.wml, in your C:/My Documents folder. Don't try running this file, however, until you create the WMLScript file that accompanies it:

```
1  <?xml version="1.0"?>
2  <!DOCTYPE wml PUBLIC "-//WAPFORUM//DTD WML 1.1//EN"
3  "http://www.wapforum.org/DTD/wml_1.1.xml">
4  <wml>

5  <!-- Card 1 -->

6    <card id="assign" title="Assignment">
7      <do type="accept" label="Go">
8      <go href="ArithValue.wmls#ShowValue('$(num)')" />
9      </do>
10      <p><b>Arithmetic Operations</b><br/><br/>
11      Enter a number. The constant is five.
12      <input name="num" type="text" format="*N"/>
13      </p>
14    </card>

15 </wml>
```

This file provides the capability to enter data and then have this data used by a WMLScript file named ArithValue.wmls (see line 8 in the previous code example).

Notice in line 8 that the variable num (created in line 12) is specified. When linking from WML to WMLScript, a WML variable can be included with the WMLScript function being called. Specifying a WML variable works similarly to the WMLBrowser.getVar built-in function you used in Chapter 10—it provides the WMLScript file access to the WML variable.

Now, let's create the WMLScript file used with this WML. Type the following code, and save it in the C:/My Documents folder (the same folder that contains your arith.wml file):

```
1    extern function ShowValue(num)
2    {

3      WMLBrowser.setVar("Value", Lang.parseInt(num));

4      var B = 5;
5      var Result;

6      Result = num  + B;
7      Dialogs.alert(num + " + 5 = " + Result);

8      Result = num  - B;
9      Dialogs.alert(num + " - 5 = " + Result);

10     Result = num  * B;
11     Dialogs.alert(num + " * 5 = " + Result);

12     Result = num  / B;
13     Dialogs.alert(num + " / 5 = " + Result);

14     Result = num  div B;
15     Dialogs.alert(num + " div 5 = " + Result);

16   };
```

The following is an explanation of the bolded areas of this code:

- Lines 6 and 7 work together. In line 6, the Results variable is set equal to the sum of user's inputted num variable. This value is then added to the B variable, which was set equal to the value 5 (see Line 4).

  In line 7, the Dialogs library (you'll learn more about this and other WMLScript libraries in Chapter 12, "Working with WMLScript Libraries") presents the user with the result of the equation in line 6.

NOTE

The built-in function used in this example is the `alert` function, which is part of the Dialogs library. As you'll learn in Chapter 12, the `alert` function enables developers to create messages that display to users.

- Lines 8–15 work in a similar fashion as lines 6 and 7. The difference is that in these lines, different types of mathematical equations are defined. For example

  - Line 8 defines the `Results` variable equal to the user's inputted num variable. The `B` variable is then subtracted from this value.

  - Line 10 defines the `Results` variable equal to the user's inputted num variable. This value is then multiplied by the `B` variable.

  - Line 12 defines the `Results` variable equal to the user's inputted num variable. This value is then divided by the `B` variable. This type of division includes a remainder.

  - Line 14 defines the `Results` variable equal to the user's inputted num variable. This value is then divided by the `B` variable. This type of division *does not* include a remainder.

Figure 11.1 displays these files on a device emulator.

NOTE

If Chapter 6, "User Input with Variables," you learned that WML allows for only the input of strings. Thus, if you want your WMLScript to perform calculations on the user-inputted data, you must convert the string into an integer.

WMLScript provides built-in functions in the Lang and Float libraries to perform the conversion of values in WMLScript. You'll learn more about these and other built-in functions in Chapter 12.

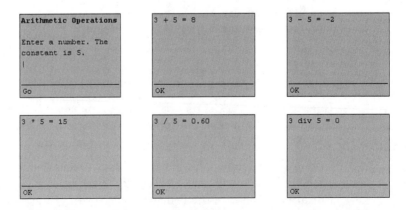

Figure 11.1   *Arithmetic operations on a device emulator.*

Looking at arithmetic operators (refer to Tables 11.2–11.4), the addition, subtraction, multiplication, and division operators should be familiar to you. However, the increment and decrement operators might not be as familiar.

The next example discusses these increment and decrement operators.

The Increment and Decrement Operators

As you work more and more in software development, you'll see that certain arithmetic operations are used more prevalently than others. An example of a common arithmetic operation is the automatic increase or decrease of a value by one.

Think about an e-mail application that tracks the number of messages received. An application can report the number of e-mails by adding 1 to a value each time a new message arrives. Such functionality is considered an increment and is made possible through the increment operator.

THE INCREMENT OPERATOR (++)

WMLScript provides similar functionality through an *increment operator* (the double-plus sign [++]). Essentially, this operator provides a shortcut for adding the value 1 to a variable's value.

To get an idea of how the increment operator works, let's try an example. First, modify the `arith.wml` file with the changes shown in the following code (marked in bold font); then, save your work as `arith2.wml` in your `C:\My Documents` folder. Do not run this file, however, until you create the WMLScript that accompanies it:

```
1   <?xml version="1.0"?>
2   <!DOCTYPE wml PUBLIC "-//WAPFORUM//DTD WML 1.1//EN"
3   "http://www.wapforum.org/DTD/wml_1.1.xml">
4   <wml>

5   <!-- Card 1 -->

6     <card id="assign" title="Assignment">
7       <do type="accept" label="Go">
8       <go href="ArithValue2.wmls#ShowValue('$(num)')" />
9       </do>
10        <p><b>Arithmetic Operations</b><br/><br/>
11        Enter a number.
12        <input name="num" type="text" format="*N"/>
13        </p>
14     </card>

15 </wml>
```

You've made two changes to this file. The first change occurs in line 8, where the filename of the WMLScript that accompanies this WML file is changed. The second change occurs in line 11, where the text is modified to only state `Enter a number`.

With your WML file ready, it's now time to write a WMLScript file that incorporates the increment operators.

Type the following WMLScript code, and save your work as `ArithValue2.wmls` in your `C:\My Documents` folder. When you've made these changes, run these files on a device emulator (see Figure 11.2):

```
1     extern function ShowValue(num)
2     {

3       WMLBrowser.setVar("Value", Lang.parseInt(num));

4       Dialogs.alert("Entered Value = " + num);

5       num++;
6       Dialogs.alert("Incremented Value = " +  num);

7     };
```

The following is an explanation of the bolded areas of this example:

- Line 5 uses the double-plus operator after the `num` variable (entered by users in the WML file). This operator increases the user's inputted value by one.

- Line 6 uses a Dialog library function to display text to the user. The text displays, followed by the incremented value of the num variable.

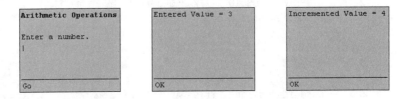

Figure 11.2   *The increment operator on a device emulator.*

THE DECREMENT OPERATOR (--)

WMLScript's decrement operator (--) works in a similar fashion as the increment operator. The difference is that, instead of increasing a value by 1, the decrement operator *decreases* a value by 1.

Let's modify the `ArithValue2.wmls` file you just created to use the decrement operator instead of the increment operator. Type the changes to this file (marked in bold font). This file works with the `arith2.wml` file.

Figure 11.3 displays these files on a device emulator:

```
1      extern function ShowValue(num)
2      {

3        WMLBrowser.setVar("Value", Lang.parseInt(num));

4      Dialogs.alert("Entered Value = " + num);

5      num--;
6      Dialogs.alert("Decremented Value = " +  num);

7      };
```

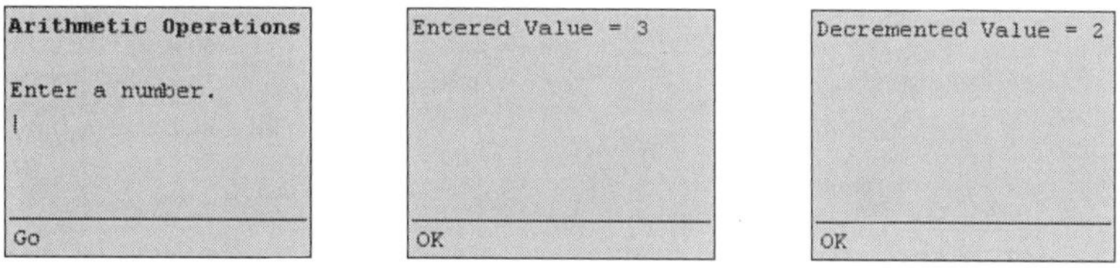

Figure 11.3   *The decrement operator on a device emulator.*

The following is an explanation of the bolded areas of this example:

- In this example, line 5 uses the decrement operator after the `num` variable (entered by users in the WML file). The decrement operator decreases the user's inputted value by 1.

- Line 6 uses the Dialog library function to display text to the user. The text that displays is followed by the decremented value of the `num` variable.

Creating Conditional Functionality with Comparison Operators

Regardless of the simplicity (or complexity) of your WMLScript application, if you're using WMLScript, you can almost guarantee that somewhere in the code is the need to compare values.

Applications often make decisions by performing tests. For example, in the application you've been creating in this book, you've written one statement that tests whether the username entered by a user is correct. A second statement tests whether the password entered by a user is in a correct format.

You might not have realized it at the time, but the statements created to perform these tests use WMLScript's comparison operators. These operators are listed in Table 11.5.

Table 11.5   The WMLScript Comparison Operators

Operation	WMLScript Operator	Description
Less than	<	Returns true if the left operand is less than the right operand
Greater than	>	Returns true if the left operand is greater than the right operand
Less than or equal to	<=	Returns true if the left operand is less than or equal to the right operand
Greater than or equal to	>=	Returns true if the left operand is greater than or equal to the right operand
Equal	==	Returns true if the operands are equal
Not equal	!=	Returns true if the operands are not equal

Comparison operators are used to do just what their name implies—compare values. Comparison operators compare two values and then generate a true or false value from this comparison. This true or false value is better known as a *Boolean result*. Comparison operators allow developers to determine whether two values are equal and then make a decision based on the results.

Looking at Table 11.1, you might notice something different between the equality and inequality symbols. Notice that the equal sign (=) doesn't represent equality. Also, notice that inequality is not represented with the less-than and greater-than signs. The reason for these new symbols is to avoid confusion in the code (this convention comes from JavaScript).

To explain, let's take a moment to look at these two operators in closer detail.

The Equality Operator (==)

Referring to Table 11.1, notice that the double equal signs (==) represent equality. The reason WMLScript uses two equal signs to represent equality is because the single equal sign is used to assign specific values.

NOTE

You looked at the assign operator earlier in this chapter, when reading about the assignment operators.

To aid in understanding, consider the `validate.wmls` WMLScript file, originally supplied in Chapter 9:

```
1  extern function checkpass()

2  {
3      var password = WMLBrowser.getVar("password");

4          if (String.length(password) != 6)
5      {
6              WMLBrowser.go("login.wml#badpass");
7      }
8          else if (String.length(password) == 6)
9      {
10              WMLBrowser.go("menu.wml#menu");
11      }

12 };
```

In the eighth line of this code, an `if`/`else if` conditional statement uses the equality operator (refer to Chapter 9 for information about the various types of WMLScript statements).

If the password value equals six characters (and thus has a Boolean value of `true`), the next line of code determines the action.

TIP

Line 3 of this WMLScript uses the assign operator, which is part of WMLScript's assignment operators. The assign operator is a single equal sign.

Try not to confuse the assign operator (=) with the equality operator (==). Remember, the assign operator *assigns* a specific value, whereas the equality operator creates a comparison to make a decision.

The Inequality Operator (!=)

In your scripting, you can use the not equal symbol (the exclamation point) to negate the value of an operator. In this case of the `validate.wmls` file created in Chapter 9, the exclamation point occurs before the single equal sign:

```
1  extern function checkpass()

2  {
3      var password = WMLBrowser.getVar("password");

4          if (String.length(password) != 6)
5      {
6              WMLBrowser.go("login.wml#badpass");
```

```
7     }
8         else if (String.length(password) == 6)
9     {
10            WMLBrowser.go("menu.wml#menu");
11    }

12 };
```

In the fourth line, the not-equal operator determines whether the variable password is equal to six characters.

The comparison operators you've discussed aren't the only ones available to developers; you can use any of those listed in Table 11.5. However, the equality and inequality comparison operators are among the most useful in creating functionality in your applications.

Realize that the examples in this book use comparison operators with Boolean (true/false) data. However, comparison operators also can use strings, integers, and floating-point data.

NOTE

Several important rules exist regarding the data available with comparison operators. Although these rules are not applicable to the application you're creating in this book, you might find this information helpful as you continue your WAP development efforts after completing this book:

- **Boolean data**—`true` is larger than `false`.

- **Integer data**—Comparisons are based on the given integer values.

- **Floating-point data**—Comparisons are based on the given floating-point values.

- **String data**—Comparisons are based on the order of character codes of the given string values.

- **Invalid data**—If at least one of the operands is invalid, the result of the comparison is invalid.

Manipulating Strings with the WMLScript String Operators

String operators provide the capability to connect string variables together (better known as *concatenating*). Two string operators are available to enable developers to concatenate strings together (see Table 11.6).

Table 11.6   The WMLScript String Operators

Operation	WMLScript Operator	Description
Addition	+	Returns the sum of combining operands. It's similar to the addition arithmetic operator, but in this case, the operands are strings.
Assignment with addition	+=	Returns the sum of combining operands, and then assigns the new value to the original operand. It's similar to the assignment with addition operator, but in this case, the operands are strings.

To get an idea of how string operators works, let's try an example.

For this example, access the `login3.wml` file you created in Chapter 10. Type the changes to this code, which are marked in bold. Then, resave this file as `login4.wml`. Be sure you save this file in your `C:\My Documents` folder:

```
1   <?xml version="1.0"?>
2   <!DOCTYPE wml PUBLIC "-//WAPFORUM//DTD WML 1.1//EN"
3   "http://www.wapforum.org/DTD/wml_1.1.xml">
4   <wml>
5   <!-- Card 1 -->
6      <card id="username" title="Username">
7        <do type="accept" label="Go">
8        <go href="validate4.wmls#checkname()"/>
9        </do>
10        <p>
11        Enter username:
12        <input name="username" type="text"/>
13        </p>
14     </card>

15 <!-- Card 2 -->
16     <card id="password" title="Password">
17       <do type="accept" label="Go">
18       <go href="validate4.wmls#checkpass()" />
19       </do>
20        <p>Enter password:
21        <input name="password" type="password"/>
22        </p>
23     </card>
24 </wml>
```

Lines 8 and 18 link to a new WMLScript file named validate4.wmls. First, save this new WML file in your C:\My Documents folder. You'll need to write the new WMLScript file before running this application.

The following WMLScript file is a modified version of the validate.3.wmls file, created in Chapter 10. The bold font marks areas of the code that have changes. Modify this code, and then save the file as validate4.wmls in your C:\My Documents folder:

```
1    extern function checkname()
2    {
3       var username = WMLBrowser.getVar("username");
4         if (String.length(username) != 5)
5       {
6           Dialogs.alert(username + " is an incorrect username format.");
7       }
8         else if (String.length(username) == 5)
9       {
10          WMLBrowser.go("login3.wml#password");
11      }
12   }

13   extern function checkpass()
14   {
15      var password = WMLBrowser.getVar("password");
16        if (String.length(password) != 6)
17      {
18          Dialogs.alert(password + " is an incorrect password format.");
19      }
20        else if (String.length(password) == 6)
21      {
22          WMLBrowser.go("menu.wml#menu");
23      }

24   };
```

The following is an explanation of the bolded areas of this code:

- Line 6 uses a WMLScript built-in function (we'll discuss these more in Chapter 12).

In this code, the parameters within this function (those areas contained within the curved brackets) are as follows:

```
Dialogs.alert(username + " is an incorrect password format.");
```

In this parameter, you've used the assignment operator to concatenate a couple of pieces to create an error message.

The parameter message consists of the following:

- The user's inputted password, as specified by the following:

  `password`

- A text message, with an empty space designated at the beginning of the message. This causes the user entered password and text message to be separated by a single space. The text message states

  `is an incorrect username format.`

All together, when accessed, the message reads as follows:

`user's username variable` (space) `is an incorrect username format.`

- Line 18 works in the same manner as line 6; however, in this line of code, the user's `password` variable is included with the text message if the format is incorrect.

Figure 11.4 displays this code on a device emulator.

NOTE

This message displays only when the user enters an incorrect username or password format.

Figure 11.4 *String operators in a WAP application.*

NOTE

This chapter has covered the most popular WMLScript operators. For a complete list of all WMLScript operators, see Appendix B.

Summary

In this chapter, you've digested a lot of information regarding the WMLScript operators. However, you've only scratched the surface of what operators can bring to your development efforts. The main point to pull away from this chapter is that WMLScript operators provide the means to add functionality and logic to your expressions. In a way, operators are the glue that holds together the code that determines what an application does and how it works.

This chapter examined how operators can further improve the functionality of your application. You looked at assignment, arithmetic, comparison, and string operators, and how they can add exciting functionality to your applications.

In the next chapter, you'll use this information and incorporate this information with WMLScript's built-in functions. As you'll see, built-in functions are useful because they provide existing functionality in which a developer does not need to write out huge lines of code.

Built-in functions are snippets of code that already exist, organized under the name of one of these functions. Functions are useful in that they provide power and added complexity to your applications, without requiring much work on the developer's part.

Working with WMLScript Libraries

In previous examples in this book, you've used several built-in functions. Built-in functions are a useful and important part of WAP development. Because they contain a number of commonly used operations, these functions enable developers to improve the quality of their applications, while easing the workload of development.

In WAP 2.0, the WMLScript language provides several useful libraries, each with its own collection of functions. The good news is that you've already used some of these libraries in the last couple of chapters.

For example, you've already used the Dialogs Library to create error messages, the WMLBrowser Library to grab variables from the WML file, and the String Library to check the length of the user's input. This chapter discusses these, as well as all other libraries and the functionality they provide.

In this chapter, you'll examine the most important functions within each library and discuss how they work. Some of the lesser-used functions are also presented, providing future reference material for you to explore as your experience with WAP development increases.

Study this chapter, and memorize the functions in it. By learning to incorporate these libraries into your code, you'll ease your development efforts while improving the functionality and power of your WAP applications.

Specifically, this chapter discusses the following:

- The syntax necessary for using built-in functions in a WAP application
- The functions of the closely related Lang and Float Libraries
- The functions of the String Library
- The functions of the URL Library
- The functions of the WMLBrowser Library
- The functions of the Dialogs Library

What Are WMLScript Libraries?

So, what exactly is a WMLScript library, anyway? WMLScript *libraries* are simply groups of built-in functions.

For the most part, these libraries contain names descriptive of the types of functions they contain. For example, the String Library contains functions that relate to the manipulation of string data. The WMLBrowser Library, on the other hand, contains functions that perform operations to the WML and WMLScript browsers.

Figure 12.1 summarizes all the function names contained in the six major WMLScript libraries.

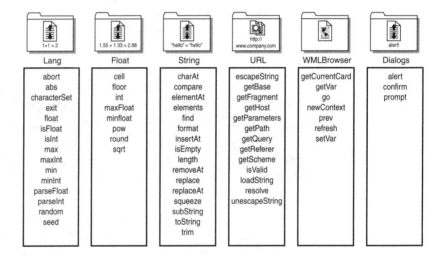

Lang	Float	String	URL	WMLBrowser	Dialogs
abort	cell	charAt	escapeString	getCurrentCard	alert
abs	floor	compare	getBase	getVar	confirm
characterSet	int	elementAt	getFragment	go	prompt
exit	maxFloat	elements	getHost	newContext	
float	minfloat	find	getParameters	prev	
isFloat	pow	format	getPath	refresh	
isInt	round	insertAt	getQuery	setVar	
max	sqrt	isEmpty	getReferer		
maxInt		length	getScheme		
min		removeAt	isValid		
minInt		replace	loadString		
parseFloat		replaceAt	resolve		
parseInt		squeeze	unescapeString		
random		subString			
seed		toString			
		trim			

Figure 12.1 *Graphical representation of WMLScript libraries and their functions.*

Built-in functions differ from user-created functions. *User-created* functions provide functionality created in blocks of code written by the developer. In contrast, *built-in* functions are previously developed operations included in the WMLScript language that contain the internal workings of blocks of code.

A good way to understand the difference between user-created and built-in functions is to think of the WMLScript libraries and their built-in functions as shortcuts—an easier way for developers to incorporate certain types of functionality in their code without having to write out lines and lines of code.

The following is a summary of each WMLScript library and the kinds of operations their functions possess:

- **The Lang Library**—Contains functions that perform arithmetic operations on integer numbers (numbers without decimal points). This library also contains two application-aborting functions and a check function to see whether a particular browser supports floating-point arithmetic.

- **The Float Library**—Contains functions that perform arithmetic operations on floating-point numbers (numbers that contain decimal points).

- **The String Library**—Contains functions that perform a variety of operations on string data.

- **The URL Library**—Contains functions that provide operations to URLs that exist either locally (within the device) or remotely (on a remote server).

- **The WMLBrowser Library**—Contains functions used to command how WML and WMLScript files work together when processed by the browser.

- **The Dialogs Library**—Contains functions to communicate information to users.

The Syntax of Built-In Functions

Before learning about the individual WMLScript libraries, let's first look at the syntax rules required for built-in functions. As you can see, no matter what you do, you just can't get away from rules in this world!

To understand the syntax of built-in functions, let's look at an example of one. This built-in function first appeared in Chapter 10, "Variables and Functions":

```
Dialogs.alert("You have entered an incorrect username format.")
```

Notice that the keyword `Dialogs` begins the function by stating from which library the function comes (in this case, the Dialogs Library).

Following the keyword `Dialogs` is a dot separator (.) and then the name of one of the library's built-in functions (in this case, the `alert` built-in function).

As is the case with all functions, open and close parentheses must follow the function name. These parentheses contain the function's arguments. In programming, an *argument* is a value that returns when the argument's function is called.

TIP

The existing name of the built-in functions must be used in your code—you can't change the name of a built-in function.

In addition, all WMLScript library functions must be in the following format:

Library.function(argument)

The Lang and Float Libraries

The Lang and Float Libraries are similar in that both contain several functions designed to perform various types of arithmetic operations. The main differences between these libraries are as follows:

- The Lang functions calculate numbers without decimals (integer numbers).

- The Float functions calculate numbers with decimals (floating-point numbers).

Working with arithmetic calculations usually requires a significant amount of processing power from the device performing the operations. Because of that, the functions within these libraries are not frequently used.

As you'll find in your development efforts, calculations of data are best performed on a server.

This is not to say that WAP applications never have a need to perform calculations on the client side. For example, many games developed for WAP devices use several of the Lang and Float functions.

The Lang Library

The Lang Library contains functions that enable arithmetic operations on integer numbers (numbers without decimals). Although both the Lang and Float Libraries contain arithmetic functions, the Lang Library is most commonly used in WAP applications. Because of this, the Lang Library contains a couple of functions not specifically related to calculations: float, exit, and abort. Table 12.1 describes these special functions in greater detail.

Table 12.1   *The Built-In Functions of the Lang Library*

Function	Syntax	Argument	Description	Example
abort	`Lang.abort(string)`	String message.	Aborts the current WMLScript (due to an error) and displays the message defined in the function's argument. The control is returned to the browser.	`Lang.abort("input error");`
abs	`Lang.abs(number)`	Integer, float, string, or Boolean number.	Returns the absolute value of the number defined in the function's argument.	`Lang.abs(7);`
characterSet	`Lang.characterSet()`	No argument is specified.	Used to return the identifier for the character set used by the device.	`Lang.characterSet();`
exit	`Lang.exit(value)`	Any data type.	Aborts the current WMLScript (not due to error) and displays the message defined in the function's argument. The control is returned to the browser.	`Lang.exit(100);`
float	`Lang.float()`	No argument is specified.	Determines whether the device supports floating-point operations.	`Lang.float();`
isFloat	`Lang.isFloat(string)`	String.	Converts the string defined in the function's argument to a floating-point number.	`Lang.isFloat("500MB");`
isInt	`Lang.isInt(string)`	String.	Converts the string into an integer number.	`Lang.isInt("500MB");`

Table 12.1 *continued*

Function	Syntax	Argument	Description	Example
max	Lang.max(*number1*, *number2*)	Integer or float.	Returns the larger of the two values defined in the function's arguments.	Lang.max(1,100);
min	Lang.min(*number1*, *number2*)	Integer or float.	Returns the smallest of the two values defined in the function's argument.	Lang.min(1,100);
minInt	Lang.minInt( )	No argument is specified.	Returns the smallest integer value that is supported by the device.	Lang.minInt( );
parseFloat	Lang.parseFloat(*string*)	Integer, float, string, or Boolean number.	Returns a string as a decimal integer.	Lang.parseFloat ("500MB");
random	Lang.random(*range*)	Integer.	Generates a random integer number. The range of the number is from zero (0) to the number defined in the function's argument.	Lang.random(100);
seed	Lang.seed	Integer.	Begins a random number generation sequence. The sequence begins with the number defined in the function's argument.	Lang.seed(10);

The Float Library

The Float Library is a continuation of arithmetic functions, specifically designed to handle numbers that contain decimal points.

At the time of this writing, not all WAP device browsers support decimal point numbers. Devices today have difficulty handling the arithmetic of numbers, let alone decimal numbers.

Table 12.2 lists the built-in functions available in the Float Library.

Table 12.2   The Built-In Functions of the Float Library

Function	Syntax	Argument	Description	Example
ceil	Float.ceil (*number*)	Floating-point number.	Returns the largest integer number available within the device. This number is not less than the floating-point number defined in the function's argument.	Float.ceil(3.12);
floor	Float.floor (*number*)	Floating-point number.	Returns the smallest integer number available within the device. This number is no less than the floating point number defined in the function's argument.	Float.floor(3.12);
int	Float.int (*number*)	Floating-point number.	Returns the integer part of the defined floating-point number specified in the function's argument.	Float.int(3.12);
maxfloat	Float. maxfloat()	No argument is specified.	Returns the largest floating-point number available within the device.	Float.maxfloat();
minfloat	Float. minfloat()	No argument is specified.	Returns the smallest floating-point number available within the device.	Float.minfloat();

Table 12.2   continued

Function	Syntax	Argument	Description	Example
pow	Float.pow (*number 1, number 2*)	Floating-point number.	Returns the value of raising the value of the first defined number to the value of the second defined number.	Float.pow(3.12, 5);
round	Float.round (*number*)	Floating-point number.	Returns the value of the defined number, rounded to the nearest whole number.	Float.round(3.12);
sqrt	Float.sqrt (*number*)	Floating-point number.	Returns the square root of the floating-point number defined in the function's argument.	Float.sqrt(3.12)

An Example of the `Lang.float` Function

If you do decide to use any of the `Float` functions in your applications, you should test the device to see whether the device's browser supports decimal arithmetic. The `float` function (from the Lang Library) provides this functionality.

To get an idea of how the Lang Library works, in this example, you add functionality that checks whether a device supports floating-point numbers. The Lang Library provides the functionality to perform this type of check.

To begin, open the `login3.wml` file created in Chapter 10. Make the following changes (marked in bold), and save the file as `lang.wml`.

NOTE

Be sure to save this file in the same location as the other files created in the Part II exercises. Doing so ensures that all the relative links will work correctly.

```
1   <?xml version="1.0"?>
2   <!DOCTYPE wml PUBLIC "-//WAPFORUM//DTD WML 1.1//EN"
3   "http://www.wapforum.org/DTD/wml_1.1.xml">
4   <wml>
5   <!-- Card 1 -->
6     <card id="floatvalidate">
7       <do type="accept" label="Float">
8       <go href="validate5.wmls#checkfloat()"/>
9       </do>
10        <p>Press the Float button to test for Float support.</p>
11    </card>
```

```
12 <!-- Card 2 -->
13   <card id="username" title="Username">
14     <do type="accept" label="Go">
15     <go href="validate5.wmls#checkname()"/>
16     </do>
17       <p>
18       Enter username:
19       <input name="username" type="text"/>
20       </p>
21   </card>
22 <!-- Card 3 -->
23   <card id="password" title="Password">
24     <do type="accept" label="Go">
25     <go href="validate5.wmls#checkpass()" />
26     </do>
27       <p>Enter password:
28       <input name="password" type="password"/>
29       </p>
30   </card>
31 </wml>
```

In this example, you've added a card at the beginning of the file. The following is an explanation of the bolded areas of the previous code:

- Line 6 begins a card that checks whether the device supports floating calculations. This card's id is floatvalidate, and its functionality occurs before all other cards within this WML file.

- Line 7 uses a DO element, with the type attribute set equal to accept. Recall that the type attribute identifies the user interface mechanism that triggers a task. The type attribute being set equal to accept means that this DO element contains functionality for the WAP device's Accept button.

  The label attribute displays the text that appears over the user interface mechanism. In this case, the label attribute is equal to the text Float. Thus, the text Float displays over the Accept button.

- Line 8 contains the GO element, which is a task element.

  The DO element requires a task element. In this example, the GO element is equal to "validate4.wmls#checkfloat()" (which is a relative URL).

  This link works in that, whenever the Accept button is clicked, the application accesses the checkfloat() function, available from the validate4.wmls file. You'll add this new function to the validate4.wmls file.

- Line 9 contains the </do> tag, which closes this first DO element.

- Line 10 uses the P element to display a message on the device screen. This message asks users to click the Float button to test the device for support of float calculations.

  The checkfloat() function you'll create in a moment contains the functionality to check whether the device does support float calculations. This function displays the username card if the device supports float calculations. Otherwise, the function displays a message stating that the device does not support float calculations.

- Line 11 closes the new floatvalidate card.

- Line 15 sets the GO task equal to the checkname() function, available from the validate4.wmls file. Whenever the Accept button is clicked, the application accesses the checkname() function.

- Line 25 also sets the GO task equal to a function; however, in this line the function is the checkpass() function. This function is also available from the validate4.wmls file. Whenever the Accept button is clicked, the application accesses the checkpass() function.

Before running this code, you also must update the WMLScript file. Open the validate4.wmls file, also created in Chapter 10. Type the following changes in the code, and resave your work as validate5.wmls. After you are done, run the lang.wml file through a device emulator:

```
1    extern function checkfloat()
2    {
3            if (Lang.float())
4        {
5            WMLBrowser.go("lang.wml#username");
6        }
7        else
8        {
9            Dialogs.alert("Device does not support decimal calculations.");
10       }
11   }

12   extern function checkname()
13   {
14       var username = WMLBrowser.getVar("username");
15         if (String.length(username) != 5)
16       {
17             Dialogs.alert("You have entered an incorrect username
         ➥format.");
18       }
```

```
19        else if (String.length(username) == 5)
20      {
21          WMLBrowser.go("lang.wml#password");
22      }
23   }

24   extern function checkpass()
25   {
26     var password = WMLBrowser.getVar("password");
27       if (String.length(password) != 6)
28     {
29          Dialogs.alert("You have entered an incorrect password
             ➥format.");
30     }
31       else if (String.length(password) == 6)
32     {
33          WMLBrowser.go("menu.wml#menu");
34     }

35   };
```

In this example, you've added a function at the beginning of the file. The following is an explanation of the bolded areas of the WMLScript file:

- Line 3 begins the `if` clause of a conditional statement. This clause uses the `Lang.float` function. The `float` function does not require arguments to be specified, thus the curved brackets can be left empty.

  In Line 3, the code states `if (Lang.float())`.

  The `Lang.float` checks the device to see whether arithmetic on floating-point numbers is acceptable. If the function is found to be true, line 5 executes.

- Line 5 uses a WMLBrowser function (you'll learn about this library in more detail later in this chapter) that directs the application back to the username card of the `lang.wml` file.

- Line 7 begins the `else` clause of the conditional statement. In this clause, if the `Lang.float` function finds that the device does not support floating-point operations, line 9 executes.

- Line 9 uses a Dialogs function (you'll learn about this library later in this chapter) to report to the user that the device does not support decimal calculations. Figure 12.2 displays this code on a device emulator.

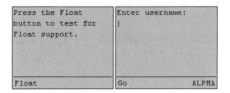

Figure 12.2 *The* lang.wml *file on a device screen.*

NOTE

This application checks whether the device supports floating calculations. If the device does support floating calculations, the username prompt displays (as is the case in Figure 12.2).

If, however, the device does not support floating calculations, the text message defined in the validate4.wmls file displays.

The String Library

The String Library is an important (and widely used) WMLScript Library that enables developers to perform a number of important operations to strings.

You'll find the String Library useful because the majority of data inputted by users from a WML file will be of the string data type. (see Chapter 6, "User Input with Variables," for more information). A *string*, by definition, is a set of characters grouped together.

The built-in functions in the String Library specify how to separate elements of a string. For example, the trim function enables developers to remove any whitespace characters from a string.

Many of these String functions use indexes. *Indexes* are a numeric way of identifying a particular character of a string. In WMLScript, each character of a string is designated a number, beginning with 0. For example, in the string ctull, the following displays a summary of that string's input numbers:

	C	T	U	L	L
Index Numbers:	0	1	2	3	4

NOTE

The first character of a string always begins with an index zero (0). Also, you'll often hear characters referred to as *elements* when discussing strings. In the previous example, the last element (the letter L) has an index of 4.

Knowledge of the functions in the String Library enables developers to perform various types of operations to strings. Table 12.3 lists the functions available in the String Library.

Table 12.3 The Built-In Functions of the String Library

Function	Syntax	Argument	Description	Example
charAt	String.charAt (string, number)	String and integer number.	Returns the character in the string that is designated by the index number. The index number is defined by the function's argument.	String.charAt ("Sales",1);
compare	String.compare (string1, string2)	String.	Returns a -1 value if the first string is smaller than the second string. Returns a 1 if the first string is larger than the second string. Returns a 0 if both strings are the same length.	String.compare ("Sales" "Mrkt");
elements	String.elements (string, separator)	String. A separator is a string character that separates string elements from one another.	Returns the number of string elements as specified by the separator.	String.elements ("Sales, Mrkt", ",");
elementAt	String.elementAt (string, index, separator)	String, integer (for index), string separator.	Returns the element in the separated string, according to the index number.	String.elementAt ("Sales, ",");
find	String.find (string, element)	String. An element is one or more characters of the entire string.	Returns the index of the first character of the string element.	String.find ("ctull", "tull");
format	String.format (string format, value)	String format.	Defines a value for a string that contains formatting specifiers.	String.format ("rate = "%d%%", 3);

Table 12.3 *continued*

Function	Syntax	Argument	Description	Example
insertAt	String.insertAt (*string, element, index, separator*)	String, integer (for index), string separator.	Inserts a string element into a separated string. The location of the insertion is specified by the index defined in the function's argument.	String.insertAt ("Sales", "TX", 5, ",");
isEmpty	String.isEmpty (*string*)	String.	Determines whether a string has a zero length. Returns a true or false value.	String.isEmpty ("Sales");
length	String.length (*string*)	String.	Used to determine the character length of a string.	String.length ("Sales");
removeAt	String.removeAt (*string, index, separator*)	String, integer (for index). string separator.	Removes a string element according to the index defined within a function.	String.removeAt ("Sales1", "a", 5, ",");
replace	String.replace (*string, oldelement, newelement*)	String, string elements.	Replaces the first string element with the second string element.	String.replace (SalesTX, TX, LA);
replaceAt	String.replaceAt (*string, element, index, separator*)	String, integer (for index), string separator.	Replaces a string element according to the index defined in the function.	String.replaceAt string ("Sales1", "2", 5, ",");
squeeze	String.squeeze (*string*)	String.	Reduces all the whitespace in a string to a single space.	String.squeeze ("Welcome, ctull");
subString	String.subString (*string, index, length*)	String, integer (for index), integer (for length of characters).	Removes a portion of a string.	String.subString ("SalesTX", 5, 2);

Recall the following code in the `validate4.wmls` file created earlier in this chapter:

```
if (String.length(username) !=5)
```

This line of code uses the String Library's `length` function to determine whether the user-inputted string does not contain a length of five characters.

In this next example, you'll modify the `validate5.wmls` file to handle instances where no username is entered (the username is left blank and contains no characters).

First, here is the `lang.wml` file again. Change the areas in bold, which now refer to a new WMLScript file you'll create in a moment. Save your changes as `string.wml`.

NOTE

Be sure to save this file in the same location as the other files created in the Part II exercises. Doing so ensures that all the relative links will work correctly.

```
1   <?xml version="1.0"?>
2   <!DOCTYPE wml PUBLIC "-//WAPFORUM//DTD WML 1.1//EN"
3   "http://www.wapforum.org/DTD/wml_1.1.xml">
4   <wml>
5   <!-- Card 1 -->
6      <card id="floatvalidate">
7         <do type="accept" label="Float">
8         <go href="validate6.wmls#checkfloat()"/>
9         </do>
10         <p>Press the Float button to test for Float support.</p>
11      </card>

12  <!-- Card 2 -->
13      <card id="username" title="Username">
14         <do type="accept" label="Go">
15         <go href="validate6.wmls#checkname()"/>
16         </do>
17         <p>
18         Enter username:
19         <input name="username" type="text"/>
20         </p>
21      </card>
22  <!-- Card 3 -->
23      <card id="password" title="Password">
24         <do type="accept" label="Go">
25         <go href="validate6.wmls#checkpass()" />
26         </do>
```

```
27        <p>Enter password:
28        <input name="password" type="password"/>
29        </p>
30     </card>
31 </wml>
```

Now that you have your WML file ready, let's revisit the `validate4.wmls` file. Type the following changes to this code. After you've made these changes, resave this file as `validate6.wmls`:

```
1    extern function checkfloat()
2    {
3        if (Lang.float())
4        {
5            WMLBrowser.go("string.wml#username");
6        }
7        else
8        {
9            Dialogs.alert("Device does not support decimal calculations.");
10       }
11   }

12   extern function checkname()
13   {
14     var username = WMLBrowser.getVar("username");
15       if (String.isEmpty(username))
16     {
17           Dialogs.alert("You must enter a username.");
18     }
19       else
20     {
21           WMLBrowser.go("string.wml#password");
22     }
23   }

24   extern function checkpass()
25   {
26     var password = WMLBrowser.getVar("password");
27       if (String.length(password) != 6)
28     {
29           Dialogs.alert("You have entered an incorrect password
           ➡format.");
30     }
31       else if (String.length(password) == 6)
32     {
```

```
33          WMLBrowser.go("menu.wml#menu");
34     }

35   };
```

The following is a summary of the bolded areas of the new `validate5.wmls` file:

- Line 5 uses a WMLBrowser function to direct the application back to the username card of the `string.wml` file.

- Line 15 begins the `if` clause of a conditional statement.

  In this example, the String Library's `length` function is used to check the length of the `username` variable. With this line of code, the `isEmpty` function is checking the `username` variable. If the variable is empty (does not contain any string characters), line 17 executes.

- Line 17 displays the `Dialog` Library's `alert` function. This function displays a message to the user, stating an incorrect username format has been entered.

- Line 19 makes up the `else` clause of a conditional statement. In this example, if the `isEmpty` function determines that the username was not left blank, the WMLBrowser Library's `go` function is executed. This function returns users to the password card of the `string.wml` file.

- Line 21 uses a WMLBrowser function (you'll learn about this library in more detail later in this chapter) that directs the application back to the username card of the `string.wml` file.

Figure 12.3 displays this application on a device emulator.

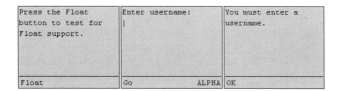

Figure 12.3 *The* `string.wml` *file on a device screen.*

NOTE

To see how this functionality works, try clicking the Accept button at the username prompt without entering any information.

The URL Library

Working with WAP now for a while, you've probably begun to see an underlying way of how these types of applications work. What you might have been noticing is that a WAP application is essentially a series of cards and functions linked together through URLs. Web applications work in a similar fashion.

To say that URLs are an important part of a WAP application is an understatement. URLs are nothing less than the driving force behind how a WAP application operates.

The WMLScript language provides several built-in functions to enhance the operations of URLs. The URL Library handles both URLs that exist either locally (within the device) and remotely (on a remote server).

As you look at the functions of WMLScript's URL Library, you'll find the operations available enable developers to manipulate various portions of a URL.

For example, consider a real-world URL:

```
http://www.yourcompany.com/cgi-bin/directory.cgi?d=1#sales1
```

A summary of the syntax of this previous URL is as follows:

```
<scheme>://network(host and port)/<path>;<parameters>?<query>#<fragment>
```

The functions of the URL Library provide developers with a means of extracting and using portions of a URL, such as the previous one. Table 12.4 summarizes the parts of a URL.

Table 12.4   The Parts of a URL

URL Part	Definition
Scheme	Represents the protocol type of the URL (for example, `http`, `https`, and so on).
Network	Represents the address of the server, as well as any login and password information necessary to connect to the server. The host and port information is contained in this network information.
Path	Represents the path (name) of the file directory.
Parameters	Represents any optional parameters that can be used. Parameters are usually a list of values, separated by the semicolon (`;`) character.
Query	Represents an optional part of the URL that is used to send arguments to a server for processing of specific information.
Fragment	Provides a reference shortcut. A fragment is used to represent a partial URL. URLs that use only the fragment portion of a URL are known as *relative* URLs.

Table 12.5 summarizes the URL Library's functions.

Table 12.5   The Built-In Functions of the URL Library

Function	Syntax	Argument	Description	Example
escapeString	URL.escapeString (*string*)	String.	Returns a new string where the escape sequences are presented with their ASCII code value.	URL.escapeString ("/yourcompany.cgi");
getBase	URL.getBase( )	No argument is specified.	Returns the absolute form of the URL for the current WMLScript file.	URL.getBase( );
getFragment	URL.getFragment (*string*)	String URL.	Returns the fragment part extracted from the URL.	URL.getFragment ("input.wml# login");
getHost	URL.getHost (*string*)	String URL.	Returns the host portion extracted from the URL.	URL.getHost ("http://www.yourcompany.com");
getParameters	URL.getParameters (*string*)	String URL.	Returns the parameters extracted from a URL.	URL.getParameters ("./logo.wbmp");
getPath	URL.getPath (*string*)	String URL.	Returns the path extracted from the URL.	URL.getPath ("http://www.yourcompany.com");
getPort	URL.getPort (*string*)	String URL.	Returns the query portion extracted from the URL.	URL.getPort (http://www.yourcompany.com :80");
getQuery	URL.getQuery (*string*)	String URL.	Returns the query portion extracted from the URL.	URL.getQuery ("http://www.yourcompany.com");
getScheme	URL.getScheme (*string*)	String URL.	Returns the scheme extracted from a URL.	URL.getScheme
isValid	URL.isValid (*string*)	String URL.	Performs a check to see if a URL has a valid syntax.	URL.isValid (http://www.yourcompany.com");
loadString	URL.loadString (*string1, string2*)	*String1* is a URL; *String2* is the text type (must start with text/).	Returns a string from a URL.	URL.loadString ("http://www.yourcompany.com", "text/plain");

The WMLBrowser Library

As you've seen from the examples in this chapter, the WMLBrowser Library contains several functions used to command how WML and WMLScript files work together when processed by the browser.

Because not all WAP devices use the same browsers, sometimes a particular browser might not be capable of interpreting these functions. In this case, the WMLScript is ignored. Table 12.6 displays the functions of the WMLBrowser Library.

Table 12.6 The Built-In Functions of the WMLBrowser Library

Function	Syntax	Argument	Description	Example
getCurrentCard	WMLBrowser. getCurrentCard()	No argument is specified.	Retrieves the URL of the current card in the browser.	WMLBrowser. getCurrentCard();
getVar	WMLBrowser.getVar (string)	String name.	Retrieves the contents of a browser variable.	WMLBrowser. getVar ("username");
go	WMLBrowser.go (string)	String URL.	Specifies a <go> task that is executed.	WMLBrowser.go ("input.wml #login");
newContent	WMLBrowser. newContent( )	No argument specified.	Clears the browser of all content.	WMLBrowser. newContent( )
prev	WMLBrowser.prev( )	No argument specified.	Specifies a WML <prev> task that is executed.	WMLBrowser.prev()
refresh	WMLBrowser. refresh( )	No argument specified.	Specifies a WML <refresh> task.	WMLBrowser. refresh( )
setVar	WMLBrowser.setVar (string1, string2)	string1 is the name of the variable. string2 is the value of the variable.	Sets a browser variable.	WMLBrowser.setVar ("password");

In this chapter, you've already addressed the most widely used functions in this library. Take a closer look at the latest version of your `validate6.wmls` file:

```
1    extern function checkfloat()
2    {
3         if (Lang.float())
4         {
5             WMLBrowser.go("string.wml#username");
6         }
7         else
8         {
9             Dialogs.alert("Device does not support decimal calculations.");
10        }
11   }

12   extern function checkname()
13   {
14     var username = WMLBrowser.getVar("username");
15       if (String.isEmpty(username))
16     {
17           Dialogs.alert("You must enter a username.");
18     }
19       else
20     {
21           WMLBrowser.go("string.wml#password");
22     }
23   }

24   extern function checkpass()
25   {
26     var password = WMLBrowser.getVar("password");
27       if (String.length(password) != 6)
28     {
29           Dialogs.alert("You have entered an incorrect password
             ➥format.");
30     }
31       else if (String.length(password) == 6)
32     {
33           WMLBrowser.go("menu.wml#menu");
34   };
```

In this WMLScript file, you've made wide use of the WMLBrowser's go function (used to send a user back to the WML file) and the getVar function (used to retrieve a variable from the WML file). Although the other WMLScript functions are valuable, you'll find that these two are the most widely used in WAP applications.

The Dialogs Library

Similar to the WMLBrowser Library, the Dialogs Library contains a number of commonly used functions. You've already seen the Dialog Library's `alert` function used widely within the examples in this chapter and throughout the last couple of chapters.

The Dialogs Library is important in that it contains functionality to communicate messages to users. Table 12.7 lists the functions of the Dialogs Library.

Table 12.7   The Built-In Functions of the Dialogs Library

Function	Syntax	Argument	Description	Example
alert	Dialogs.alert (*string*)	String message.	Displays a warning message to the user.	Dialogs.alert ("Incorrect Format.");
confirm	Dialogs.confirm (*string1, string2, string3*)	*string1* represents a message. *string2* represents the yes option. *string3* represents the no option.	Requests a yes or no response from the user.	Dialogs.confirm ("Accept?", "OK", "Cancel");
prompt	Dialogs.prompt (*string1, string2*)	*string1* represents a message. *string2* represents a default entry if the user does not enter information.	Retrieves a string from the user.	Dialogs.prompt ("Username", "no username entered");

The following is the `validate6.wmls` file, created earlier in this chapter. Of the available functions within the Dialogs Library, you'll find that the `alert` function is used the majority of the time.

The other Dialogs functions, while useful, are better handled within the WML file:

```
1    extern function checkfloat()
2    {
3        if (Lang.float())
4      {
5          WMLBrowser.go("string.wml#username");
6      }
```

```
 7         else
 8      {
 9          Dialogs.alert("Device does not support decimal calculations.");
10      }
11   }

12   extern function checkname()
13   {
14      var username = WMLBrowser.getVar("username");
15        if (String.isEmpty(username))
16      {
17          Dialogs.alert("You must enter a username.");
18      }
19        else
20      {
21          WMLBrowser.go("string.wml#password");
22      }
23   }

24   extern function checkpass()
25   {
26      var password = WMLBrowser.getVar("password");
27        if (String.length(password) != 6)
28      {
29          Dialogs.alert("You have entered an incorrect password
            ➥format.");
30      }
31        else if (String.length(password) == 6)
32      {
33          WMLBrowser.go("menu.wml#menu");
34      }

35   };
```

Summary

You should pat yourself on the back—you've come a long way since the beginning of this book, acquiring a variety of WAP development knowledge to use in your development efforts.

This chapter has examined some of the built-in functions available in the WMLScript language. You've learned about the differences between built-in functions and user functions. You've also explored the syntax required for correctly using built-in functions in a WAP application.

This chapter then visited each of the WMLScript libraries, discussing the various types of operations that each provides through its built-in functions. You then delved into some examples, employing the most commonly used functions in your development efforts. Hopefully, this chapter has whet your appetite for WMLScript libraries, demonstrating how WMLScript libraries can further enhance an application without much work from the developer.

In the next chapters, you'll begin exploring even more advanced topics in the world of WAP development, including the integration of your development efforts to an existing database and the use of Active Server Pages (ASPs) to generate WAP content from a remote server.

Your future awaits—turn the page!

Part III Examples

The following code is a continuation of the application created at the end of Part II, "Static WAP Development." In this exercise, you add a WMLScript file that provides client-side checks for your application. You also modify a couple of your WML files so that they link to this WMLScript file correctly.

Remember to save all these files in the same directory (such as `C:\My Documents`).

If you have any questions about any portion of this code, refer to Part II. Figure III.1 shows these files on a device screen.

login.wml

You created this file in the Part II exercises. However, now you'll modify how this file accesses a WMLScript file. After you make the changes, resave this file as `login.wml`.

One of the changes you will make is with the links. Instead of linking to cards in the deck, you'll create links to the `validate` WMLScript file (which you'll create in a moment). The changes are marked in bold.

The other change to this file is the removal of the `format` attributes related to the username and password inputs. Recall from Part II that these attributes validate whether a user's input is in a correct format. You can remove this attribute because the WMLScript file will now handle this validation:

```
<?xml version="1.0"?>
<!DOCTYPE wml PUBLIC "-//WAPFORUM//DTD WML 1.1//EN"
"http://www.wapforum.org/DTD/wml_1.1.xml">
<wml>
<!-- Card 1 -->
   <card id="username" title="Username" ontimer="#message">
     <timer name="nametime" value="$nametime"/>
       <do type="accept" label="Go">
       <go href="validate.wmls#checkname()"/>
       </do>
         <p>
         <anchor title="Go"><go href="#set"/>Settings</anchor><br/>
         Enter username:
         <input name="username" type="text"/>
         </p>
   </card>

<!-- Card 2 -->
   <card id="password" title="Password">
     <do type="accept" label="Go">
```

```
      <go href="validate.wmls#checkpass()"/>
    </do>
      <p>Enter password:
      <input name="password" type="password"/>
      </p>
  </card>

<!-- Card 3 -->
  <card id="message" title="Message">
    <do type="accept" label="Go">
    <go href="home.wml"/>
    </do>

    <do type="option" label="Settings">
    <go href="#set"/>
    </do>

      <p>Expired input time limit. Login again?</p>
  </card>

<!-- Card 4 -->
  <card id="set" title="Settings">
    <do type="accept" label="Go">
    <go href="#username"/>
    </do>
      <p>Set input time:
      <input name="nametime" format="*N"/>
      </p>
  </card>

</wml>
```

validate.wmls

The last version of this file was created in this chapter, with the
validate6.wmls file. The only change you need to make now is to remove
the checkfloat() function.

NOTE

You won't be creating any float calculations in your application. Therefore, you don't
need to test the device for support of floating numbers.

```
extern function checkname()
{
    var username = WMLBrowser.getVar("username");
      if (String.isEmpty(username))
    {
```

```
            Dialogs.alert("You must enter a username.");
    }
       else
    {
       WMLBrowser.go("login.wml#password");
    }
}

extern function checkpass()
{
   var password = WMLBrowser.getVar("password");
     if (String.length(password) != 6)
   {
       Dialogs.alert("You have entered an incorrect password format.");
   }
     else if (String.length(password) == 6)
   {
       WMLBrowser.go("menu.wml#menu");
   }
};
```

To test this application, begin running it from the `splash.wml` file. Clear your emulator's cache before testing this new code.

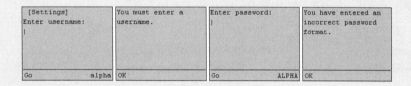

Figure III.1 *The Part III example on a device screen (new functionality).*

Part IV

Dynamic WAP Development

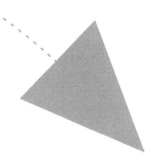

WAP Development with ASP

The WAP development you've completed thus far has been an excellent example of client-side applications (programs that perform functionality on the device). In this chapter, you'll widen your development knowledge by learning how to incorporate server-side technology into your WAP applications.

If you recall from Chapter 9, "Introduction to WMLScript," server-side technology allows applications to perform advanced operations on a remote server and then send the results back to a WAP device. Server-side functionality can bring a whole new range of capabilities to your WAP applications, enabling you to create powerful functionality on a Web server and then send the results back to a device.

Today, several server-side technologies are available for your development efforts. In this book, you explore Microsoft's Active Server Pages (ASP) to create server-side functionality within your WAP applications.

This chapter discusses the following:

- Understanding what ASP is and how it works
- Configuring your Web server test environment to use ASP
- Creating a dynamic ASP page

A total treatment on the subject of ASP is beyond the scope of this book. However, you'll find the following chapters an excellent introduction to the subject of ASP development. You'll also find the information in these chapters useful in learning to incorporate it into your WAP development efforts.

Where Did Server-Side Technologies Come From?

ASP is a good solution for server-side development for a number of reasons. ASP has been around for a while, is used widely throughout the wired Web, and is constant and stable. ASP enables developers to easily tweak other file types (such as WML or HTML files) so that it's recognized as an Active Server Page and capable of performing from a remote server.

You'll learn about all this later in this chapter. However, before jumping in head first with ASP, let's take a look at where all this ASP stuff came from in the first place. To do that, let's turn our attention to WAP's big brother—the Web.

Static Pages

In Chapter 1, "What Is WAP Development?" you learned about the wired Internet and its humble beginnings as a posting board for static pages. Over the course of a couple of years, the popularity of the Internet grew. In due course, the technology surrounding the Internet improved to keep up with user interest. As a result, these static pages became increasingly interesting, including things such as flowering colored graphics, the use of tables, and different text characteristics such as different fonts and effects.

Yet, even with all these improvements, the awful truth was that Web pages were still static—they displayed information and the only functionality included was the capability for one page to link to another page. Figure 13.1 displays a graphical representation of how static pages interact with a server. This figure summarizes both wired and wireless pages.

The Common Gateway Interface

Eventually, users of the wired Internet wanted more from their Web experience than simple static pages. No matter how flashy a static page looked—users wanted more.

To meet the demands of users, the Common Gateway Interface (CGI) was created. CGI is a specification that enables developers to create applications. These CGI applications provide a way to process data from a Web (or WAP) page, often providing dynamic feedback for users. CGI applications are an example of a server-side technology and are still used by many developers today.

Figure 13.1 *Graphical representation of wired and wireless static pages.*

NOTE

CGI applications are often written in the programming language Perl. However, other possible programming languages for CGI applications include C, Java, and Visual Basic.

However, one problem with this technology is that each time a CGI application executes, a new process starts on the Web server. As a result, busy Web servers that are running several CGI processes eventually begin to slow down drastically. If you have a hundred users using a CGI application at one time, a hundred CGI applications are firing off simultaneously! Eventually, under this much activity, even the most powerful Web servers begin to bog down.

Application Programming Interfaces

In the world of the Web (and WAP), speed is everything. No one likes to wait around for some application to return data—this is one of the criticisms of CGI applications.

As an alternative to CGI, another possibility in the arena of server-side development is the use of a server's Application Programming Interface (API).

APIs are a set of tools (such as routines and protocols) that provide developers with the ability to build software applications. Most operating systems (such as Windows) provide an API for developers to create applications that work in an operating environment.

NOTE

Often, developers use a variation of APIs designed directly for Web servers. Two of the most popular APIs available for Web servers are Internet Server APIs (ISAPI) for Microsoft's Internet Information Server (IIS) and Netscape Server APIs (NSAPI) for Netscape Web servers.

Both enable developers to create server-side functionality that's much more efficient than CGI.

In some regards, APIs are more efficient than CGI applications. This is because CGIs do not require the firing of separate programs each time a different request is sent to a Web server.

Unfortunately (there's always a downside to everything, isn't there), APIs aren't the easiest programs to create. APIs involve creating several different interfaces to connect Web pages to a Web server. They're also difficult to maintain. What developers needed was a server-side technology that worked like APIs but was also easy to learn, use, and maintain.

The answer to this developer's dilemma was the development of Active Server Pages by Microsoft.

Active Server Pages to the Rescue

Active Server Pages (ASP) work by embedding additional code within the Web (or WAP page). This additional code (written in a popular scripting language such as JavaScript or VBScript) allows for a client's browser to directly access and view files that reside on a remote server.

ASPs also allow the Web server to send information back to a client's browser—in a format that can be read directly by the browser. For example, an ASP might send some output information back to a WAP device, with the data in a WML format.

NOTE

Check out Microsoft's online MSDN information center for the latest information regarding Active Server Pages. The URL for this resource is http://msdn.microsoft.com/library/.

Once at this URL, select Web Development, Server Technologies, Active Server Pages from the table of contents on the left side of the screen. You also can type **ASP** in the search field available from this page.

To begin using ASP, you first must set up a Web server for testing purposes. To date, there is no way to test ASP files without a live connection to the Internet. Thus, you'll need the following to start developing server-side technologies:

- An Internet connection
- A Web server

In this book, you learn to set up Microsoft's Personal Web Server on your PC to simulate the interaction between a remote server and your WAP device.

Configuring Your Test Environment

WAP developers today can find an almost endless number of Web servers available for their development efforts. In fact, the variety of Web servers available can leave you scratching your head, wondering which one works best for your needs.

For the purposes of this book, we'll stick with Web servers designed for the Windows operating systems. Table 13.1 provides a summary of the various Windows operating systems and the Web servers that are available for each.

Table 13.1 *Web Servers Associated with Operating Systems*

Web Server	Company	Operating System
Internet Information Server 4.0 (IIS 4.0)	Microsoft	Windows NT 4.0
Internet Information Server 5.0 (IIS 5.0)	Microsoft	Windows 2000/XP
Personal Web Server 4.0 (PWS 4.0)	Microsoft	Windows 95/98/NT/2000/XP

These three are not the only Web servers available today—far from it. However, because you're only creating a test environment at this stage of the game, any of these Web servers will meet your needs equally well.

Windows XP and 2000 provide both these Web servers at the time of installation (and are also located on the installation CD). However, if you are using an older operating system, you might find these Web servers available for free download from the Microsoft Web site (www.microsoft.com).

TIP

For users of older Microsoft operating systems, to download one of these Web servers from the Web, go to the Downloads section of the Microsoft site.

Then, perform a search for *NT Option Pack* for Windows 95. Be sure that you are searching for *All Downloads*. The download should display at the bottom of the page as a hyperlink.

continues

continued

Select the hyperlink. An NT Option Pack download page displays. You now can choose the correct operating system for the download of the option pack.

Microsoft has a tendency to move its downloads around from time to time. If you can't find one of these on the Web, consider upgrading your operating system to one of the versions that includes the Web servers with installation.

NOTE

You might notice that the Windows Me operating system is missing from Table 13.1. This is not a mistake. Microsoft does not support PWS in this product.

Installing PWS

This book uses PWS for all its examples. PWS is a good product to use to begin familiarizing yourself with how Web servers work and how to develop applications for use with Web servers.

CAUTION

Avoid using PWS as an actual Web server. Although PWS is great for developing and testing applications, because of its stripped-down nature, it also has many security holes.

PWS is not a good Web server to use in any type of real-world environment. IIS, Apache, or any other variety of web server will better meet the needs of your development efforts.

You also might want to incorporate a firewall (especially a good idea for developers working with any type of server-side development). Firewalls prevent the unauthorized access to or from private networks. Firewalls can consist of only hardware, only software, or a combination of both.

Performing a search on *firewalls* on any search engine will provide sufficient information on finding the right firewall product for you.

To install PWS onto your PC, follow these steps:

1. Check your operating system installation CD for PWS (available with Windows NT, 2000, and XP). If you are not using an older operating system, you can download PWS from the Microsoft site. See the previous tip for more information.

2. Run the PWS `setup.exe`. A splash page first displays, followed by an Agreement Terms page (see Figure 13.2). Read through this page, and then click the Accept button to accept these terms.

    A setup page then displays. Click the Next button to continue through the setup process.

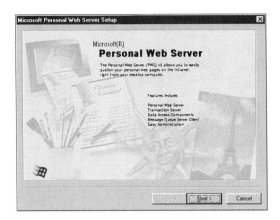

Figure 13.2   *The PWS setup page.*

3. A page then displays asking which type of install you want to perform (see Figure 13.3). Click the Typical button.

Figure 13.3   *The PWS installation options.*

4. PWS then designates a default home page for the Web site. You can change this as desired. For the examples in this book, you'll use the PWS default home location, which is C:\Inetpub\wwwroot (see Figure 13.4).

Figure 13.4 *The PWS default home directory.*

5. The PWS setup then begins the install. After the installation is complete, you must restart your computer.

Starting the PWS

After you've successfully installed your Web server, go to the Start menu and select Personal Web Manager. Depending on the operating system you're using, the location of this can vary from one version to another. Figure 13.5 shows the Personal Web Manager page that displays.

Figure 13.5 *The Personal Web Manager page.*

To start your Web server, simply click the Start button.

Testing Your PWS

To see whether your Web server is working correctly, you can simulate accessing your computer as if it were a Web site. Open a Web browser and in the URL line type **localhost**. Figure 13.6 shows the page that should display.

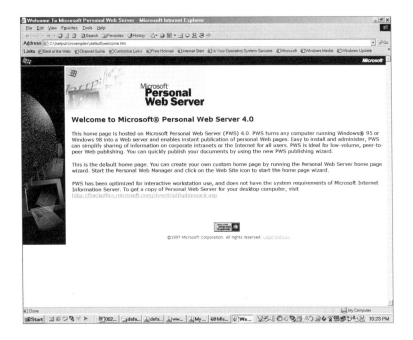

Figure 13.6   *Your* localhost's *default Web page.*

If Your PWS Is Not Working Correctly

Getting a Web server up and running (even if it is only Personal Web Server) can be somewhat of a daunting task. If your PWS does not seem to be working correctly, check the following:

1. Be sure you've installed (or downloaded) the correct NT option pack for your operating system.

2. Be sure you've started the Web server by clicking the Start button.

3. If PWS has loaded correctly, but you are not able to find the default page, try these steps:

   3.1. In the Personal Web Manager, double-click the Advanced icon located at the right of the screen.

   3.2. Double-click Home from the Virtual Directory that displays.

3.3. An Edit Directory screen displays (see Figure 13.7). The Directory field displays the location of your default Web page (the home page of your Web site that uses PWS). This directory location can be whatever you want. For the purposes of this book, you'll use the default location, which is `C:\Inetpub\wwwroot`.

TIP

After you start the PWS, the main page displays your home page as a hyperlink. By selecting that hyperlink, you are taken to that page's folder (through Windows Explorer).

Figure 13.7 *Checking the default page location in PWS.*

3.4. Click the Cancel button on the Edit Directory screen.

3.5. Open your Windows Explorer, and physically check to see whether a `default.asp` page exists within the location of your site (located at `C:/inetpub/wwwroot`).

If there isn't a `default.asp`, don't sweat it! You'll learn how to create an ASP page in a moment and how to view it from a WAP device. However, the fact that this page doesn't exist is why you are not seeing the result of Figure 13.6.

If a `default.asp` file already exists, you might want to move it to another location so that you don't overwrite it when you create this new file.

TIP

If you are still not able to get your PWS up and running, check out the PWS help documentation provided during installation. You can also access the Microsoft Knowledge Base (located on its Web site) to aid you in troubleshooting.

Adding MIME Types in PWS

In Chapter 2, "Tools of the Trade," you learned about adding Multipurpose Internet Mail Extensions (MIME) types.

MIME types provide header information that comes down with every file sent from a Web server to a browser; they are a specification for the format of data that can be sent over the Internet.

The easiest way to add MIME types to PWS is to open Windows Explorer. Then, select View, Folder Options from the toolbar. If you need a refresher on setting up this information, refer to Chapter 2.

Writing Your First ASP

Now that you've gotten a Web server up and running, your test environment is ready. To get the hang of how ASPs work, let's try our hand at one to ensure your Web server is running correctly.

In this code, you create a WAP application that does the following:

- Allows a WML card to sit on the Web server, not on the remote user's device. Thus, when a user accesses the remote Web server, the WML card page first displays.

- The WML card will actually be an Active Server Page that dynamically displays the server's time to the user.

First, type the changes to this new code. Save the file as `default.asp` and save this file in the `C:\Inetpub\wwwroot` directory. If another `default.asp` file already exists in this directory, you might want to move it to another location for now. Here's the code:

```
1    <%Response.ContentType = "text/vnd.wap.wml" %>
2    <?xml version="1.0"?>
3    <!DOCTYPE wml PUBLIC "-//WAPFORUM//DTD WML 1.1//EN"
4    "http://www.wapforum.org/DTD/wml_1.1.xml">
5    <wml>
6      <card id="default" title="Welcome">
7         <p align="center">Logging into system<br/><br/>
8         The time is now <% = time() %>
9         </p>
10     </card>
11  </wml>
```

The following is an explanation of the bolded areas of this code:

- Line 1 begins and ends with the <%...%> delimiters. In ASP, you use delimiters to embed a scripting language within a file. In this example, you use the delimiters to embed VBScript within your WML file.

NOTE

VBScript is the default scripting language for ASP. Therefore, if you're using VBScript, you do not need to declare it in your code.

If you want to use another scripting language for ASP (such as JavaScript or Perl), you must first define it in your code. To do this, simply type the following line before all your other code:

```
<% @LANGUAGE="language" %>
```

In this line of code, *language* stands for the scripting to use in the ASP file. For example, if you wanted to use JavaScript as your scripting language, you would type

```
<% @LANGUAGE="JavaScript" %>.
```

- Within the delimiters in line 1, you've included the following:

```
<%Response.ContentType = "text/vnd.wap.wml" %>
```

This line of code uses an object included in ASP 3.0. ASP objects are similar to WMLScript libraries: They're functions built into the VBScript code. Table 13.2 lists all the ASP 3.0 objects.

Table 13.2   ASP 3.0 Objects

Object	Functionality
Application	Allows multiple users to share information in an application.
ASPError	Allows the viewing of errors in an ASPScript.
Request	Enables data to be retrieved from a Web server.
Response	Enables a request for data to be sent to the Web server. It provides control over which data and data types can be sent, as well as when and how the data is sent.
Session	Enables information regarding users to be stored on the Web server.
Server	Provides additional functionality regarding the Web server.

Each of the objects in Table 13.2 contains a number of functions. The object's function is listed after the period separator. Thus, just as was the case with WMLScript libraries, ASP objects have the following syntax:

```
Object.function(parameter)
```

The following continues the explanation of the code:

- In line 1, the function used is ContentType. This function enables us to define the type of data to be sent when a request is sent to the Web server.

Because your application is a WAP application, you've defined the data type to be sent as text/vnd.wap.wml, which is the MIME type for WML.

- You've added additional code in the eighth line. This line of code contains the text The time is now, followed by the VBScript function time(). This function returns the current time of the Web server's internal clock.

  In the examples in this book, the Web server you're using exists on our PC, the time returned is that of your PC's system clock.

NOTE

Remember to save this file in C:\Inetpub\wwwroot. This simulates the file residing on a remote server.

When you're ready to run your application, access the http://localhost file from your device emulator. Figure 13.8 displays the results of this example on a device emulator.

CAUTION

You must access the ASP file via the Web server. In other words, be sure you type out the entire http://localhost address, rather than just the default.asp file.

For example, if you saved the default.asp file in your My Documents folder, typing **file://c:/My Documents/default.asp** would produce an error. This is because the device tries to interpret the ASP file in HTML rather than WML. To avoid any errors, be sure you access the ASP file through a Web server.

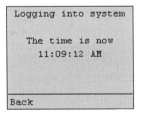

Figure 13.8   *The* default.asp *file from a device emulator.*

This page will act as your default page in our home site. In the next chapters, you'll look at incorporating ASP into our applications by requesting and retrieving data from a database.

Summary

This chapter covered Active Server Pages and began with a review of the history behind ASPs, looking at the evolution of the Web as a basis for this information. ASPs are a server-side technology. In other words, their functionality occurs on a Web server, not on the client (in our case, not on the WAP device).

The chapter then discussed configuring a Web server test environment. The test environment created is one that resides on your PC, along with all the other WAP development tools. This chapter also discussed using Microsoft's Personal Web Server, a tool that's available for free download from the Microsoft Web site.

After installing the test environment and configuring your PC to recognize WAP files, you then created your first dynamic ASP page. In this example, you've created a WML card that is accessible from WAP devices, even though it resides on a Web server. This WML card is dynamic and reports the time of the Web server's system clock when accessed.

In the next chapters, we'll further discuss using ASP in mobile applications. In the next chapter, you'll create a database and then use ASP to send and retrieve information from this database, all from a WAP device.

An Introduction to DBMS Development

Most business applications today require some type of data storage. Database Management Systems (DBMS) play an essential role in providing a means for users to store, retrieve, modify, and delete information.

Today, the use of DBMS has extended into the realm of the mobile world, with users wanting to access data wirelessly from their devices.

This chapter discusses database application development. In this chapter, you'll look at the parts of a database and the technology required to access data through WAP. You'll then create a database and learn how to manipulate this information. You also will use these DBMS skills in Chapter 15, "Accessing Database Content from WAP Devices," where you'll couple this newfound knowledge with WAP development.

This chapter covers the following:

- The concepts behind a database

- Creating a database

- An introduction to the Structural Query Language, the language used to retrieve and modify information in a database

The concept of database application development is vast and that could easily fill an entire book. In this chapter, though, you'll concentrate on the most important concepts of databases and database development.

What Is a Database Management System?

A *database management system* is an application that enables users to control and maintain the information in a database. Just as its name implies, a DBMS is a software program that manages a database.

To understand how DBMS works, you need to learn the concepts behind a database. This book examines *relational databases*—the type of database most widely used with DBMS. The next sections discuss the characteristics of relational databases.

Databases

Databases are similar to a powerful electronic filing cabinet. At their most basic level, databases enable users to add, modify, or delete information.

However, databases provide much more functionality than simply manipulating data. A database can allow authorized users to view specific information. Databases can also back up data automatically and on any type of time interval desired.

Perhaps the most advantageous aspect of databases is that they enable data changes to apply throughout all the areas of the system. Consider the scenario that takes place when you go to the doctor. You're often required to fill out several forms, sometimes in triplicate. Many times, the information you're filling out is the same for all three forms. Your name never changes, and your address never changes.

With a database, if you were filling out this information, you would fill your name in once. Then, any area that required your name would be able to reference it. This is how databases work, and this is partly why they are so useful.

Tables

Databases consist of several tables (also known as *entities*). Using the filing cabinet analogy, if databases are like filing cabinets, tables are like the folders that hold information.

Tables consist of *records* and *fields*. To explain these concepts, let's use the idea of an employee table as an example.

RECORDS

In an employee table, each employee is a record. Records contain several pieces of information, such as the employee's computer username, password, department, and so on. The horizontal rows of the table represent records. Figure 14.1 displays an example of some database records.

Records

empl_id	username	password	dept	fname	lname
1	ctull	232456233	IT	Chris	Tull
2	kthom	563221542	Acct	Keith	Thompson
3	jlidd	123556456	Sales	John	Liddy
4	nther	669845123	Mrkt	Nicole	Theriot
5	jsmit	556123245	Plant	John	Smithy
6	mblue	362115326	Sales	Matt	Blue
7	kandr	889456781	Mrkt	Kevin	Andrzejewski
8	bthom	561234569	IT	Brad	Thompson
9	dwass	663956452	Acct	Dave	Wassenich
10	gyoun	663123652	Plant	George	Young
(AutoNumber)		0			

Figure 14.1   *Database records in a table.*

Fields

Fields contain the specific information related to a record. *Fields* are the columns on a table and contain information about one specific type of data. For example, in the employee table, username might contain data in one type field, password might contain data in another field, dept might contain data in a third field, and so on. Figure 14.2 shows an example of database fields.

Fields

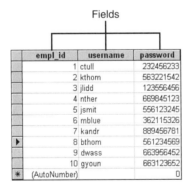

empl_id	username	password
1	ctull	232456233
2	kthom	563221542
3	jlidd	123556456
4	nther	669845123
5	jsmit	556123245
6	mblue	362115326
7	kandr	889456781
8	bthom	561234569
9	dwass	663956452
10	gyoun	663123652
(AutoNumber)		0

Figure 14.2   *Database fields in a table.*

Creating a Database

Before you can incorporate WAP into a DBMS, you first must create a database. In this book, all the examples use Microsoft Access because this database is the most affordable one and has the least amount of hardware requirements.

The following steps describe creating a Microsoft Access database from scratch:

1. Select the Start menu, and then select Programs, Microsoft Access.

2. Select the Blank Access Database option, and click OK (see Figure 14.3).

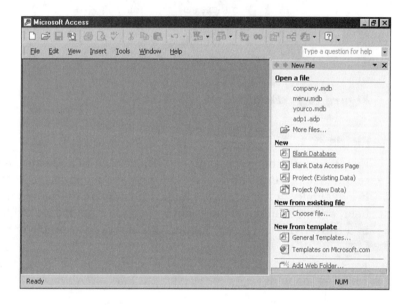

Figure 14.3 *Creating a new database in Microsoft Access.*

3. Save the database as company.mdb in your My Documents folder. You've now successfully created a database.

NOTE

If a Login dialog box displays, refer to your Access help documentation on removing this login information. The reason you should remove this information is that in the coming chapters, you'll create database user authentication in your WAP application and you will not need Access to perform this check for you.

After you save the database, you'll notice an Option Screen displays. Keep this screen open—you'll need it for the rest of this chapter.

Creating the Employee Table

In the DBMS you're creating, you need to create only one table: the employee table.

Creating tables in Access is easy. However, realize that most databases do not contain the graphical interface of Access. Most databases require developers to create tables using the Structured Query Language (SQL). Chapter 15 discusses creating tables using SQL in more detail.

The following steps describe one way of creating tables in Microsoft Access:

1. Double-click the Create Table in Design Mode. Figure 14.4 shows this Access option screen.

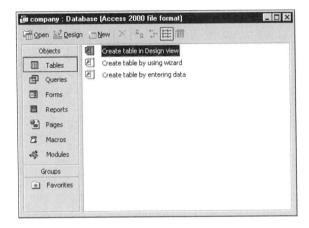

Figure 14.4 *The Microsoft Access option screen.*

2. A Table design screen appears (see Figure 14.5). Table 14.1 summarizes the information to enter in this design screen.

Table 14.1 *Employee Table Design Information*

Field Name	Data Type	Field Size*
empl_id	AutoNumber	Long integer
username	Text	5
password	Text	6
dept	Text	10
fname	Text	30
lname	Text	30

*Located at the bottom-left side of the screen

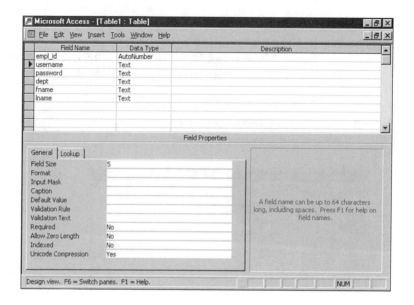

Figure 14.5 *The Microsoft Access design screen.*

3. You must assign a primary key to one of these rows. To do this, right-click the empl_id row; then, select Primary Key from the drop-down list.

NOTE

In the world of databases, a *key* is a field used to sort data. For example, if you wanted to sort records by username, the username field would be a key.

Most DBMS enable you to have more than one key so that you can sort records in different ways. One type of key that must be present is a primary key. *Primary* keys must hold a unique value for each record.

Incidentally, a *foreign key* identifies records in different tables. You won't be using foreign keys in this book.

4. Select File, Save As from the toolbar, and save the table as tblEmpl. You can now close the design screen.

TIP

You should create table names that are descriptive, yet not overly wordy. A good rule of thumb is to begin table names with the prefix *tbl*. Doing so helps other developers realize what type of database object that data is coming from (data can also come from things such as queries and views).

ADDING TEST DATA TO THE EMPLOYEE TABLE

Now that you've created your first database table, you need to enter some test data records. To do this, double-click the tblEmpl table.

You should add some test data to your table. Test data is necessary to ensure that an application is working correctly. Figure 14.6 shows the tblEmpl table with some test data.

Feel free to add more test data to this table if you want. You also might want to add fields to this table. Additional fields might consist of the employee's first name and last name, the employee's address information, the employee's phone extension, or other contact information.

empl_id	username	password	dept	fname	lname
1	ctull	232456	IT	Chris	Tull
2	kthom	563221	Acct	Keith	Thompson
3	jlidd	123556	Sales	John	Liddy
4	nther	669845	Mrkt	Nicole	Theriot
5	jsmit	556123	Plant	John	Smithy
6	mblue	362115	Sales	Matt	Blue
7	kandr	889456	Mrkt	Kevin	Andrzejewski
8	bthom	561234	IT	Brad	Thompson
9	dwass	663956	Acct	Dave	Wassenich
10	gyoun	663123	Plant	George	Young
0					

Record: I◀ ◀ | 10 | ▶ ▶I ▶∗ | of 10

Figure 14.6 *The tblEmpl table with test data.*

Retrieving Information from a Database

So, you've created a database and table. Now you're ready to learn how to view and modify information in your database.

Microsoft Access makes viewing and modifying information easy by creating a graphical interface for your data. In other words, with Microsoft Access, all you need to do is double-click the name of a table. The information in that table displays, enabling you to view and modify data directly. Figure 14.7 displays an example of this table view in Microsoft Access.

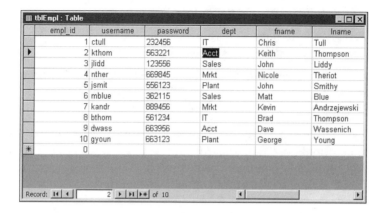

Figure 14.7 *Microsoft Access's table view.*

Unfortunately, most databases do not contain Access's graphical interface. Therefore, to view and modify most databases, you must use SQL.

SQL is important to DBMS developers because it provides the means to manipulate data. However, it does not contain the capability to create front-end application objects, such as forms and procedures.

SQL is used in conjunction with another development language. As you'll see in the next chapter, you use SQL with VBScript to access data (all available from your WAP device).

However, before you can run, you have to learn to walk. Before you can access data from a WAP device, you must first understand SQL.

An Introduction to the Structured Query Language

SQL is the language used with most relational databases today. Although the SQL syntax for different databases might differ slightly, the topics covered in this chapter are relevant to most relational databases.

Familiarizing yourself with SQL is important and useful, and it is especially important if you want to continue in the realm of database development.

Viewing Data with the SELECT Statement

One of the main functions of a database is to supply users with data. SQL's SELECT keyword provides this capability, enabling users to view database data.

The following is an example of the syntax of a SELECT query:

```
SELECT the records you want
FROM a table
WHERE the data meets a certain criteria;
```

NOTE

Similar to the syntax found in WMLScript, you must end each of your SQL statements with a semicolon.

Let's look at the SELECT statement in action to see how it really works:

1. Be sure you're still in the company.mbd database. If not, open this database again.

2. Select Queries from the list of objects (see Figure 14.8).

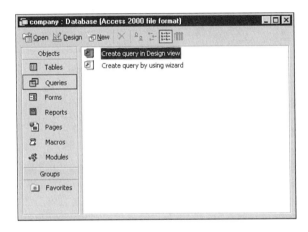

Figure 14.8   *The query options on the option screen.*

3. Double-click the Create Query in Design View option. A Query Design screen displays. Click the Close button on the Show Table Display screen. Your screen should look similar to Figure 14.9.

4. Click the SQL button from the toolbar, or right-click in the gray area and select the SQL View option from the drop-down menu. A query screen displays.

5. Type the following code into this query screen:

```
SELECT *
FROM tblEmpl;
```

Your screen should look similar to Figure 14.10.

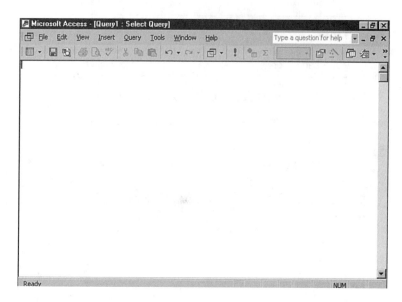

Figure 14.9 *The query design screen.*

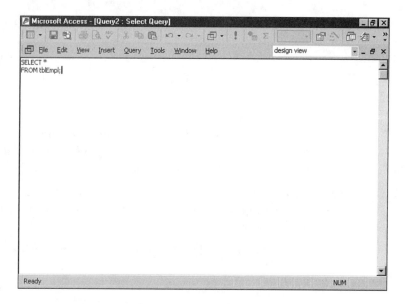

Figure 14.10 *The* SELECT *statement in the query screen.*

To run a query, click the exclamation icon located on the toolbar. You also can select Query, Run from the menu bar. In this example, the asterisk (*) indicates that all fields are to display from the tblEmpl table. Therefore, when you run this query, all records in this table display.

TIP

To start a different query, select View, SQL View from the menu bar. You're returned to the Query screen, where you can type in a new SQL statement.

Of course, you can specify specific fields to include within a query. Specifying field criteria returns a smaller result set of records.

The next example displays a SELECT statement that returns an employee's first name. Type the following code in the query screen. You can omit the reference numbers. These reference numbers for explanation purposes only.

Run this code when you're ready. Figure 14.11 shows the results of this new SELECT statement:

```
1 SELECT fname
2 FROM tblEmpl
3 WHERE username='ctull';
```

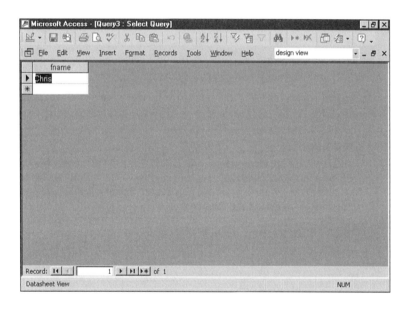

Figure 14.11 *The result of the SELECT statement.*

The following is an explanation of the previous code:

- The first line uses the SELECT keyword, followed by the field from which to view data. In this example, the data you want to view is from the fname field. In other words, you want the result of this query to display the first name of an employee.

- The second line uses the FROM keyword to specify from which table to select data. In this example, the data is selected from the tblEmpl table.

- The third line uses the WHERE keyword to specify any criteria on a field. Specifying criteria reduces the number of records returned. In this example, you've specified for the statement to return only records in which the username field is equal to a value of ctull.

Adding Data with the INSERT Statement

In the previous section, you learned how to select data from a company database. However, selecting data is only one type of functionality that users require. Users must also have the ability to add new records.

To add records to a database, you must use INSERT statements. The INSERT statement enables users to add a new record into a table. The syntax of the INSERT statement is as follows:

```
INSERT INTO the name of the database object &
(the name of the fields to populate with data)
VALUES the values of the data to populate;
```

This syntax is much easier to understand in action. Type the following code into the query screen (do not type in the reference numbers), and run the code. Figure 14.12 shows the results of this statement.

NOTE

When you run this statement in Access, a message displays. This message states that you're about to append rows into the database. The message also states that you can't undo changes. You can click the Yes button. Because you're adding a record, it's acceptable to append the database.

```
1 INSERT INTO tblEmpl (username, password, dept, fname, lname)
2 VALUES ('jsurr', '458965', 'IT', 'Jon', 'Surrells');
```

The following is an explanation of this INSERT statement:

- The first line uses the INSERT INTO keyword to specify the table to which to add data. In this example, you've specified to add data to tblEmpl.

  After referring to the table, the curved brackets specify to which fields to add data. This example lists the username, password, dept, fname, and lname fields. These are the fields in the tblEmpl table that are to have data added to them.

- The second line uses the VALUES keyword, which specifies the values to enter into the fields (listed in line 1).

  By default, SQL assigns each value listed to the fields in order.

After you've run the code, minimize the query screen and return to the option screen. Select the Tables object from the main menu. Then, double-click the tblEmpl table to view the data. Notice that a new record exists in this table (see Figure 14.12).

empl_id	username	password	dept	fname	lname
1	ctull	232456	IT	Chris	Tull
2	kthom	563221	Acct	Keith	Thompson
3	jlidd	123556	Sales	John	Liddy
4	nther	669845	Mrkt	Niki	Theriot
5	jsmit	556123	Plant	John	Smithy
6	mblue	362115	Sales	Matt	Blue
7	kandr	889456	Mrkt	Kevin	Andrzejewski
8	bthom	561234	IT	Brad	Thompson
9	dwass	663956	Acct	Dave	Wassenich
10	gyoun	663123	Plant	George	Young
11	jsurr	458965126	IT	Jon	Surrells
0					

Figure 14.12 *The results of the INSERT statement.*

Modifying Data with the UPDATE Statement

Besides viewing and adding information, users also need to be able to modify information in their databases. UPDATE statements enable users to change existing information in a database table.

The following is the syntax of the UPDATE statement:

```
UPDATE the database object
SET the changes that take place within the database fields
WHERE the data meets a certain criteria;
```

The following is an example of the UPDATE statement in action. Type the following code in the query screen, and then run it. Figure 14.13 shows this code in detail.

NOTE

When you run this statement in Access, a message displays. This message states that you're about to update rows into the database. The message also states that the changes cannot be undone. You can click the Yes button. Because you are modifying a record, it is acceptable to update the database.

```
1 UPDATE tblEmpl
2 SET fname = 'Niki'
3 WHERE username = 'nther';
```

The following is an explanation of this UPDATE statement:

- The first line uses the UPDATE keyword to specify the table in which to modify data. In this example, you've specified to modify data in the tblEmpl table.

- The second line assigns which fields to modify. In this example, the fname field is set equal to Niki. Thus, this line of code states that the field fname is to change to Niki.

- The third line uses the WHERE keyword to designate which records are to contain the change. In this example, the third line of code states that all usernames equal to nther are to have the fname field data changed to Niki.

empl_id	username	password	dept	fname	lname
1	ctull	232456	IT	Chris	Tull
2	kthom	563221	Acct	Keith	Thompson
3	jlidd	123556	Sales	John	Liddy
4	nther	669845	Mrkt	Niki	Theriot
5	jsmit	556123	Plant	John	Smithy
6	mblue	362115	Sales	Matt	Blue
7	kandr	889456	Mrkt	Kevin	Andrzejewski
8	bthom	561234	IT	Brad	Thompson
9	dwass	663956	Acct	Dave	Wassenich
10	gyoun	663123	Plant	George	Young
11	jsurr	458965126	IT	Jon	Surrells
0					

Figure 14.13   *The results of the UPDATE statement.*

Deleting Data with the DELETE Statement

The final SQL functionality discussed in this chapter is the capability to delete records. As you'll see, deleting records is an easy statement to write. However, you should use caution when creating the ability for users to delete records.

CAUTION

After a record is deleted from a database, it's gone for good. There are means for retrieving deleted records (such as using backup data), but these methods are usually time-consuming and not always reliable.

By design, most DBMSs don't allow for the deletion of data, except for information such as notes about a person. Most DBMSs use a design in which records are marked as inactive rather than deleted.

The proper handling of deletion is important, especially as your DBMS development efforts become more involved.

The syntax for a DELETE statement is as follows:

```
DELETE FROM the name of a database object
WHERE the data meets a certain type of criteria;
```

To see the DELETE statement in action, type the following code in the query screen (without the reference numbers). Then, run this statement. Figure 14.14 shows the results of this statement.

```
1 DELETE FROM tblEmpl
2 WHERE username = 'gyoun';
```

NOTE

When you run this statement in Access, a message displays stating that you're about to delete rows in the database. The message also states that the changes can't be undone. You can click the Yes button. Because you're deleting a record, it's acceptable to make deletions to the database.

The following is an explanation of this DELETE statement:

- The first line uses the DELETE FROM keyword to specify the table from which to delete a record. In this line of code, the table data is deleted from is tblEmpl.

- The second line uses the WHERE keyword to specify the criteria of records to delete data. In this example, the username is set equal to gyoun. Thus, any records with the username gyoun are deleted.

empl_id	username	password	dept	fname	lname
1	ctull	232456	IT	Chris	Tull
2	kthom	563221	Acct	Keith	Thompson
3	jlidd	123556	Sales	John	Liddy
4	nther	669845	Mrkt	Niki	Theriot
5	jsmit	556123	Plant	John	Smithy
6	mblue	362115	Sales	Matt	Blue
7	kandr	889456	Mrkt	Kevin	Andrzejewski
8	bthom	561234	IT	Brad	Thompson
9	dwass	663956	Acct	Dave	Wassenich
10	gyoun	663123	Plant	George	Young
11	jsurr	458965126	IT	Jon	Surrells
0					

Figure 14.14 *The results of the DELETE statement.*

TIP

If the table you're deleting records from is open when you're running the query, you must close the table and then open it again to see your changes.

Summary

In this chapter, you've learned several important skills required for development with relational databases. You've learned about a number of concepts regarding databases and DBMS.

This chapter also introduced you to the Structured Query Language, the language used for nearly every relational database on the market today. You learned how to use SQL to manipulate data, including the viewing, adding, editing, and deleting of records.

In the next chapter, you'll use much of this newfound information to create a WAP application that interacts with a relational database. You'll use all the technologies presented in this book—WML, WMLScript, ASP, and SQL—to create a robust WAP application that, from a WAP device, accesses and manipulates data.

We've covered a lot of ground throughout this book, perhaps more than you've realized. Chapter 15 will put all these concepts together, showing you just how far you've come.

Accessing Database Content from WAP Devices

Chapter 14, "An Introduction to DBMS Development," covered a great deal of information about DBMS development. This chapter takes that information and incorporates it with the WAP skills you've practiced throughout this book.

In this chapter, you'll more closely examine connecting WAP devices to databases—one of the hottest areas in wireless development today. In this chapter, you'll also create ASP pages using VBScript and ActiveX Data Objects, both of which you'll learn about in this chapter. You'll then learn how to access these ASP pages from your WAP device, calling them from a WML deck.

Specifically, this chapter covers the following topics:

- Understanding and creating an Open Database Connectivity Data Source Name (ODBC DSN) for your database. An ODBC DSN provides the means for your Active Server Pages (ASP) to connect and identify information from your database.

- Understanding and creating ActiveX Data Objects (ADO) to use in your ASP pages. ADOs provide the capability to access data from a server. You'll create a WAP application that uses ADO to access data from a Web server.

Using an ODBC DSN to Connect to Your Database

In Chapter 14, you created the company database and then populated this database with data. Sure, you can access this data directly by opening the database, but what if you want to access the data by some other means, such as an application? To access database information from an application, you must create a means for the application to connect to and identify your database.

One possible solution for developers is to connect an application to a database using an ODBC DSN. Let's take a moment to dissect this acronym and understand what ODBC DSN is all about.

Using Open Database Connectivity

ODBC stands for open database connectivity, which is software that enables applications to access a variety of databases. In fact, at the time of this writing, ODBC currently supports drivers for more than 55 of the most widely used databases on the market.

Before ODBC, different types of databases (such as Access, Oracle, SQL Server, and Apache) required different means for applications to access data. ODBC has standardized the means for which applications can access a database. Thus, most popular databases support an ODBC driver. Microsoft Windows supplies many of these drivers in its Windows software.

In this chapter, you'll use an ODBC connection to access the company database from an ASP page.

Using an ODBC Data Source Name

A *data source name (DSN)* is a system name given to a database. DSNs are used when connecting to a database. As you'll see, you'll use a DSN with your ODBC connection.

"But why does a database need a DSN when the database already has a name?" you might ask. The reason is because several arguments are required to connect to a database. Without a DSN, you would need to define all these arguments every time you wanted to connect to a database.

A DSN removes the need to define all these arguments by creating a system name that groups all the arguments together. Thus, when you create a DSN for a database, you're actually bundling a bunch of arguments under one name (the data source name). Whenever this DSN is called, all the arguments associated with it are executed.

CREATING A **DSN** FOR THE COMPANY DATABASE

Now that you're familiar with the concepts behind ODBC DSN, let's create one. You must create an ODBC DSN for your WAP application to use data from the company database.

The following steps describe how to create an ODBC DSN in a Windows environment. The examples in this book use a Microsoft Access database.

NOTE

Depending on the type of database for which you're creating an ODBC DSN, the following steps can differ. Refer to your database documentation for more information about creating an ODBC DSN for a particular database.

---

1. Select the Start menu, and then select Settings, Control Panel. Double-click the Data Sources (ODBC) icon. The name of this icon can differ slightly, depending on the operating system you are using. When the icon is selected, the ODBC Data Source Administrator screen displays.

NOTE

On some Windows versions the ODBC icon might not be visible from your Control Panel. This can be due to the Control Panel displaying in a summary. Make sure your Control Panel is showing all icons.

A hyperlink to the left of the Control Panel screen provides the ability to toggle from summary to detail of all aspects of the screen.

---

2. Select the System DSN tab, and then click the Add button. The Create New Data Source screen displays (see Figure 15.1).

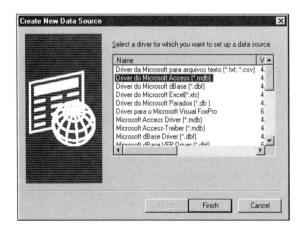

Figure 15.1   *The Create New Data Source screen.*

3. Select the Microsoft Access driver if you're using an Access database (the examples use Access). If you're using another type of database, select the appropriate database driver from the list.

4. After you've selected the appropriate database driver, click the Finish button.

NOTE

Most databases provide ODBC drivers with the installation of the database. However, if you need to obtain a particular driver, most are available for free download from the database company's Web site. You also can perform a search on any search engine for a list of other areas to obtain ODBC drivers if needed.

---

5. The ODBC Microsoft Access Setup screen displays, as shown in Figure 15.2.

Figure 15.2 *The ODBC Microsoft Access Setup screen.*

6. Type in **company** in the Data Source Name field. Then, click the Select button. Select the location of the company database you created in the last chapter, and click the OK button.

In the examples in the last chapter, the database was saved in the My Documents folder. Your screen should look similar to Figure 15.3.

7. After you've typed in a DSN and selected the location of your database, click the OK button. You should see the company data source name in the ODBC Data Source Administrator screen (see Figure 15.4).

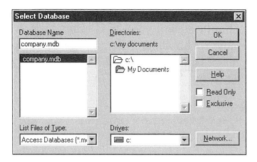

Figure 15.3 *Creating the data source name for the company database.*

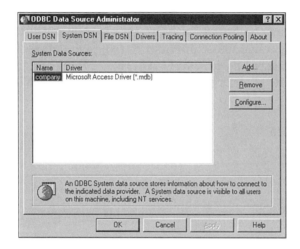

Figure 15.4 *The company DSN.*

CAUTION

When selecting the correct driver for Microsoft Access, you might find different language versions of the same driver. For most of you reading this book, you should select the English version driver. Be sure the driver looks like the one selected in Figure 15.4.

Retrieving Information from a WAP Application

Now that you've created a means for your application to connect to and identify with your database, let's focus our attention on creating the functionality to access data from the database.

Because accessing data from a device requires greater amounts of memory and processing, you should design your WAP applications to retrieve information using server-side technology. Thus, in the examples in this chapter, you'll create an ASP page that processes the data of your database and then sends the results back to the WAP device (in a WML format).

To process data from an ASP page, you'll use a combination of ASP and server components. The server components you'll use are known as ActiveX Data Objects, better known as ADO.

ADOs are groups of objects that provide the capability to perform several actions against a database.

Using ActiveX Data Objects

ADO is Microsoft's solution for interfacing to multiple databases. Before ADO, developers had to use different tools and languages to interface with different databases and platforms. ADO eases things for developers, providing a single data interface to create complete database solutions.

Eight ADO objects are available for developers:

- Connection
- Command
- Recordset
- Record
- Stream
- Parameter
- Field
- Property

Although all ADO objects are useful, in this book you'll use only the Connection objects. As you become more familiar with database development, you'll find uses for all the ADO objects. However, at this stage of the game, it's better to learn only the information you need.

TIP

Check out Microsoft's MSDN site at http://msdn.microsoft.com for excellent information regarding ADO. Once at this site, access the Data Access topic in the table of contents to find information regarding ADO.

Connecting to a Database Using the `Connection` Object

The `Connection` object creates an open connection to a data source. It's through this connection that you can access and manipulate information from a database.

The `Connection` object contains several methods. In this book, you'll use the `Open`, `Close`, and `Execute` methods. Table 15.1 summarizes some of the most common methods of the `Connection` object.

NOTE

The terms *objects* and *methods* might be new to you, but you've used these types of things before when you used the WMLScript libraries.

Objects essentially serve the same purpose as WMLScript libraries. Objects are self-contained entities that consist of procedures to manipulate data.

Methods are essentially built-in functions, grouped with a particular object. They're procedures that are executed from in an object.

The reason for the different terminology is that ADO borrows its functionality from object-oriented programming languages (such as Java and Visual C++). In this book, we've mainly used procedural programming languages.

Don't worry too much about the differences between structural and object-oriented programming languages—it's not necessary to delve into these distinctions for the purposes of this book.

---

*Table 15.1   The Common Methods of the **Connection** Object*

Method	Description
Open	Opens a connection to a data source
Execute	Executes some type of command (be it a query, statement, procedure, or provider-specific text)
Close	Closes an open object and any dependent objects

NOTE

To view all information regarding ADO objects (including all methods), check out the Microsoft MSDN site at `http://www.msdn.microsoft.com`.

Once at the site, locate the table of contents toward the left frame of the Web page. Select MSDN, `Access Data Access`, SDK Documentation, Microsoft ActiveX Data Objects, ADO Programmer's Reference, ADO API Reference, ADO Objects, Connection Object (ADO), Properties, Methods, and Events.

I know what you're thinking: Whew!

Don't worry, finding these links aren't as daunting as they might seem. The MSDN site is set up for easy navigation. If you have some trouble finding information, you also can type a keyword in the Search field located on this page.

You'll write this page so that it's accessible from your WAP device. Save the following code as menu.asp, and save this file in the C:\Inetpub\wwwroot directory.

TIP

The location of your Web server's index files is contained in a file location referred to as a Web server's *document root*.

For instance, in the examples in this book, the C:\Inetpub\wwwroot file location is considered your Web server's document root.

To run this code, access the http://localhost/menu.asp URL from your emulator. You must access all ASP files in this manner, being sure to type them after the forward slash after localhost. This is only required when working with individual files:

CAUTION

In case you're wondering, the ADO objects are installed with Microsoft Operating Systems and stored in the C:\Program Files\Common Files\System\ADO directory.

Before running any of these scripts, find the adovbs.inc file in these files and copy it into your C:\Inetpub\wwwroot directory. This will ensure that your test Web server has access to the proper ADO objects.

If you can't find this file, you can also download this file as part of Microsoft's Microsoft Data Access Components (MDAC). At the time of this writing, this file is accessible from http://www.microsoft.com/data/download.htm.

```
1   <% Response.ContentType = "text/vnd.wap.wml" %>
2   <?xml version="1.0"?>
3   <!DOCTYPE wml PUBLIC "-//WAPFORUM//DTD WML 1.1//EN"
4   "http://www.wapforum.org/DTD/wml_1.1.xml">
5   <wml>
6     <card id="menu" title="Menu">
7       <p>You are connected
8       <%
9       dim dbConn

10      set dbConn = Server.CreateObject("ADODB.Connection")
11      dbConn.open("dsn=company")

12      dbConn.Close
13      set dbConn = Nothing

14      %>
15      </p>
16    </card>
17 </wml>
```

Because several aspects of this code are new to you, let's look at the bold lines of this code:

- Line 1 uses the ContentType method of the ASP's Response object. If you recall from Chapter 13, "WAP Development with ASP," ContentType enables developers to define the type of data sent when a request is sent to the Web server.

  In this line of code, the data type is defined to be sent as text/vnd.wap.wml. This data type represents the MIME type used for WML.

- Line 8 begins the ASP script by using the start delimiter (<%).

- Line 9 uses VBScript's dim keyword to declare variables at the beginning of your code. It's usually a good programming practice to use the dim keyword at the beginning of your ASP scripts. Doing so helps you (as well as others reading your code) keep track of the different variables used in a script.

- Line 10 uses the VBScript set keyword to declare a variable (just as the var keyword is used to set variables in WMLScript). In Line 10, the variable identifier created is dbConn.

TIP

dbConn is a common variable identifier used by developers when creating a variable that represents database connection information (in other words, how the application connects to the database).

In this line of code, you associate the dbConn variable with the ASP's CreateObject method. This method is part of ASP's Server objects.

Recall from Table 15.1 that this method creates an instance for ADO objects. If you want to use the methods of an ADO object, you must include this method.

In this Connection object, you've specified ADODB.Connection. This creates an ADO Connection object on the server. You are now able to use any of the ADO's Connection methods until this Connection object is closed.

- Line 11 uses the Open method of ASP's Connection object (listed as the dbConn variable because of line 10, where the dbConn variable is set equal to the instance of Connection object).

  The Open method sets the DSN equal to the name of the database DSN company. This is the DSN you created earlier in this chapter.

- Line 12 closes the Connection object. It's usually a good practice to close any ADO object you've opened in your scripts.

- Line 13 sets the dbConn variable equal to Nothing. This frees up memory used by the Connection object. Again, this is another good practice for any ADO object you've opened in your scripts.

- Line 14 uses an ending deliminator (%>) to close your ASP script.

Figure 15.5 displays this file on a device screen.

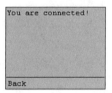

Figure 15.5   *The menu.asp file on a device emulator.*

Congratulations! You've now connected to a database residing on a remote server—all from a WAP device. This is no small task, and you're now entering the exciting and in-demand realm of DBMS development. Not to be dramatic, but you're also entering a new developmental frontier—a frontier that is widely unexplored and uncharted today.

Lewis and Clark eat your heart out.

Selecting a Set of Records with SQL

Of course, now that you've connected to a database, you'll need to incorporate functionality that allows you to retrieve user-defined information from your database.

To better define the retrieval of values in this application, let's first return to the login.wml file created at the end of Part II, "Static WAP Development."

To get an idea of how to incorporate SQL into your WAP applications, let's add to the menu.asp file created earlier in this chapter. Type the following code, and save your work as menu2.asp. Be sure to save this file in the C:\Inetpub\wwwroot directory:

```
1   <% Response.ContentType = "text/vnd.wap.wml" %>
2   <?xml version="1.0"?>
3   <!DOCTYPE wml PUBLIC "-//WAPFORUM//DTD WML 1.1//EN"
4   "http://www.wapforum.org/DTD/wml_1.1.xml">
5   <wml>
6     <card id="menu" title="Menu">
7       <p>
8       <%
9       dim dbConn, sql, empl
```

```
10      set dbConn = Server.CreateObject("ADODB.Connection")
11      dbConn.open("dsn=company")

12      sql = "SELECT * FROM tblEmpl WHERE username='ctull' AND password=
        ➥'232456'"

13      set empl = dbConn.Execute(sql)

14      if empl.EOF then
15        Response.Write "You have entered an invalid login."
16      else
17        Response.Write "Welcome, " & empl("fname")
18      end if

19      empl.Close
20      dbConn.Close
21      set empl = Nothing
22      set dbConn = Nothing

23      %>
24      </p>
25    </card>
26 </wml>
```

In this example two lines have been added. The following is an explanation of the new code created in this example:

- Line 9 adds variables to the dim statement. In this code, three variables to use throughout this script are listed: dbConn, sql, and empl.

- Line 12 creates the variable identifier empl_sql. This variable is equal to a SQL SELECT statement. In this SELECT statement, an asterisk (*) represents all records. Thus, the way this SQL statement functions is that all records from the tblEmpl table are selected.

  Notice that you do not need to use the set keyword when defining a variable that defines a SQL statement. You must use the set keyword only when creating variables that use ASP objects.

- Line 13 creates the variable identifier empl. This variable is set equal to the execute method (from ADO's Connection object). This method executes the sql variable (as designated in the object's argument).

  This SQL is executed for the dbConn variable, which is equal to the DSN company. The dbConn variable's DSN is defined in line 11 of this code.

- Lines 14–18 use an if/else statement. In this code, line 14 states that if no records are found from the query, the ASP Response object writes the message You have entered an invalid login to the device.

Line 17 presents the else clause of this statement. If a record is found, the Response object writes the message Welcome, along with the fname field from the record. Thus, if the username and password are authenticated, the user's first name (as recognized by the company data) displays.

- Lines 19 and 20 close the objects associated with the empl and dbConn variables.

- Lines 21 and 22 clear the memory used by the objects associated with the empl and dbConn variables.

Try running this code from a device emulator. You'll see the same result as the menu.asp file created earlier in this chapter. Don't be disappointed—your query worked. However, you must add some more functionality to actually view the results of your query.

There always has to be a catch, doesn't there?

Figure 15.6 displays this file on a device emulator.

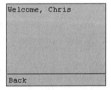

Figure 15.6 *The menu2.asp file on a device emulator.*

Currently, the application performs a query to view the first name of the employee with the username ctull and password 223456. If you have not entered this information into the company database (see Chapter 14), the application returns an Invalid Login message. Figure 15.7 displays this application if the record is not found.

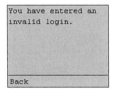

```
You have entered an
invalid login.




Back
```

Figure 15.7   *The* menu2.asp *file not finding a record.*

User-Defined Retrieval of Database Values

You're now getting to the exciting stuff—pulling all the information you've learned in this book together. You'll now see some of the exciting dynamic capabilities made possible through combining WAP with other exciting technologies (such as ASP).

In the previous example, you created functionality that pulls data from the remote database. But who wants to log on as ctull all the time (especially, if you're not that user)?

In this next example, you add some lines of code to dynamically allow the card to display a user's first name. In this example, after the query is executed and the results selected, you use some ASPs to define the user's personal information from the company database.

To begin, you first must modify the login.wml file created in Part III, "Advanced WAP Development." The bold font represents modified areas of this file. When you're finished with the changes, save this file as loginASP.wml in the C:\My Documents folder.

By the way, don't try running this example until you also create the ASP file that accompanies it.

NOTE

At the end of the Part IV exercise, you'll learn why some of the files should reside in the C:\My Documents folder and others should reside on the remote server.

Essentially, those files that reside in the C:\My Documents represent files that reside in the WAP device.

```
1   <?xml version="1.0"?>
2   <!DOCTYPE wml PUBLIC "-//WAPFORUM//DTD WML 1.1//EN"
3   "http://www.wapforum.org/DTD/wml_1.1.xml">
4   <wml>
5   <!-- Card 1 -->
6      <card id="username" title="Username" ontimer="#message">
7         <timer name="nametime" value="$nametime"/>
```

```
8         <do type="accept" label="Go">
9         <go href="#password"/>
10        </do>
11          <p>
12          <anchor title="Go"><go href="#set"/>Settings</anchor><br/>
13          Enter username:
14          <input name="username" type="text" maxlength="5"/>
15          </p>
16      </card>

17 <!-- Card 2 -->
18      <card id="password" title="Password">
19        <do type="accept" label="Go">
20        <go method="post" href="http://localhost/menu3.asp">
21          <postfield name="username" value="$username"/>
22          <postfield name="password" value="$password"/>
23        </go>
24      </do>
25          <p>Enter password:
26          <input name="password" type="password" maxlength="6"/>
27          </p>
28      </card>

29 <!-- Card 3 -->
30      <card id="message" title="Message">
31        <do type="accept" label="Go">
32        <go href="home.wml"/>
33        </do>

34        <do type="option" label="Settings">
35        <go href="#set"/>
36        </do>

37          <p>Expired input time limit. Login again?</p>
38      </card>

39 <!-- Card 4 -->
40      <card id="set" title="Settings">
41        <do type="accept" label="Go">
42        <go href="#username"/>
43        </do>
44          <p>Set input time:
45          <input name="nametime" format="*N"/>
46          </p>
47        </card>

48 </wml>
```

The following in an explanation of the bolded lines of this code:

- Line 9 changes the link from the validate.wmls file to the password card located in this deck. The reason for this is that you'll create validation functionality in this deck that's similar to the functionality found in the validate.wmls file.

- Line 14 adds the maxlength attribute to the username input field. This attribute defines that the username input can't be more than five characters.

- Line 20 uses the method attribute of the GO element. This element allows users to send information using the post value.

- Lines 21 and 22 use the POSTFIELD element of WML. This WML element was mentioned briefly in Chapter 6, "User Input with Variables." This element specifies a field and value to be sent to a URL (all through the GO element).

  In this example, the URL specifies that the username and password data entered by the user is to be sent to the URL http://localhost/menu3/asp. You might recognize this URL as that of your Web server test environment.

- Line 26 adds the maxlength attribute to the password input field. This attribute defines that the password input can't be more than six characters.

Now that you have an understanding of the login functionality of this WML deck, let's turn our attention to our ASP file. You'll need to make only a couple of adjustments to the menu2.asp file created earlier in this chapter. These changes are marked in bold font.

After you finish making these changes, save the new file as menu3.asp in the C:\Inetpub\wwwroot directory:

```
1   <% Response.ContentType = "text/vnd.wap.wml" %>
2   <?xml version="1.0"?>
3   <!DOCTYPE wml PUBLIC "-//WAPFORUM//DTD WML 1.1//EN"
4   "http://www.wapforum.org/DTD/wml_1.1.xml">
5   <wml>
6       <card id="menu" title="Menu">
7         <p>
8         <%
9         dim dbConn, sql, empl

10        set dbConn = Server.CreateObject("ADODB.Connection")
11        dbConn.open("dsn=company")
```

```
12      sql = "SELECT * FROM tblEmpl WHERE username='"&Request.Form
        ➡("username")&"'
13      AND password='"&Request.Form("password")&"'"

14      set empl = dbConn.Execute(sql)

15      if empl.EOF then
16        Response.Write "You have entered an invalid login."
17      else
18        Response.Write "Welcome, " & empl("fname")
19      end if

20      empl.Close
21      dbConn.Close
22      set empl = Nothing
23      set dbConn = Nothing

24      %>
25      </p>
26    </card>
27 </wml>
```

The following is an explanation of the bolded areas of this code:

- Line 12 uses the Request object to retrieve values sent from the client to the server. When using the POST element to send data (like you did with the login.wml file), you must use ASP's form method.

CAUTION

Although lines 12 and 13 split up the sql statement, you should ensure that you type the code on lines 12 and 13 all together on one line.

Figure 15.8 displays this code on a device emulator.

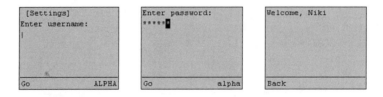

Figure 15.8   *Retrieving data from a WAP device.*

Testing WAP Decks on an Actual WAP Device

At some point in your development efforts, you'll eventually want to see your applications operate on an actual device. Testing your applications on a wireless emulator is acceptable for development purposes. However, before deploying your application in a real-world setting, you must test it on an actual WAP gateway and WAP device.

Although these topics in themselves could fill another book (there's an idea!), I'll discuss the options available for developers in taking their development efforts from a wireless emulator to an actual WAP device.

WAP GATEWAYS

The first issue you must consider is the WAP gateway (recall from Chapter 1, "What Is WAP Development?" that the WAP *gateway* is the device that translates wireless data into a format that a wired server recognizes, and vice versa).

Typically, as a developer, you have two options when testing and deploying an actual WAP application. You can purchase and use a private gateway, or you can use a public gateway.

Obviously, each option has advantages and disadvantages. A private gateway provides developers with more access control and security. However, having your own WAP gateway also requires more expense and more administration time on the owner's part.

Public gateways, on the other hand, are cost-effective and require less administrative attention (and therefore are less time-consuming). However, what you gain in these areas is offset by what you ultimately lose in the control of how the gateway operates.

Several WAP gateways are available, and most of the major mobile device manufacturers sell WAP gateways.

To find out how to use a public WAP gateway, check to see whether your company or mobile network provider offers these services. If not, you might be able to find a WAP hosting service you can subscribe to.

WAP DEVICES

After you've found a WAP gateway, you must purchase a WAP phone. You'll then need to configure the WAP device for use with the WAP gateway. Your

WAP device and mobile network provider will have information about this. For the most part, you must configure the following on your WAP device:

- **A dial-up number**—This establishes a connection with the ISP, the call type that your service provider uses, and any user authentication that's required.

- **The IP address and port number**—This is for the WAP gateway you're using.

- **The default WAP page**—This loads when accessing wireless services.

After you've performed these steps, you're ready to load WML decks into your WAP device. The first thing you must do is have your WML decks loaded on the WAP gateway you're using. You grab these decks from the gateway and place them in your device.

Although each device is slightly different, the overall method is to find the WAP Settings area on the WAP device. This area is usually located in a System Info area of the device.

From here, you then must select the URL Location area of your device, which enables you to specify the URL of the WML deck you want to load into your device. These steps enable you to load decks into your device.

Where to Go from Here...

You've come a long way in learning the technologies involved for real-world WAP development. By now, you probably have a strong understanding of the WML language and are familiar with the possibilities of WMLScript, ADO, and ASP in creating exciting and usable WAP applications.

You now have a strong foundation to build on if you want to expand on the areas covered in this book or pursue other existing areas of WAP development, including incorporating VoiceXML and even Java technologies into your development efforts. Keep plugging away, and remember that the only way to learn how to develop is by doing.

Part IV Examples

It's now time to take the experience and knowledge you've gained in this book and pull it all together. After piecing these files together, feel free to experiment, perhaps exploring different areas of ASP and ADO to add to this application, or perhaps incorporating some WMLScript into your files.

Before you begin, let's summarize how this application works. First, a default.asp page resides on a remote Web server. To begin the application, users access this page from their WAP devices. The page presents users with a title page and dynamically states the time of the Web server.

A timer resides in the default.asp file and, after a period of five seconds, takes users to the splash.asp Login button, which allows users to log in to the system.

After users click the Login button, a splash page displays (splash.wml) followed by a brief title page (title.wml). Both of these use timers; therefore, users don't need to have any interaction with this portion of the application.

After the title.wml file displays, users are taken to the home.wml page, which displays menu options, such as Login and Help. By selecting the Login option, users are taken to the Login.wml file.

The login.wml file asks users to enter their usernames and password information, and then it posts this information back to the remote server. The menu.asp file receives this information and checks it against the company database to see whether this data exists.

If the data does exist in the database, users are given a personalized welcome message. If the data does not exist, an invalid login message displays.

Figure IV.1 displays a graphical representation of the workflow of this application.

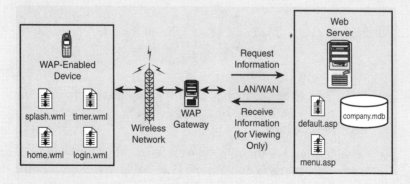

Figure IV.1 *The workflow of the user authentication WAP application.*

The following sections summarize all the code you'll use. Save files that are to reside on the Web server in the c:\inetpub\wwwroot directory, and save files that are to reside on the client in the c:\My Documents directory.

default.asp

To begin, you must use the default.asp file created in Chapter 14, "An Introduction to DBMS Development." In this file, you add a DO element that enables users to initiate the login process to the system application.

Type the following changes to the default.asp file; then, save your changes. You should save this file in the C:\Inetpub\wwwroot directory. Figure IV.2 displays this file on a device screen:

```
<%Response.ContentType = "text/vnd.wap.wml" %>
<?xml version="1.0"?>
<!DOCTYPE wml PUBLIC "-//WAPFORUM//DTD WML 1.1//EN"
"http://www.wapforum.org/DTD/wml_1.1.xml">
<wml>
   <card id="default" title="Default">
     <do type="Options" label="Login">
     <go href="file://c:/My Documents/splash.wml"/>
     </do>
       <p align="center">Logging into system<br/><br/>
       The time is now <% = time() %>
       </p>
   </card>
</wml>
```

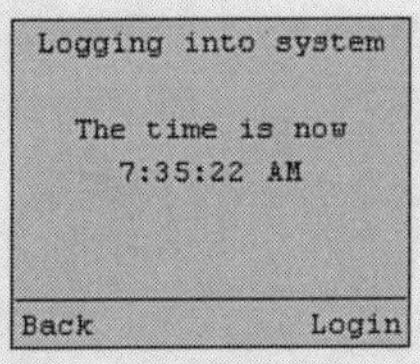

```
Logging into system

  The time is now
    7:35:22 AM



Back              Login
```

Figure IV.2   *The* default.asp *file on a device emulator.*

splash.wml

This file acts as the first page of the application you are building. This file contains the same code as the splash.wml file created in Part II, "Static WAP Development."

Be sure you save this file, as well as the wbmp files you created, in the C:/My Documents folder. Figure IV.3 displays these files on a device screen:

```
<?xml version="1.0"?>
<!DOCTYPE wml PUBLIC "-//WAPFORUM//DTD WML 1.1//EN"
"http://www.wapforum.org/DTD/wml_1.1.xml">
<wml>

<!-- Card 1 -->
   <card id="splash25" title="Splash" ontimer="#splash50">
     <timer name="splashlogo25" value="5"/>
       <p align="center">
       <img src="logo25.wbmp" alt=""/>
       </p>
   </card>

<!-- Card 2 -->
   <card id="splash50" title="Splash" ontimer="#splash75">
     <timer name="splashlogo50" value="5"/>
       <p align="center">
       <img src="logo50.wbmp" alt=""/>
       </p>
   </card>

<!-- Card 3 -->

   <card id="splash75" title="Splash" ontimer="#splash100">
     <timer name="splashlogo75" value="5"/>
       <p align="center">
       <img src="logo75.wbmp" alt=""/>
       </p>
   </card>

<!-- Card 4 -->
   <card id="splash100" title="Splash" ontimer="#splash125">
     <timer name="splashlogo100" value="5"/>
       <p align="center">
       <img src="logo.wbmp" alt=""/>
       </p>
   </card>

<!-- Card 5 -->
   <card id="splash125" title="Splash" ontimer="timer.wml">
     <timer name="splashlogo125" value="5"/>
       <p align="center">
       <img src="logo125.wbmp" alt=""/>
       </p>
   </card>

</wml>
```

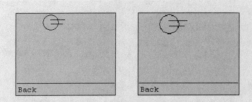

Figure IV.3 *The* splash.wml *file on a device emulator.*

timer.wml

This file works with the splash.wml file and presents a title page for a couple of seconds before moving on to the home.wml file. This code was created at the beginning of Chapter 8, "Incorporating Timers into WAP Applications."

You should save this file in your C:\My Documents folder. Figure IV.4 displays this file on a device screen:

```
<?xml version="1.0"?>
<!DOCTYPE wml PUBLIC "-//WAPFORUM//DTD WML 1.1//EN"
"http://www.wapforum.org/DTD/wml_1.1.xml">
<wml>
    <card id="splash" title="Splash" ontimer="home.wml">
      <timer name="splashlogo" value="50"/>
        <p align="center">Yourcompany.com
        <img src="logo.wbmp" alt="Yourcompany.com"/>
        </p>
    </card>
</wml>
```

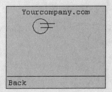

Figure IV.4 *The* timer.wml *file on a device emulator.*

home.wml

You first created this file at the end of Part II. This code is similar, but you'll make a couple of changes. Be sure you save this file in your C:\My Documents folder. Figure IV.5 displays this file on a device screen:

```
<?xml version="1.0"?>
<!DOCTYPE wml PUBLIC "-//WAPFORUM//DTD WML 1.1//EN"
"http://www.wapforum.org/DTD/wml_1.1.xml">
<wml>
   <template>
     <do type="options" label="Help">
     <go href="#help"/>
     </do>

     <do type="accept" label="Home">
     <go href="#home"/>
     </do>
   </template>

<!-- Card 1 -->
   <card id="home" title="Home">
     <p align="center"><b>Welcome to the yourcompany.com system.</b>
       <table columns="2">
         <tr>
           <td>Option 1:</td>
             <td><anchor title="Go"><go href="login.wml"/>Login</anchor>
             ➥<br/></td>
         </tr>
         <tr>
           <td>Option 2:</td>
           <td><anchor title="Go"><go href="#help"/>Help</anchor><br/></td>
         </tr>
       </table>
     </p>
   </card>

<!-- Card 2 -->
   <card id="help" title="Help">
     <p>Please contact your system administrator at 800.555.1212</p>
   </card>
</wml>
```

Figure IV.5 *The* home.wml *file on a device emulator.*

login.wml

This file's last incarnation was as loginASP.wml, created in this chapter. However, you should modify the area in bold font as follows. The change you make are to rename the menu3.asp file to simply menu.asp. You should save this file in your C:\My Documents folder. Figure IV.6 displays this file on a device screen:

```
<?xml version="1.0"?>
<!DOCTYPE wml PUBLIC "-//WAPFORUM//DTD WML 1.1//EN"
"http://www.wapforum.org/DTD/wml_1.1.xml">
<wml>
<!-- Card 1 -->
   <card id="username" title="Username" ontimer="#message">
     <timer name="nametime" value="$nametime"/>
       <do type="accept" label="Go">
       <go href="#password"/>
       </do>
         <p>
         <anchor title="Go"><go href="#set"/>Settings</anchor><br/>
         Enter username:
         <input name="username" type="text" maxlength="5"/>
         </p>
   </card>

<!-- Card 2 -->
   <card id="password" title="Password">
     <do type="accept" label="Go">
     <go method="post" href="http://localhost/menu.asp">
       <postfield name="username" value="$username"/>
       <postfield name="password" value="$password"/>
     </go>
     </do>
       <p>Enter password:
       <input name="password" type="password" maxlength="6"/>
       </p>
   </card>
```

```
<!-- Card 3 -->
   <card id="message" title="Message">
     <do type="accept" label="Go">
     <go href="home.wml"/>
     </do>

     <do type="option" label="Settings">
     <go href="#set"/>
     </do>

       <p>Expired input time limit. Login again?</p>
   </card>

<!-- Card 4 -->
   <card id="set" title="Settings">
     <do type="accept" label="Go">
     <go href="#username"/>
     </do>
       <p>Set input time:
       <input name="nametime" format="*N"/>
       </p>
   </card>

</wml>
```

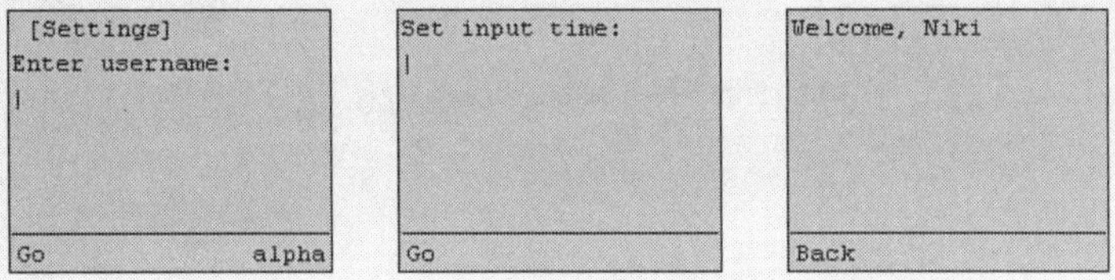

Figure IV.6 The `login.wml` file on a device emulator.

menu.asp

This file was named `menu3.asp` in the examples in Chapter 15, "Accessing Database Content from WAP Devices." However, for ease of reading, let's rename this file `menu.asp`. Be sure to save this file in your `C:\Inetpub\wwwroot` directory. Figure IV.7 displays this file on a device screen.

CAUTION

As mentioned in Chapter 15, you should ensure that your SQL statement resides all in one line when typed on your text editor. This will avoid any problems when your ASP script runs the SQL.

```
<% Response.ContentType = "text/vnd.wap.wml" %>
<?xml version="1.0"?>
<!DOCTYPE wml PUBLIC "-//WAPFORUM//DTD WML 1.1//EN"
"http://www.wapforum.org/DTD/wml_1.1.xml">
<wml>
   <card id="menu" title="Menu">
     <p>
     <%
     dim dbConn, sql, empl

     set dbConn = Server.CreateObject("ADODB.Connection")
     dbConn.open("dsn=company")

     sql = "SELECT * FROM tblEmpl WHERE username='"&Request.Form("username")
     ➥&"'
     AND password='"&Request.Form("password")&"'"

     set empl = dbConn.Execute(sql)

     if empl.EOF then
        Response.Write "You have entered an invalid login."
     else
        Response.Write "Welcome, " & empl("fname")
     end if

     empl.Close
     dbConn.Close
     set empl = Nothing
     set dbConn = Nothing

     %>
     </p>
   </card>
</wml>
```

```
Enter password:
*****█



Go              alpha
```

Figure IV.7   *The menu.asp file on a device screen.*

Part V

Reference

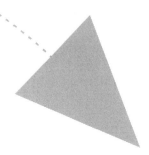

Appendix A

WML Reference

This book uses the WML 1.1 specification within all examples. To date, this specification is the most stable version of WML and is the most widely accepted language for both older and new WAP devices.

NOTE

The latest WML specifications are available from the WAP Forum Web site (http://www.wapforum.org). To find these specifications, select the This Site link at the top of the page.

Under the What Is WAP heading, find the white papers associated with the Wireless Application Environment. You'll find the latest specifications for WML in this area of the site.

This appendix first presents a quick reference of the WML 1.1 language presented within this book and then follows with a more detailed reference of the WML elements and their attributes. The quick reference section groups the elements alphabetically, and the detailed reference section groups the elements by their functionality.

WML Quick Reference

The following pages provide a quick summary of the WML elements. These elements are listed in alphabetical order.

NOTE

The available WML elements might differ slightly, depending on the browser being used by the WAP device. The following list presents the standard WML elements available within WAP browsers at the time of this writing.

For more information, check the WML specification available from the WAP Forum.

WML Elements

Element	Description	Syntax	Attributes	Chapter Reference
ANCHOR	Enables users to select and navigate throughout a WAP application.	`<anchor>` *content* `</anchor>`	accesskey href title	Chapter 5
ACCESS	Provides the functionality that restricts unauthorized users from accessing content-sensitive information.	`<head>` `<access/>` `</head>`	domain path	Chapter 3
B	Creates a bold font.	`<b>`*content* `</b>`	None	Chapter 4
BIG	Creates a big font.	`<big>`*content* `</big>`	None	Chapter 4
BR	Forces the insertion of a line break into the text.	`<p>`*content* ` </p>`	None	Chapter 4
CARD	A single WML unit, which may contain information such as text to present to the user, instructions for gathering user input, and so on. WML cards are to a WAP application as pages are to a Web site or screens are to PC applications.	`<card>` *content* `</card>`	id newcontext onenterbackward onenterforward ontimer ordered title	Chapter 3

Chapter Element	Description	Syntax	Attributes	Reference

DO	Enables developers to associate actions with a user interface mechanism. Like the ANCHOR element, the DO event must be associated with a task.	`<do>`
		    `content`
		`</do>`
			`label`
			`name`
			`optional`
			`type`
				Chapter 5

EM	Creates emphasis on the font.	`<em>content` `</em>`	None	Chapter 4

GO	Specifies forward navigation to a URL. This element is the most widely used task element.	`<go href=URL/>`
		`content</go>`
			`href`
			`send referer`
			`method`
			`accept-charset`
			`enctype`
				Chapter 5

HEAD	Contains information relating to the deck as a whole, including metadata and access control elements.	`<head>`
		    `content`
		`</head>`
			None	Chapter 3

I	Creates an italicized font.	`<i>content` `</i>`	None	Chapter 4

IMG	Provides the ability to display images within WAP applications.	`<img>`
		    `content`
		`</img>`
			`align`
			`alt`
			`height`
			`hspace`
			`localsrc`
			`src`
			`vspace`
			`width`
				Chapter 7

INPUT	Enables developers to create a place in applications for users to enter data.	`<input>`
		    `content`
		`</input>`
			`accesskey`
			`emptyok`
			`format`
			`maxlength`
			`name`
			`size`
			`tabindex`
			`title`
			`type`
			`value`
				Chapter 6

META	Provides information to the browser about meta information. Meta information tells a device to treat the data in a specific way.	`<head>`
		`<meta/>`
		`</head>`
			`content`
			`forua`
			`name`
			`property`
			`schema`
				Chapter 3

Chapter Element	Description	Syntax	Attributes	Reference
NOOP	Specifies that nothing is performed, and it is used to shadow deck-level tasks provided from the TEMPLATE element. This element is useful for overriding deck-level DO elements.	`<noop/>`	None	Chapter 5

ONEVENT	Enables developers to create intrinsic navigational events; in other words, events that are not triggered by the user but by an internal processing event from the device.	`<onevent>`
		  content
		`</onevent>`
			type	Chapter 5

OPTGROUP	Provides a method for grouping options in a list neatly when you need to create lists that use a couple levels.	`<select>`
		`<optgroup>`
		  content
		`</optgroup>`
		`</select>`
			title	Chapter 6

OPTION	Creates the options that exist within a selection list.	`<select>`
		`<optgroup>`
		`<option>`
		  content
		`</option>`
		`</optgroup>`
		`</select>`
			onpick
			title
			value
				Chapter 6

P	Controls how all text displays on a WAP device's screen.	`<p>`
		  content
		`</p>`
			align
			mode
				Chapter 4

POSTFIELD	Defines values that may be passed to a remote server. This element is used in conjunction with the GO element.	`<postfield`
		`name="`*label*`"`
		`value=`
		variable`/>`
			name
			value
				Chapter 5,
				Chapter 15

PREV	Declares a previous task, indicating navigation to the previous URL recorded in the device's history.	`<prev>`
		  content
		`</prev>`
			None	Chapter 5

Chapter Element	Description	Syntax	Attributes	Reference
REFRESH	Refreshes the specified variables to their initial or updated values.	`<refresh>` `content` `</refresh>`	None	Chapter 5
SELECT	Enables developers to create a list of options for user selections.	`<select>` `content` `</select>`	iname ivalue multiple name tabindex title value	Chapter 6
SETVAR	Enables developers to define variables associated with one of the WML task elements.	`<setvar>` `content` `</setvar>`	name value	N/A
SMALL	Creates a small font.	`<small>content` `</small>`	None	Chapter 4
STRONG	Creates a strong emphasis on the font.	`<strong>` `content` `</strong>`	None	Chapter 4
TABLE	Enables the display of information in a columnar form. This element must have a beginning tag and an ending tag.	`<table>` `content` `</table>`	align title columns	Chapter 4
TD	Creates the content within the table rows. This element is specified between the beginning and ending tags of the TR element.	`<table><tr>` `<td></td>` `</tr>` `</table>`	None	Chapter 4
TEMPLATE	Specifies deck-level actions that apply to all cards in the deck.	`<template>` `content` `</template>`	onenterbackward onenterforward ontimer	Chapter 5
TIMER	Provides a method for executing a task automatically after a period of user inactivity.	`<timer>content` `</timer>`	name value	Chapter 8

Chapter Element	Description	Syntax	Attributes	Reference
TR	Creates rows within a table. This element must be specified between the beginning and ending tags of the TABLE element.	`<table><tr>` `</tr></table>`	None	Chapter 4
U	Creates an underlined font.	`<u>content` `</u>`	None	Chapter 4
WML	Starts and ends a deck, and encloses all cards.	`<wml>` `content` `</wml>`	None	Chapter 3

WML Detail Reference

The following text provides further detail regarding the WML elements and their attributes. For further information regarding the WML language specification, visit the WAP Forum site (`www.wapforum.org`) for the latest white paper specifications for WML.

General Syntax

The following syntax tips present some general syntax rules:

- **All WML tags must be enclosed in the brackets (< >).**

- **WML elements must follow the open brackets directly without spaces**—Tabs, blanks, carriage returns, and line feeds are treated as spaces.

- **WML is (in comparison to HTML and other markup languages) case sensitive**—All WML elements must be in lowercase. Thus, `<tag>` is the correct syntax for a WML element, whereas `<TAG>` is an incorrect syntax and will produce errors within your code.

- **Two types of tag syntaxes are found within WML**—These are paired and standalone. *Paired* tags must contain a beginning tag and an ending tag (paired tags must be in the form `<tag>...</tag>`). *Standalone* tags (in the format of `<tag/>`) can appear anywhere within the code and do not require a closing tag.

- **When using interlocked tags, the tags must be closed in the reverse order of opening (this is the case with most XML languages)**—For example, `<tag_a><tag_b>...</tag_b></tag_a>`.

- **Some WML elements have attributes**—Attributes add functionality to the element. When including attributes with a paired element tag, the attribute is included only in the beginning tag. You do not need to restate the attribute in the ending tag—for example, `<tag attribute="abc">...</tag>`. If you are including an attribute with a standalone tag, it must include the trailing slash behind the attribute—for example, `<tag attribute="abc"/>`.

- **Similar to other markup languages, documents are referenced through the use of a uniform resource locator (URL)**—The syntax of the URL is `method://server[:port]/[path/][file][#cards]`.

  The only allowed method is `http`—Other methods, such as `mailto` or `tel:` links, are not allowed.

In addition, there are two types of URLs: relative and absolute. These are summarized as follows:

- **Relative URL**—Creates a link to a card that exists in the same WML deck. In other words, the card being linked to must be in the same directory (be it on a device or on a remote server) as the card that contains the link.

- **Absolute URL**—Navigates between servers and helps to access another file (be it a WML deck or some other file type) that's located in another directory. Absolute URLs are necessary when your applications need to access files that reside on a remove server.

URLs can be abbreviated with the hash mark (#) to refer to cards in the same WML deck.

Decks and Cards

Every WAP application consists of at least one deck and one card. Thus, the following is a summary of the elements used in some degree with every WAP application you create.

DOCUMENT PROLOGUE (CHAPTER 3)

Every WML deck must contain a document prologue. Compilers on the device, WAP gateways, and remote servers all use document prologues to interpret your code. Developers must include the XML document prologue at the top of every WML deck, like so:

```
<?xml version="1.0">
<!DOCTYPE wml PUBLIC "-//WAPFORUM//DTD WML 1.1//EN"
"http://www.wapforum.org/DTD/wml_1.1.xml">
```

The following is an explanation of the previous code:

- The first line of the prologue designates the XML version of the WAP server and WML compiler. WAP servers and WML compilers use XML to interpret your code. These servers and compilers then transform this information back into WML, so that a WAP device can display the information.

- The second line of the prologue defines the version of WML used. This line of code states that you'll use WML version 1.1. in your applications.

- The third line specifies the location of the WML document type definition (DTD). In this prologue, you'll reference the WAP Forum's site. Any additional extensions or information for the WAP server or compiler are available from this site.

The WML Element (Chapter 3)

The WML element defines a deck of cards and encloses all information and cards within the deck. At least one card must be displayed per WML deck.

SYNTAX

The following is the syntax of the WML element:

```
<wml>
   <card>
     content
   </card>
</wml>
```

ATTRIBUTES

The WML element has no attributes.

The CARD Element (Chapter 3)

The CARD element is a single WML unit that can contain information such as text to present to the user, instructions for gathering user input, and so on. WML cards are to a WAP application as pages are to a Web site or screens are to a PC application.

SYNTAX

The following is the syntax of the CARD element:

```
<wml>
   <card attribute>
     content
   </card>
</wml>
```

Table A.1 presents the attributes of the CARD element.

*Table A.1   Attributes of the **CARD** Element*

Attribute	Required	Description
id	No	Specifies a name for the card. For easier programming, avoid using an id longer than eight characters.
newcontext	No	A true or false (Boolean) value that specifies whether the device should initialize the context whenever the card is loaded. The default value is false.
onenterbackward	No	Specifies the URL to open if the user navigates to this card through a PREV task (discussed in Chapter 5).
onenterforward	No	Specifies the URL to open if the user navigates to this card through a GO task. (discussed in Chapter 5).
ontimer	No	Specifies the URL to open if a specified TIMER element expires.
ordered	No	A true or false (Boolean) value that specifies the organization of the card content. The default is true.
title	No	Specifies a brief text label for the card.

The TEMPLATE Element (Chapter 5)

This specifies deck-level actions that apply to all cards in the deck.

SYNTAX

The following is the syntax of the TEMPLATE element:

```
<wml>
  <template attribute>
    content
  </template>
</wml>
```

ATTRIBUTES

Table A.2 presents the attributes of the TEMPLATE element.

*Table A.2 The **TEMPLATE** Element's Attributes*

Attribute	Required	Description
onenterbackward	No	Specifies the URL to open if the user navigates to this card through a PREV task
onenterforward	No	Specifies the URL to open if the user navigates to this card through a GO task
ontimer	No	Specifies the URL to open if a specified TIMER element expires

The HEAD Element (Chapter 3)

This element contains information relating to the deck as a whole, including metadata and access control elements.

SYNTAX

The following is the syntax for the HEAD element:

```
<head>
  content
</head>
```

ATTRIBUTES

There are no attributes for the HEAD element. However, the HEAD element must contain at least one META element or one ACCESS element.

The ACCESS Element (Chapter 3)

The ACCESS element provides the functionality that restricts unauthorized users from accessing content-sensitive information.

SYNTAX

The following is the syntax for the ACCESS element:

```
<head>
  <access attribute/>
</head>
```

ATTRIBUTES

Table A.3 presents the attributes of the ACCESS element.

*Table A.3 Attributes of the **ACCESS** Element*

Attribute	Required	Description
domain	Yes	The URL domain of other WML decks that can access the cards within the current deck. The default value is the domain of the current deck.
path	Yes	The URL root of other WML decks that can access the cards in the current WML deck.

The META Element (Chapter 3)

The META element provides information to the browser about meta information. Meta information tells a device to treat the data in a specific way.

SYNTAX

The following is the syntax of the META element:

```
<head>
  <meta attribute/>
</head>
```

ATTRIBUTES

Table A.4 presents the attributes of the META element.

Table A.4   *META Element Attributes*

Attribute	Required	Description
content	Yes	Specifies the metadata value to assign to the property
forua	Yes	A true or false value that specifies whether the content is intended for the device's browser (rather than a proxy server or some other program)
name	Yes	The property name that represents the meta information
property	Yes	Used in place of the name attribute to specify information the browser should interpret as an HTTP header
schema	No	Form or structure used to interpret the property value

Text Elements

The WML language by nature is a text formatting language. Several WML text elements can be used to influence the display of text, including the use of special characters and character encoding. Note that how these elements are rendered depends partially on the wireless device being used.

The P Element (Chapter 4)

The P element controls how all text displays on a WAP device's screen.

SYNTAX

The following code snippet presents the syntax of the P element:

```
<p attribute>
   content
</p>
```

Table A.5 presents the attributes of the P element.

Table A.5   **P** *Element Attributes*

Attribute	Required	Description
align	No	Specifies the line alignment relative to the display area. If no value is specified, the align attribute defaults the line to left alignment. This attribute can be equal to left, right, or center.
mode	No	Specifies whether the display should automatically wrap or split text so that is always viewable from the display. The nowrap value uses another mechanism, such as horizontal scrolling, to display long lines of text. If no value is specified, the default value is wrap.

The BR Element (Chapter 4)

The BR element forces the insertion of a line break into the text.

SYNTAX

The following code snippet presents a summary of the syntax of the BR element:

```
<p>
   content<br/>
</p>
```

ATTRIBUTES

There are no attributes for the BR element.

The B Element (Chapter 4)

This creates a bold font.

SYNTAX

The following is a summary of the syntax of the B element:

```
<wml>
  <card>
    <p>
    Press <b>OK</b>.
    </p>
  </card>
</wml>
```

ATTRIBUTES

There are no attributes for the B element.

The BIG Element (Chapter 4)

The BIG element creates a big font.

SYNTAX

The following code snippet presents the syntax of the BIG element:

```
<wml>
  <card>
    <p>
    Press <big>OK</big>.
    </p>
  </card>
</wml>
```

Attributes

There are no attributes for the BIG element.

The EM Element (Chapter 4)

The EM element creates emphasis on the font.

SYNTAX

The following code snippet presents the syntax of the EM element:

```
<wml>
  <card>
    <p>
    Press <em>OK</em>.
    </p>
  </card>
</wml>
```

ATTRIBUTES

There are no attributes for the EM element.

The I Element (Chapter 4)

The I element creates an italicized font.

SYNTAX

The following presents the syntax of the I element:

```
<wml>
  <card>
    <p>
    Press <small>OK</small>.
    </p>
  </card>
</wml>
```

ATTRIBUTES

There are no attributes for the I element.

The STRONG Element (Chapter 4)

This element creates a strong emphasis on the font.

SYNTAX

The following code snippet presents the syntax of the STRONG element:

```
<wml>
  <card>
    <p>
    Press <strong>OK</strong>.
    </p>
  </card>
</wml>
```

ATTRIBUTES

There are no attributes for the STRONG element.

The U Element (Chapter 4)

This element creates an underlined font.

SYNTAX

The following code snippet presents the syntax for the U element:

```
<wml>
  <card>
    <p>
    Press <u>OK</u>.
    </p>
  </card>
</wml>
```

ATTRIBUTES

There are no attributes for the U element.

Tables

Tables in WML are similar to those found in all other XML languages; essentially, they require rows and column definitions. One important difference is the required presence of the definition of columns. Other differences are that the nesting of tables in not allowed, and there is no special table header cell tag.

The TABLE Element (Chapter 4)

This element enables the display of information in a columnar form and must have a beginning tag and an ending tag.

SYNTAX

The following presents the syntax of the TABLE element:

```
<table attribute>
   row and data declarations
</table>
```

ATTRIBUTES

Table A.6 presents the attributes of the TABLE element.

Table A.6   ***TABLE*** *Element Attributes*

Attribute	Required	Description
align	No	Specifies the text alignment relative to the column. If you do not specify an align attribute, the text is automatically left aligned. It must be equal to left, right, or center.
title	No	Specifies a label for the table.
columns	No	Specifies the number of columns for the row set. Specifying a zero value for this attribute is not allowed.

The TD Element (Chapter 4)

Creates rows within a table. This element must be specified between the beginning and ending tags of the TABLE element.

SYNTAX

The following presents the syntax of the TD element:

```
<table attribute>
   <td>Row 1</td>
</table>
```

ATTRIBUTES

There are no attributes for the TD element.

The TR Element (Chapter 4)

Creates the content within the table rows. This element is specified between the beginning and ending tags of the TABLE element.

The following presents the syntax of the TR element:

```
<table attribute>
  <td>Row 1</td>
    <tr>Row content</tr>
</table>
```

ATTRIBUTES

There are no attributes for the TR element.

Hypertext Links

In WAP applications, a URL provide the path to which cards navigate. WML provides elements that provide the functionality for cards to connect to other cards and files, whether they are both contained within the same deck or on different networks and servers.

The ANCHOR Element (Chapter 5)

Enables users to select and navigate throughout a WAP application.

SYNTAX

The following presents the syntax of the ANCHOR element:

```
<anchor attribute>task text</anchor>
```

> **TIP**
>
> Some developers like to abbreviate the ANCHOR element by using the A element.
>
> The A element is an abbreviation of an ANCHOR element that uses the GO element only. For example, consider in the table.wml code (created in Chapter 4). Line 11 could have been shorted by using the A element.
>
> ```
>     . . . <a href="#login" title="Go">Login</a> . . .
> ```
>
> This element contains the same attributes as the ANCHOR element (summarized in Table A.7).

ATTRIBUTES

Table A.7 presents the attributes of the ANCHOR element.

Table A.7 ***ANCHOR** Element Attributes*

Attribute	Required	Description
accesskey	No	Specifies a number (0–9) that is displayed to the left of the link. Users can press that keypad number, hash mark (#), or asterisk (*) to make a selection.

Table A.7   continued

Attribute	Required	Description
href	Yes	Specifies the designation URL.
title	No	Specifies a label for the card. This label can be used for bookmarked text, pop-ups, or other uses.

Events

WAP devices also have the capability to incorporate other navigational functionality into your applications. Two WML elements are available for creating navigational events besides the ANCHOR element. These other elements are as follows:

- **The DO element**—Provides the capability to incorporate functionality into your WAP applications through a WAP device's user interface (such as the device buttons).

- **The ONEVENT element**—Provides the capability to incorporate functionality into your WAP application through intrinsic events (such as internal processing events).

The DO Element (Chapter 5)

This enables developers to associate actions with a user interface mechanism. Like the ANCHOR element, the DO event must be associated with a task.

SYNTAX

The following code snippet presents the syntax of the DO element:

```
<do attribute>
  <go href="/foo"/>
</do>
```

ATTRIBUTES

Table A.8 presents the attributes of the DO element.

Table A.8   DO Element Attributes

Attribute	Required	Description
label	No	Specifies a textual string used as a display label.
name	No	Specifies an element name that enables card-level binding to override deck-level binding.
optional	No	Specifies that the device should ignore this element if set to true. The available values are true and false. The default is false.

Table A.8   continued

Attribute	Required	Description
type	Yes	Specifies the device mechanism associated with this attribute. Several `type` attributes are available that can define the type of action the `DO` event executes. These are as follows:

`accept`—Affirms acknowledgement

`prev`—Backward history navigation

`help`—Request for help

`reset`—Clears and resets the current state

`option`—Request for options or additional operations

`delete`—Deletes item or choice

`unknown`—Generic type

The ONEVENT Element (Chapter 5)

This element enables developers to create intrinsic navigational events—in other words, events that are not triggered by the user but by an internal processing event from the device.

SYNTAX

The following presents the syntax of the ONEVENT element:

```
<onevent attribute>task</onevent>
```

ATTRIBUTES

Table A.9 presents the attributes of the ONEVENT element.

*Table A.9   **ONEVENT** Element Attributes*

Attribute	Required	Description
type	Yes	Specifies the device mechanism associated with this attribute. Several `type` attributes are available that can define the type of action the `ONEVENT` event executes. These are as follows:

`onenterbackward`—Specifies the URL to load when a card is entered by backward navigation

`onenterforward`—Specifies the URL to load when a card is entered by forward navigation or by a bookmark or direct entry

`ontimer`—Specifies the URL to load when a card's timer expires

`onpick`—Clears and resets the current state

Tasks

Anchors and events are always associated with some sort of task (such as "got to another link," "refresh the screen," and so on). WML contains a number of task elements you can use in conjunction with your anchors or events.

The GO Element (Chapter 5)

The GO element specifies forward navigation to a URL. This element is the most widely used task element.

SYNTAX

The following code snippet presents the syntax of the GO element:

```
<go attribute>
  content
</go>
```

ATTRIBUTES

Table A.10 presents the attributes of the GO element.

Table A.10   GO Element Attributes

Attribute	Required	Description
href	Yes	Specifies the URL to open.
send referer	No	Specifies whether the device should send the deck URL in the URL request. Values can be true or false.
method	No	Specifies the HTTP submission method. Methods can be either post or get.
accept-charset	No	Specifies the character encoding that an application can handle.
enctype	No	Specifies the content type used to submit a parameter to the sever (when the value of method is post).

The NOOP Element (Chapter 5)

This specifies that nothing is performed and is used to shadow deck-level tasks provided from the TEMPLATE element. This element is useful for over-riding deck-level DO elements.

SYNTAX

The following presents the syntax of the NOOP element:

```
<noop/>
```

ATTRIBUTES

There are no attributes for the NOOP element.

The PREV Element (Chapter 5)

This element declares a previous task, indicating navigation to the previous URL recorded in the device's history.

SYNTAX

The following presents the syntax of the PREV element:

```
<prev>content</prev>
```

ATTRIBUTES

There are no attributes for the PREV element.

The REFRESH Element (Chapter 5)

This refreshes the specified variables to their initial or updated values.

SYNTAX

The following presents the syntax of the REFRESH element:

```
<refresh>content</refresh>
```

ATTRIBUTES

There are no attributes for the REFRESH element.

Posting Data

WML enables users to transcode variable data and then pass this data to a remote URL. To perform this functionality, users may use the POSTFIELD element, in conjunction with the GO element.

The POSTFIELD Element (Chapters 5 and 15)

This element defines values that can be passed to a remote server.

SYNTAX

The following presents the syntax of the POSTFIELD element:

```
<go method="post" href="URL">
  <postfield name="label" value="variable"/>
</go>
```

ATTRIBUTES

Table A.11 presents the attributes of the POSTFIELD element.

Table A.11 **POSTFIELD** *Element Attributes*

Attribute	Required	Description
name	Yes	Specifies the label that identifies the field
value	Yes	Specifies the value for a variable

User Input

WML enables users to input information in two ways: by entering text or by selecting the items from a list. Whatever method you choose, remember that limiting the amount of text users must enter and letting them chose items from lists is the most preferable design for your wireless applications.

The INPUT Element (Chapter 6)

This enables developers to create a place in applications for users to enter data.

SYNTAX

The following presents the syntax of the INPUT element:

```
<input attribute/>
```

ATTRIBUTES

Table A.12 presents the attributes of the INPUT element.

Table A.12 **INPUT** *Element Attributes*

Attribute	Required	Description
accesskey	No	Specifies a number (0–9), a hash mark (#), or an asterisk (*) that displays to the left of a link. Users can press one of these buttons.
emptyok	No	Specifies whether this field can be left blank. The only values available for this attribute are true and false. The default value is false.
format	No	This attribute enables developers to specify the format of characters that can be inputted. For example, with format masks, you can specify whether the user can input upper- or lowercase characters, the number of characters allowed for input, and so on. Formatting masks are covered in the next example of code.
maxlength	No	Specifies the maximum field length available for user input. The default value is unlimited characters allowed.

Table A.12 *continued*

Attribute	Required	Description
name	Yes	Specifies the name of the variable (remember, variables are the placeholder that contains the user's inputted data).
size	No	Specifies the width of the input field (in characters).
tabindex	No	Specifies the tabbing position in a card.
title	No	Specifies a title that can be displayed by the browser (depending on the WAP device being used).
type	No	Specifies whether the input field is a text or password input field. The default value is text.
value	No	The initial value of the field. This attribute is used only if the variable specified in the name attribute has no value.

The SELECT Element (Chapter 6)

The SELECT element enables developers to create a list of options for user selections.

SYNTAX

The following code snippet presents the syntax of the SELECT element:

```
<select attribute>
  content
</select>
```

ATTRIBUTES

Table A.13 is a summary of the attributes of the SELECT element.

Table A.13   **SELECT** *Element Attributes*

Attribute	Required	Description
iname	No	Specifies the index number of the default option.
ivalue	No	Specifies the default index number value.
multiple	No	Specifies whether multiple selections can be made. The available values are true and false. The default value is false.
name	Yes	Specifies the name of the variable to contain the value of the selected <option>.
tabindex	No	Specifies the tabbing position in a card.
title	No	Specifies the field value.
value	No	Specifies the default value for the variable.

The OPTGROUP Element (Chapter 6)

The OPTGROUP element provides a method for grouping options in a list neatly when you need to create lists that use a couple of levels.

SYNTAX

The following presents the syntax of the OPTGROUP element:

```
<select>
  <optgroup attribute>content</optgroup>
</select>
```

ATTRIBUTES

Table A.14 presents the attributes of the OPTGROUP element.

Table A.14 **OPTGROUP** *Element Attribute*

Attribute	Required	Description
title	No	Title for the group. If this attribute is used, it should be unique in a card to avoid confusion.

The OPTION Element (Chapter 6)

The OPTION element creates the options that exist within a selection list.

SYNTAX

The following presents the syntax of the OPTION element:

```
<select>
  <option attribute>
    content
  </option>
</select>
```

ATTRIBUTES

Table A.15 presents the attributes of the OPTION element.

Table A.15 **OPTION** *Element Attributes*

Attribute	Required	Description
onpick	No	Specifies the URL to navigate to upon option selection
title	No	Specifies an optional title
value	No	Specifies the value to be returned if the option is selected

Variables

WML provides the flexibility to parameterize its content, allowing variables to be used to improve caching behavior and better user interaction. Only one kind of data type is available within the WML language: strings. In addition, only text (including attribute values) can be substituted. No substitution of any other WML element or their attributes can occur.

Throughout the examples in this book, you've used the name attribute of elements to define your variables. However, the WML specification also provides the SETVAR element, should you want to define variables outside an element. Often, the SETVAR element is used to clear any variable data from the cache.

The SETVAR Element (Not Covered in This Book)

The SETVAR element enables developers to define variables associated with one of the WML task elements.

SYNTAX

The following presents the syntax of the SETVAR element:

```
<setvar attribute/>
```

ATTRIBUTES

Table A.16 presents the attributes of the SETVAR element.

Table A.16 **SETVAR** *Element Attributes*

Attribute	Required	Description
name	Yes	Specifies the variable name
value	Yes	Specifies the value to be assigned to the variable

Images

Images provide several advantages for both users and developers of an application. Images provide symbolic meanings to application functionality, making software easier and more fun to use. Images convey meanings, often better than lines of text can.

WML provides an element that allows developers to incorporate images into WAP applications. However, use images sparingly. Not all device browsers support images at the time of this writing.

The IMG Element (Chapter 7)

The IMG element provides the capability to display images within WAP applications.

SYNTAX

The following code snippet presents the syntax of the IMG element:

```
<img attribute/>
```

ATTRIBUTES

Table A.17 presents the attributes of the IMG element.

Table A.17 *The Attributes of the **IMG** Element*

Attribute	Required	Description
align	No	Represents where the image is aligned relative to the current line of text. The available entries for this attribute are top, middle, or bottom.
alt	Yes	Specifies the text that displays if the device has a problem displaying the image (for example, if images are not supported on the device or the device can't find the image).
height	No	Represents a height setting for the image. Several devices do not support this attribute.
hspace	No	Represents the amount of empty space to the left or right of the image. The default setting for this attribute is 0.
localsrc	No	Represents the name of a known icon that exists within the device's browser.
		Even if a localsrc icon is used, users must include the localsrc attribute within their code.
src	Yes	Specifies the URL of the image displayed.
vspace	No	Represents the amount of empty space above or below the image. Several devices do not support this attribute.
width	No	Represents a width setting for the image. Several devices do not support this attribute.

Timers

WML enables timers, which enables developers to have an event occur without the user explicitly having to activate a control, to be declared within a WML card. Timeouts are specified in units of tenth of a second; however, some browsers might round this timeout to some other precision internally.

The TIMER Element (Chapter 8)

The TIMER element provides a method for executing a task automatically after a period of user inactivity.

SYNTAX

The following code snippet presents the syntax of the TIMER element:

```
<timer attribute/>
```

ATTRIBUTES

Table A.18 is a detailed summary of the attributes of the TIMER element.

*Table A.18 The Attributes of the **TIMER** Element*

Attribute	Required	Description
name	No	Specifies the name of the variable to be set with the value of the timer. The variable named by the name attribute will be set with the current timer value when the card is exited or when the timer expires.
value	No	Specifies the default value of the variable named in the name attribute. This attribute sets the timeout period upon timer initialization.

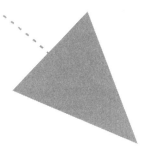

Appendix B

WMLScript Reference

In this book, you've used WMLScript to provide client-side functionality for WAP applications. This appendix presents information from Chapter 9, "Introduction to WMLScript"; Chapter 10, "Variables and Functions"; and Chapter 11, "Operators in WMLScript."

NOTE

The latest WMLScript specifications are available from the WAP Forum Web site (`http://www.wapforum.org`). To find these specifications, click the This Site link at the top of the page.

Under the What Is WAP heading, find the white papers associated with the Wireless Application Environment. You'll find the latest specifications for WMLScript in this area of the Web site.

The following is a summary of topics presented within this appendix:

- **WMLScript syntax**—Case sensitivity, comments, whitespace, semi-colons, and opening and closing brackets. Chapter 9 contains more detailed information about these topics.

- **Data types**—Boolean, float, integer, invalid, and string. Chapter 10 contains more detailed information about these topics.

- **Reserved words**—Several keywords are used by the WMLScript language. These keywords are called reserved words and can't be used when declaring programming constructs. Chapter 10 contains more detailed information about these topics.

- **Statements**—Expression, block, if, while, for, break, and variable statements. Chapter 9 contains more detailed information about these topics.

- **Variables, functions, and pragmas**—The programming constructs that provide functionality to statements. Chapter 10 contains more detailed information about these topics.

- **Naming conventions**—The rules for the naming of variable and function identifiers. Chapter 10 contains more detailed information about these topics.

- **Declarations**—Declaration of variables, internal and external functions, and pragmas. Chapter 10 contains more detailed information about these topics.

- **Operators**—Computational, logical, bitwise, and assignment operators. Chapter 11 contains more detailed information about these topics.

WMLScript Syntax (Chapter 9)

Syntax in WMLScript refers to the rules required for forming functionally correct code. The following are the syntax topics discussed in Chapter 9:

- Case sensitivity

- White space

- Comments

- Semicolons

Case Sensitivity

WMLScript interprets upper- and lowercase characters differently. This is especially critical when declaring function or variable identifiers.

Example

The following are all different variable names, due to WMLScript's case sensitivity:

- `variable`

- `Variable`

- `VARIABLE`

White Space

The term *white space* refers to things such as spaces, tabs, and new lines that appear in code. Because WMLScript ignores white space, users can use any number of spacing elements to improve the readability of their code.

WMLScript recognizes all spacing elements as a single space. Users can enter as many line breaks, spaces, or tabs as they want in their code.

Example

Here's a code sample with white space (for good readability):

```
extern function checkpass()
   {
   var password = WMLBrowser.getVar("password");

     if (String.length(password) != 6)
   {
       WMLBrowser.go("login.wml#badpass");
   }
     else if (String.length(password) == 6)
   {
       WMLBrowser.go("menu.wml#menu");
   }

};
```

Comments

Text ignored by the application when the code is executed is called a *comment*. Comments are usually included to help explain the code's functionality.

Two types of comment forms are available in WMLScript:

- Comments using /*
- Comments using //

Example

```
/* This is a legit comment form. */

/*
This is also
a legit comment form.
*/

// This is a legit comment form.

//This is also
//a legit comment
//form.
```

Semicolons

Semicolons are required at the end of all statements and separate one statement from another. Statements are the lines of code that direct a computer to perform some specified action.

Example

```
extern function checkpass()

    {
    var password = WMLBrowser.getVar("password");

/*The semicolon in the previous line ends one statement*/

    if (String.length(password) != 6)
    {
        WMLBrowser.go("login.wml#badpass");

/*The semicolon in the previous line ends another statement*/

    }
    else if (String.length(password) == 6)
    {
        WMLBrowser.go("menu.wml#menu");

/*The semicolon in the previous line ends yet another statement*/

    }

};

/*The semicolon at the end of this code ends the statement that contains
➥multiple statements*/
```

Opening and Closing Brackets (Chapter 9)

WMLScript uses three types of brackets in statements:

- Curly brackets
- Parentheses
- Square brackets

These brackets are summarized as follows.

CURLY BRACKETS

Curly brackets are used to contain WMLScript statements. Any statement enclosed by curly brackets is considered a block statement.

The following code represents a block statement:

```
{
        WMLBrowser.go("login.wml#badpass");
}
```

PARENTHESES

Parentheses are used to contain a function's arguments. Functions perform some type of action and can be procedure code written by a developer or a built-in library. Here's an example:

```
if (String.length(password) == 6)
```

SQUARE BRACKETS

Square brackets ([ ])are used with operators to create computational formulas. Here's an example of an operator that uses square brackets:

```
var calc = [3+2] + 7
```

Data Types (Chapter 10)

WMLScript allows for the use of five different data values. However, at the time of writing, not all browsers support the float data type (see Table B.1).

Table B.1   WMLScript Data Types

Data Type	Description	Example
Boolean	Values represented by either `true` or false. These values are case sensitive.	`true` `false`
Float	A number in the IEEE single-precision format in the range from 3.40282347E+38 to 1.17549435E-38. These numbers can contain a decimal point and an exponent part. Note that not all WMLScript interpreters support floating-point numbers.	`.32` `100e5` `.55E+15`
Integer	A whole number in the range from -2147483648 to 2147483647. Integers can include octals (numbers that start with 0), decimals (numbers that start with a nonzero digit), or hexadecimal values (numbers that start with the sequence 0x).	`1992` `013422` `0x31e5`
Invalid	Represents values that aren't any of the previous data types. This value is typically used in error conditions.	`5/0` (can't divide by 0) `3/(2/0)` (can't divide 0)
String	Any combination of characters, including numbers, text, or symbols. Either single or double quotation marks can enclose strings.	`"This is an acceptable string."` `'This is also an acceptable string.'`

Reserved Words (Chapter 10)

Several keywords are used by the WMLScript language. These keywords are called *reserved* words and can't be used when declaring programming constructs. The following list contains words reserved by WMLScript:

access	div=	header	private	use
agent	do	http	public	user
break	domain	if	return	var
case	else	import	sizeof	void
continue	enum	in	struct	while
catch	equiv	isvalid	super	with
class	export	lib	switch	
const	extends	meta	this	
debugger	extern	name	throw	
default	finally	new	try	
delete	for	null	typeof	
div	function	path	url	

Statements (Chapter 9)

Statements make up the set of commands executed in WMLScript. These commands provide the functionality to an application. A *statement* is a set of functions or variables that evaluates to a single value. This value can be a number, string, or logical value. Table B.2 lists WMLScript's available statements.

Table B.2   *WMLScript Statements*

Statement	Definition	Example
Expression	Used in all WMLScript operations that perform some sort of calculation. These statements are covered in Chapter 11.	var message = message + "The password must be 6 digits."
Block	A statement that is enclosed by curly brackets.	{ WMLBrowser.go ("login.wml#badpass"); }

Table B.2   continued

Statement	Definition	Example
if	A statement that enables you to conditionally perform one of two operations. These statements use a Boolean (true or false) data type to determine the value of the condition.	`if String.length` `(password ==6)`

while	A statement that performs the action of a statement, as long as an expression remains true.	`while (x > 10)`
		`{`
		some sort of action
		`}`

for	This statement enables users to use up to three optional statements. In most cases, all three statements are used and work in the following manner:
	
	The first statement initializes a variable.
	
	The second statement executes the third statement as long as it is true.
	
	The third statement performs some type of operation.
		`for`
		`(var a = 0, a > 10)`
		`{x +=1;`
		some sort of action
		`}`

break	A statement that ends the while or for loop. This statement then executes statements following the ended loop.	`while (x > 10)`
		`{`
		some sort of action
		`if (10==x)`
		`break;`
		`}`

Variables	These statements declare variables. All variables in WMLScript files must be declared before they can be used. Variables can be declared inside or outside a block statement.	`var password =`
		`WMLBrowser.getVar`
		`("password");`

Functions, Variables, and Pragmas (Chapter 10)

The programming constructs that provide functionality to statements are as follows:

- Variables
- Functions
- Pragmas

Variables

Variables are essentially areas in applications where you can store user-inputted data. Variables represent data and provide a temporary storage area for data.

Example

```
var password = WMLBrowser.getVar("password");
```

Functions

Functions are named portions of a program that perform specific tasks. In other words, functions are a type of procedure or routine.

Functions can be either user-created or one of the built-in WMLScript libraries. See Chapter 12, "Working with WMLScript Libraries," for information about WMLScript's libraries and built-in functions. Also, you can find a summary of WMLScript's libraries and subsequent built-in functions in Appendix C, "WMLScript Libraries."

Example

```
Dialogs.alert("You have entered an incorrect username format.")
```

Pragmas

Pragmas control the ability to specify characteristics of metadata, such as how, when, and by whom a particular set of data was collected or how the data is formatted.

Three types of metadata can be defined by pragmas in a WAP device. Table B.3 lists the available pragmas in WMLScript.

Table B.3   Pragmas Available in WMLScript

Pragma	Description	Example
access	Enables a user to protect a file's content. This pragma specifies which URLs can call the external function in an access-controlled compilation unit.	`use access domain "yourcompany.com/ apps/scripts";`
meta	Specifies how the originating servers, connecting servers, and user agents use information.	`use meta name "Submitted";`
url	Specifies the location (URL) of an external WMLScript file. This pragma gives this external file a local name.	`use url NameofScript "http://www. yourcompany.com/ app/scripts"`

Naming Conventions

When declaring variables and functions, you must follow a couple of rules in naming their identifiers. These rules are as follows:

- The variable or function identifier can't be a reserved word.

- The identifier can't contain any blank spaces.

- The identifier's first character can be only a letter of the alphabet (either upper- or lowercase), a number, or an underscore.

Example

The following are valid identifier declarations:

```
variable1
```

```
_function
```

The following are invalid identifier declarations:

```
variable 1
```

```
function
```

TIP

Remember, programming constructs are case sensitive. Thus, a variable identified as `VARIABLE` differs from a variable identified as `variable`. Keep this in mind when naming your programming construct identifiers.

Operators (Chapter 11)

Operators are used to compare some type of condition with a variable and then evaluate a value as directed by the expression. WMLScript enables several operator types. The following is a list of operators provided with WMLScript:

- Assignment operators

- Arithmetic operators

- Logical operators

- String operators

- Comparison operators

- Array operators

- Comma operators

- Conditional operators
- `typeof` operators
- `isvalid` operators

Assignment Operators

Assignment operators are useful for setting variables to some value. Table B.4 lists the WMLScript assignment operators.

Table B.4   The WMLScript Assignment Operators

Operation	WMLScript Operator
Assign.	=
Add (numbers)/concatenate (strings) and assign.	+=
Subtract and assign.	-=
Multiply and assign.	*=
Divide and assign.	/=
Divide (integer division) and align.	div=
Remainder or modulus and assign. The sign of the results equals the sign of the dividend.	%=
Bitwise left-shift and assign.	<<=
Bitwise right-shift with sign and assign.	>>=
Bitwise right-shift zero file and assign.	>>>=
Bitwise AND and assign.	&=
Bitwise XOR and assign.	^=
Bitwise OR and assign.	|=

Arithmetic Operators

Arithmetic operators are used to provide some type of calculation. Arithmetic operators always take numerical values as their operands and return a single numeric value. WMLScript supports basic, complex, and unary arithmetic operators. Tables B.5–B.7 list the different WMLScript arithmetic operators.

NOTE

Arithmetic operators perform both *unary* and *binary* calculations. Unary calculations involve calculations with only one values, and binary calculations involve calculations with two or more values.

Table B.5   The Basic Binary WMLScript Arithmetic Operators

Operation	WMLScript Operator	Description
Add (numbers)/ concatenate (strings)	+	Returns the sum of adding operands
Subtract	-	Returns the remainder of deducting one operand from another
Multiply	*	Returns the product of multiplying two operands together
Divide	/	Returns the quotient of dividing one operand from another (provides a remainder)
Integer division	div	Returns the quotient of dividing one operand from another when handling integers (does not provide a remainder)

Table B.6   The Complex Binary WMLScript Arithmetic Operators

Operation	WMLScript Operator
Remainder	%
Bitwise left-shift	<<
Bitwise right-shift with sign	>>
Bitwise &	&
Bitwise OR	|

Table B.7   The Unary WMLScript Arithmetic Operators

Operation	WMLScript Operator
Plus	+
Minus	-
Pre- or post-decrement	- -
Pre- or post-increment	++
Bitwise NOT	~

Logical Operators

Logical operators are a means to evaluate operands to determine the result of an overall operation. Table B.8 lists the WMLScript logical operators.

Table B.8   The WMLScript Logical Operators

Operation	WMLScript Operator	Description
Logical AND	&&	Returns true if both operands are true; otherwise, returns false.
Logical OR	||	Returns true if one of the operands is true; if both are false, it returns false.
Logical negation (not)	!	Returns false if its single operand can be converted to true; otherwise, it returns false.

String Operators

String operators provide the ability to connect (better known as *concatenating*) string variables together. Two string operators are available to enable developers to concatenate strings (see Table B.9).

Table B.9   The WMLScript String Operators

Operation	WMLScript Operator	Description
Addition	+	Returns the sum of combining operands. Similar to the addition arithmetic operator; however, in this case, the operands are strings.
Assignment with addition	+=	Returns the sum of combining operands and then assigns the new value to the original operand. Similar to the assignment with addition operator, but in this case, the operands are strings.

Comparison Operators

Comparison operators compare two values and then generate a true or false value from this comparison. This true or false value is better known as a *Boolean* result. Comparison operators enable developers to determine whether two values are equal and then make a decision based on your results. Table B.10 lists the WMLScript comparison operators.

Table B.10   The WMLScript Comparison Operators

Operation	WMLScript Operator	Description
Less than	<	Returns true if the left operand is less than the right operand
Greater than	>	Returns true if the left operand is greater than the right operand
Less than or equal to	<=	Returns true if the left operand is less than or equal to the right operand
Greater than or equal to	>=	Returns true if the left operand is greater than or equal to the right operand
Equal	==	Returns true if the operands are equal
Not Equal	!=	Returns true if the operands are not equal

Array Operators

In the world of development, an *array* is a series of objects that are of the same size and shape. Objects contained in an array are called *array elements*. Array elements can be of anything that has a defined data type (such as integers, characters, and so on).

At the time of this writing, WMLScript doesn't provide support for conventional arrays. However, the behavior of conventional arrays can be mimicked through the use of some of the WMLScript string functions, such as the String.elementAt function (see Appendix C for more information).

Comma Operators

Comma operators use the comma to combine several strings into one expression. Table B.11 summarizes how the WMLScript comma operators work.

Table B.11   The WMLScript Comma Operators

Operation	WMLScript Operator	Functionality
Combine strings	,	If (x = 1, y = 2) then functionality

Conditional Operators

Conditional operators assign values to expressions based on the Boolean result of the initial statement. The following is an example of how these operators work:

```
Result = operand1 ? operand2 : operand3
```

In this statement, *operand1* is the condition being evaluated. If the condition is true, the *Result* is the value of *operand2*. If the condition is false, the *Result* is the value of *operand3*. Table B.12 lists the WMLScript conditional operators.

Table B.12   The WMLScript Conditional Operators

Operation	WMLScript Operator	Functionality
if	?	*operand1 ? operand2*
else	:	*operand1 : operand3*

typeof Operators

typeof operators return an integer value that describes the given expression. To use this operator, simply use the typeof keyword in an expression. The following is an example of a typeof operator in action:

```
var String = "12345"
var datatype = typeof String;
```

In this example, the result of this expression is 2. Table B.13 lists the basic data types returned by the WMLScript typeof operator.

*Table B.13   The WMLScript **typeof** Operators*

Operator	Operations
Integer	0
Floating-point	1
String	2
Boolean	3
Invalid	4

isvalid Operators

isvalid operators check the validity of a given expression. Only if the expression is invalid will this expression return a value of false. The following is an example of a isvalid operator in action:

```
var String = "12345"
var Test = isvalid (1/0);
```

In this example, the result of this expression is false because of the zero divider.

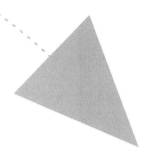

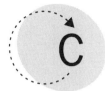

WMLScript Libraries

WMLScript provides a number of libraries that contain built-in functions. These built-in functions can be used by developers within their applications. This appendix is broken into two sections. The first section summarizes all WMLScript Libraries and the functions they contain. The second section provides a more detailed view on each of the functions within each library.

The following is a summary of each of the WMLScript Libraries discussed within this appendix:

- **The Lang Library**—Contains functions that perform arithmetic operations on integer numbers (numbers without decimal points). This library also contains an application aborting function and a check function to see whether a particular browser supports floating-point arithmetic (see the following Float Library for more information).

- **The Float Library**—Contains functions that perform arithmetic operations on floating-point numbers (numbers that contain decimal points).

- **The String Library**—Contains functions that provide functions used to perform a variety of operations on string data.

- **The URL Library**—Contains functions that provide operations to URLs that exist either locally (within the device) or remotely (on a remote server).

- **The WMLBrowser Library**—Contains functions used to command how WML and WMLScript files work together when processed by the browser.

- **The Dialogs Library**—Contains functions to communicate information to users.

Syntax of Built-In Functions

A built-in function (a function that resides within one of the WMLScript Libraries) must use the following format when included within WMLScript code:

```
Name of WMLScript Library.Name of built-in function(parameters)
```

Built-in functions must include

- The library name that it is included within.

- A dot separator.

- The name of the built-in function (cannot be changed by developer).

- Any arguments that are to be included with the function. These must be included within the curved brackets.

Summary of WMLScript Libraries and Their Functions

The following is a summary of WMLScript Libraries and the functions associated with them. More detailed definitions follow these summaries.

The Lang Library

The Lang Library contains functions that perform arithmetic operations on integer numbers (numbers without decimal points). This library also contains an application aborting function and a check function to see whether a particular browser supports floating-point arithmetic (see the following section, "Float Library," for more information). These are the functions in this library:

- abort—Aborts the current WMLScript (due to an error) and displays the message that is the function's argument. The control is returned to the browser.

- abs—Returns the absolute value of the number specified in the function's argument.

- characterSet—Used to return the identifier for the character set used by the device.

- exit—Aborts the current WMLScript (not due to error) and displays the message that is the function's argument. The control is returned to the browser.

- float—Used to determine whether the device supports floating-point operations.

- `isFloat`—Used to return whether the string specified in the function's argument can be converted to a floating-point number.

- `isInt`—Used to return whether the string can be converted into an integer number.

- `max`—Used to return the larger of the two values specified in the function's argument.

- `min`—Used to return the smallest of the two values specified in the function's argument.

- `minInt`—Used to return the smallest integer value that is supported by the device.

- `parseFloat`—Used to return a string as a decimal integer.

- `random`—Used to generate a random integer number. The range of the number ranges from zero (0) to the number specified in the function's argument.

- `seed`—Used to begin a random-number generation sequence. The sequence begins with the number specified in the function's argument.

The Float Library

The Float Library contains functions that perform arithmetic operations on floating-point numbers (numbers that contain decimal points):

- `ceil`—Returns the largest integer number available with the device. This number is no less than the floating-point number specified in the function's argument.

- `floor`—Returns the smallest integer number available within the device. This number is no less than the floating-point number specified in the function's argument.

- `int`—Returns the integer part of the specified floating-point number specified in the function's argument.

- `maxfloat`—Returns the largest floating-point number available within the device.

- `minfloat`—Returns the smallest floating-point number available within the device.

- `pow`—Returns the value of raising the value of number 1 to the specified value of number 2.

- `round`—Returns the value of the specified number, rounded to the nearest whole number.

- sqrt—Returns the square root of the floating-point number specified in the function's argument.

The String Library

The String Library contains functions that perform a variety of operations on string data:

- charAt—Returns the character within the string that is designated by the index number. The index number is defined by the function's argument.

- compare—Returns a -1 value if the first string is smaller than the second string. Returns a 1 if the first string is larger than the second string. Returns a 0 if both strings are the same length.

- elementAt—Returns the number of string elements as specified by the separator.

- find—Returns the index of the first character of the string element.

- format—Defines a value for a string that contains formatting specifiers.

- insertAt—Inserts a string element into a separated string. The location of the insertion is specified by the index defined in the function's argument.

- isEmpty—Determines whether a string has a zero length. Returns a true or false value.

- length—Determines the character length of a string.

- removeAt—Removes a string element according to the index defined within a function.

- replace—Replaces the first string element within the second string element.

- replaceAt—Replaces a string element according to the index defined within the function.

- squeeze—Reduces all the white space within a string to a single space.

- subString—Removes a portion of a string.

- toString—Returns a string representation of the passed argument.

- trim—Removes all white space at the beginning and end of a string.

The URL Library

The URL Library contains functions that provide operations to URLs that exist either locally (within the device) or remotely (on a remote server):

- escapeString—Returns a new string where the escape sequences are presented with their ASCII code values.

- getBase—Returns the absolute form of the URL for the current WMLScript file.

- getFragment—Returns the fragment part extracted from the URL.

- getHost—Returns the host portion extracted from the URL.

- getParameters—Returns the parameters extracted from a URL.

- getPath—Returns the path extracted from the URL.

- getPort—Returns the port number extracted from the URL.

- getQuery—Returns the query portion extracted from the URL.

- getReferer—Returns the smallest relative URL to the resource that called the WMLScript file.

- getScheme—Returns the scheme extracted from a URL.

- isValid—Performs a check to see whether a URL has a valid syntax.

- loadString—Returns a string from a URL.

- resolve—Converts a relative URL into an absolute URL.

- unescapeString—Undoes the URL escaping on a string. Performs the opposite operation of the escapeString function.

The WMLBrowser Library

The WMLBrowser Library contains functions used to command how WML and WMLScript files work together when processed by the browser:

- getCurrentCard—Retrieves the URL of the current card in the browser

- getVar—Retrieves the contents of a browser variable

- go—Specifies a <go> task that is executed

- newContent—Clears the browser of all content

- prev—Specifies a <prev> task that is executed

- refresh—Specifies a <refresh> task

- setVar—Sets a browser variable

The Dialogs Library

The Dialogs Library contains functions to communicate information to users:

- alert—Displays a warning message to the user
- confirm—Requests a yes or no response from the user
- prompt—Retrieves a string from the user

Detail of WMLScript Libraries and Their Functions

The following presents a more in-depth discussion of the functions found within their respective WMLScript Libraries. You can also check out the latest specifications of WMLScript at the WAP Forum Web site (www.wapforum.org).

The Lang Library

The Lang Library contains a number of arithmetic functions that allow for the calculation of integers. The Lang Library also contains two functions used to end the processing of an arithmetic function, as well as a function to test a device to see whether floating-point number calculations are supported (see Table C.1).

Table C.1 Lang Library Functions

Function	Syntax	Argument	Description
abort	Lang.abort(*string*)	String message.	Aborts the current WMLScript (due to an error) and displays the message that is the function's argument. The control is returned to the browser.
abs	Lang.abs(*number*)	Integer, float, string, or Boolean number.	Returns the absolute value of the number specified in the function's argument.
characterSet	Lang.characterSet()	No argument specified.	Used to return the identifier for the character set used by the device.
Exit	Lang.exit(*value*)	Any data type.	Aborts the current WMLScript (not due to an error) and displays the message that is the function's argument. The control is returned to the browser.

Table C.1 *continued*

Function	Syntax	Argument	Description
float	Lang.float()	No argument specified.	Used to determine whether the device supports floating point operations.
isFloat	Lang.isFloat(*string*)	String.	Used to return whether the string specified in the function's argument can be converted to a floating-point number.
isInt	Lang.isInt(*string*)	String.	Used to return whether the string can be converted into an integer number.
max	Lang.max(*number1*, *number2*)	Integer or float.	Used to return the larger of the two values specified in the function's argument.
min	Lang.min(*number1*, *number2*)	Integer or float.	Used to return the smaller of the two values specified in the function's argument.
minInt	Lang.minInt( )	No argument specified.	Used to return the smallest integer value supported by the device.
parseFloat	Lang.parseFloat (*string*)	Integer, float, string, or Boolean number.	Used to return a string as a decimal integer.
random	Lang.random(*range*)	Integer.	Used to generate a random integer number. The range of the number ranges from 0 to the number specified in the function's argument.
seed	Lang.seed	Integer.	Used to begin a random-number generation sequence. The sequence begins with the number specified in the function's argument.

The Float Library

The Float Library is a continuation of arithmetic functions, regarding numbers that contain decimal points (see Table C.2). Often, many game applications developed for wireless devices use the Float Library. At the time of this writing, not all wireless device browsers support decimal point numbers.

Table C.2   Float Library Functions

Function	Syntax	Argument	Description
ceil	Float.ceil(*number*)	Floating-point number.	Returns the largest integer number available with the device. This number no less than the floating-point number specified in the function's argument.
floor	Float.floor(*number*)	Floating-point number.	Returns the smallest integer number available within the device. This number is no less than the floating-point number specified in the function's argument.
int	Float.int(*number*)	Floating-point number.	Returns the integer part of the specified floating-point number specified in the function's argument.
maxfloat	Float.maxfloat()	No argument is specified.	Returns the largest floating-point number available within the device.
minfloat	Float.minfloat()	No argument is specified.	Returns the smallest floating-point number available within the device.
pow	Float.pow(*number1, number2*)	Floating-point number.	Returns the value of raising the value of number 1 to the specified value of number 2.
round	Float.round(*number*)	Floating-point number.	Returns the value of the specified number, rounded to the nearest whole number.
sqrt	Float.sqrt(*number*)	Floating-point number.	Returns the square root of the floating point number specified in the function's argument.

The String Library

The built-in functions available within the String Library are important, in that they allow developers to perform a number of important operations to strings.

Strings, by definition, are a set (or array) or characters that are grouped together. The length of a string is the number of characters within the array.

The functions within the String Library are used mainly to specify which elements of a string can be separated (see Table C.3). For example, the trim function enables developers to remove any white space characters from a string.

Table C.3   *String Library Functions*

Function	Syntax	Argument	Description
charAt	String.charAt (*string, number*)	String and integer number.	Returns the character within the string that is designated by the index number. The index number is defined by the function's argument.
Compare	String.compare (*string1, string2*)	String.	Returns a -1 value if the first string is smaller than the second string. Returns a 1 if the first string is larger than the second string, and returns a 0 if both strings are the same length.
elements	String.element (*string, separator*)	String. A *separator* is a string character that separates string elements from one another.	Returns the number of string elements as defined by the separator.
elementAt	String.elementAt (*string, index, separator*)	String, integer (for index), string separator.	Returns the element in the separated string, according to the index number.
find	String.find(*string, element*)	String, string element.	Returns the index of the first character of the string element.
format	String.format (*string, value*)	String.	Defines a value for a string that contains formatting specifiers.
insertAt	String.insertAt (*string, element, Index, separator*)	String, integer (for index), string separator.	Inserts a string element into a separated string. The location of the insertion is specified by the index defined in the function's argument.
isEmpty	String.isEmpty (*string*)	String.	Determines whether a string has a zero length. Returns a true or false value.
length	String.length(*string*)	String.	Determines the character length of a string.
removeAt	String.removeAt (*string, index, separator*)	String, integer (for index), string separator.	Removes a string element according to the index defined within a function.
replace	String.replace (*string, oldelement, newelement*)	String, string elements.	Replaces the first string element within the second string element.

Table C.3 continued

Function	Syntax	Argument	Description
replaceAt	String.replaceAt (*string, element, index, separator*)	String, integer (for index), string separator.	Replaces a string element according to the index defined within the function.
squeeze	String.squeeze (*string*)	String.	Reduces all the white space within a string to a single space.
subString	String.subString (*string, index, length*)	String, integer (for index), integer (for length of characters).	Removes a portion of a string.
toString	String.toString (*value*)	Any data type.	Returns a string representation of the passed argument.
trim	String.trim (*string*)	String.	Removes all white space at the beginning and end of a string.

The URL Library

The URL Library contains a number of functions, shown in Table C.4, that provide operations to handle URLs that exist either locally (within the device) or remotely (on a remote server). In other words, the URL Library contains the functionality in regard to absolute and relative URLs (see Chapter 5, "Navigation Using WML," for more information).

Table C.4 URL Library Functions

Function	Syntax	Argument	Description
escapeString	URL.escapeString (*string*)	String.	Returns a new string where the escape sequences are presented with their ASCII code values.
getBase	URL.getBase()	No argument is specified.	Returns the absolute form of the URL for the current WMLScript file.
getFragment	URL.getFragment (*string*)	String URL.	Returns the fragment part extracted from the URL.
getHost	URL.getHost (*string*)	String URL.	Returns the host portion extractedfrom the URL.
getParameters	URL.getParameters (*string*)	String URL.	Returns the parameters extracted from the URL.
getPath	URL.getPath (*string*)	String URL.	Returns the path extracted from the URL.
getPort	URL.getPort (*string*)	String URL.	Returns the port number extracted from the URL.

Table C.4   continued

Function	Syntax	Argument	Description
getQuery	URL.getQuery (*string*)	String URL.	Returns the query portion extractedfrom the URL.
getReferer	URL.getReferer()	No argument is specified.	Returns the smallest relative URL to the resource that called the WMLScript file.
getScheme	URL.getScheme (*string*)	String URL.	Returns the scheme extracted from the URL.
isValid	URL.isValid (*string*)	String URL.	Performs a check to see whether a URL has a valid syntax.
loadString	URL.loadString (*string1, string2*)	*string1* represents a URL; *string2* represents the text type (must start with keyword text).	Returns a string from a URL.
resolve	URL.resolve (*string1, string2*)	*string1* represents a base URL; *string2* represents a revolving URL.	Converts arelative URL into an absolute URL.
unescapeString	URL.unescapeString (*string*)	String URL.	Undoes the URL escaping on a string. Performs the opposite operation of the escapeString function.

The WMLBrowser Library

The WMLBrowser Library contains a number of functions used to command how WML and WMLScript files work together when processed by the browser (see Table C.5). Because not all wireless devices use the same browsers, sometimes a particular browser might not be capable of interpreting these functions. In this case, the WMLScript is ignored.

Table C.5   WMLBrowser Library Functions

Function	Syntax	Argument	Description
getCurrentCard	WMLBrowser. getCurrentCard()	No argument is specified.	Retrieves the URL of the current card in the browser.
getVar	WMLBrowser.getVar (*string*)	String name.	Retrieves the contents of a browser variable.
go	WMLBrowser.go (*string*)	String URL.	Specifies a GO task that is executed.

Table C.5   continued

Function	Syntax	Argument	Description
newContent	WMLBrowser. newContent()	No argument is specified.	Clears the browser of all content.
prev	WMLBrowser.prev()	No argument is specified.	Specifies a PREV task that is executed.
refresh	WMLBrowser. refresh()	No argument is specified.	Specifies a REFRESH task.
setVar	WMLBrowser.setVar (*string1*, *string2*)	*string1* represents the name of the variable; *string2* represents the value of the variable.	Sets a browser variable.

The Dialogs Library

The Dialogs Library contains functions that enable the application to provide communication to users (see Table C.6).

Table C.6   Dialogs Library Functions

Function	Syntax	Argument	Description
alert	Dialogs.alert(*string*)	String message.	Displays a warning message to the user.
confirm	Dialogs.confirm (*string1*, *string2*, *string3*)	*string1* represents a message; *string2* represents the yes option; *string3* represents the no option.	Used to request a yes or no response from the user.
prompt	Float.maxfloat()	Floating-point number.	Returns the integer part of the floating-point number specified in the function's argument.
maxfloat	Dialogs.prompt (*string1*, *string2*)	*string1* represents a message; *string2* represents a default entry if the user does not enter information.	Retrieves a string from the user.

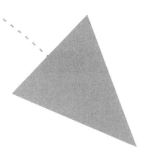

Troubleshooting Your WAP Application

Hopefully, you've been successful in getting your WAP applications up and running. However, generating WAP content correctly sometimes can be difficult. You might encounter some pitfalls along the way in your development efforts. This appendix contains some of the tips and suggestions to answer some of the more common troubleshooting problems you might experience.

continues

Setting Up Your Development Environment

Before you can develop WAP applications, you first must create a development environment. For the exercises in this book you'll need the following set of tools:

- A PC with one of the following Windows operating systems:
    - Windows 95, 98, or Millennium (Me)
    - Windows NT 4.0
- Windows 2000 Professional, Advanced Server, or Datacenter Server
- A text editor
- WAP device-emulator
- WBMP Image Tool
- WBMP Image Tool
- Web Server
- Microsoft Access 97 or higher

Text Editors

Table D.1 displays information about text editors available for your development efforts.

Table D.1   Available Text Editors for WAP Development

Text Editor	Company	Available From	Cost
Notepad	Microsoft	Installed with Windows operating systems	Included with cost of OS.
TextPad	Helios	`http://textpad.com`	Around $30. Also available as shareware from the Web site.
HomeSite	Allaire	`http://www.allaire.com`	Around $90. A free 30-day trial version is available from the Allaire Web site.

WAP Device Emulators

WAP device emulators enable developers to develop and test applications without the use of an actual WAP device. Table D.2 displays information about some of the most widely available WAP device emulators.

Table D.2   Available Device Emulators for WAP Development

Device Emulator	Company	Available From	Cost
Openwave SDK	Openwave	http://www.openwave.com	Available for free download if you register at the Web site.
Nokia Mobile Internet Toolkit	Nokia	http://www.nokia.com	Available for free download if you register at the Web site.
Ericsson WapIDE	Ericsson	http://www.ericsson.com	Available for free download if you register at the Web site.
Motorola Applications Development Kit	Motorola	http://www.motorola.com	Available for free download if you register at the Web site.
Yospace Smartphone Emulator	Yospace	http://www.yospace.com	Around $99. Users may download an evaluation version by first registering at the Web site.
Brew SDK	Qualcomm	http://www.qualcomm.com	Available for free download if you register at the Web site.
Cold Fusion Studio	Allaire	http://www.allaire.com	Around $500 for a single-user license. A free evaluation version is available from the Web site.

WBMP Image Tools

To incorporate images into your WAP applications, you'll need to use some sort of image editing tool. Several image tools are available, including

- Image converter programs (see Table D.3)

- Online converter pages (see Table D.4)

- Plug-ins for existing graphic software (see Table D.5)

Tables D.3–D.5 summarize the different image tools available for WAP development.

Table D.3   Available Image Converter Programs for WAP Development

Image Editing Tool	Company	Available From	Cost
Image Magick	ImageMagick Studio, LCC	http://www.imagemagick.org	Freeware.
Pic2wbmp	Ginco New Media	http://www.ginco.de/wap	Freeware.

Table D.3   continued

Image Editing Tool	Company	Available From	Cost
WAPDraw	Jarno Kyh	`http://www.phnet.fi/public/jiikoo`	Around $20. Also available as shareware from the Web site.
WAPPictus	CheckIT	`http://www.checkit.cz/`	Free (first must fill out contact information).
Wap Tiger BMP Converter	WAPTiger	`http://wap.infotiger.de/download/html`	Freeware.

Table D.4   Available Online Converter Pages for WAP Development

Online Converter	Company	Available From	Cost
Applepie Online Image Converter	Applepie Solutions	`http://www.applepiesolutions.com`	Free
Dwbmp	Morpheme	`http://www.morpheme.co.uk`	Free for non-commercial use
WAPuSeek Online Coverter	wapuseek	`http://wapuseek.com`	Free
WAP Tiger Online Converter	Wap Tiger	`http://wap.infotiger.de/download/html`	Free

Table D.5   Available Plug-Ins for Graphic Software

Plug-In	Company	Available From	Cost
Photoshop or Paintshop plug-ins (for Windows)	RCP	`http://www.rcp.co.uk`	Free (must have Photoshop 5.x or Paintshop Pro already installed)
Photoshop plug-ins (for Macintosh)	Creation Flux	`http://www.creationflux.com`	Free (must have Photoshop 5.x already installed)

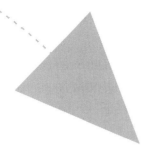

Appendix E

Wireless Development Resources

The following are some excellent reference sites on the Web to obtain further information about wireless development.

The topic of wireless development is a broad and diverse field, one which we have only touched the surface of with this book. These sites will provide further information if you want to find out more about any of the topics mentioned in this book.

Wireless Development Resources

- **InformIT.com**—Its URL is `http://www.informit.com`, and it provides a variety of great articles and tutorials on a variety of mobile/wireless development subjects. This site is an excellent source for all areas of information regarding the IT world today.

- **Anywhereyougo.com**—Its URL is `http://www.anywhereyougo.com`, and it provides many great services and information, including news, book reviews, newsletters, online WAP testing services (free of charge), new WAP tools, discussion groups, wireless development tutorials, and a lot more.

- **The Apion WAP Tutorial**—Its URL is `http://www.iec.org/tutorials/wap/`, and it provides an excellent introductory guide to WAP. A PDF version of this tutorial is available at `www.webproforum.com`.

- **Gelon.net**—Its URL is `http://www.gelon.net`, and it provides several links, tutorials, book reviews, hosting, and more. There's also a plethora of information at this site for a number of different wireless development topics.

- **Nokia** (`http://www.nokia.com`), **Ericsson** (`http://www.ericsson.com`), **Openwave** (`http://www.openwave.com`), **and Motorola** (`http://www.motorola.com`)—These all provide excellent developer's tools, forums, training classes, and many services and aids aimed at the wireless developer. I highly recommend that you register at all these sites (again, registration is free) to have access to the great amount of information made available.

- **TheFeature.com**—Its URL is `http://www.thefeature.com`, it is dedicated to information about mobile technologies, and it is run by Nokia.

- **The WAP Forum**—Its URL is `http://www.wapforum.org`, and it provides information about the latest WAP specifications. To find white papers on the WAP specifications, click the This Site link at the top of the page. Under the What Is WAP heading, you'll find links to various white papers and specifications regarding WAP technology.

- **The WAP Group**—Its URL is `http://www.thewapgroup.com`, and it provides a valuable network of professionals. This site provides a great reference of development knowledge regarding WAP technologies.

- **WAP.NET**—Its URL is `http://www.wap.net`, and it provides a number of resources for the wireless developer.

- **WAPuSeek**—Its URL is `http://www.wapuseek.com`, and it provides a number of WAP articles, tools, links, and an excellent developer's area.

- **Wireless Developer Network**—Its URL is `http://www.wirelessdevnet.com`, and it provides a comprehensive resource for developers, including tutorials, articles, and product reviews.

Wireless News

- **WirelessWeek.com**—Its URL is `http://www.wirelessweek.com`, and it is the online site of *Wireless Week* magazine.

- **WirelessInternetMag.com**—Its URL is `http://www.wirelessinternetmag.com`, and it is the online site of *Wireless Internet* magazine.

- **Unstrung.com**—Its URL is `http://www.unstrung.com`, and it is a wireless business, technology, and lifestyle site.

- **IBC Telecoms**—Its URL is `http://www.ibctelecoms.com`, and it provides information about telecom industry events. This site provides conference papers that are available for download, including the WAP Congress material.

- **IT Works**—Its URL is `http://www.itworks.be/WAP`, and it provides the latest information on wireless technology and WAP. This site also contains an excellent links page to other WAP sites.

- **MobileStart**—Its URL is `http://www.mobilestart.com`, and it is a great news site that provides information about issues in the mobile computing industries.

- **MobileWAP**—Its URL is `http://www.mobilewap.com`, and it provides all kinds of information regarding the Wireless Application Protocol, including current white papers and reports. This site also contains several excellent links to other related sites.

- **Palowireless**—Its URL is `http://www.palowireless.com`, and it provides the latest information on WAP news, products, and events.

- **WAPsight**—Its URL is `http://www.wapsight.com`, and it provides a set of news links and up-to-date coverage of WAP information and industry news.

- **Links2Mobile**—Its URL is `http://www.links2mobile.com`, and it provides a comprehensive set of links to mobile communication Internet sites.

- **Mobic**—Its URL is `http://www.mobic.com`, and it provides general WAP and other wireless industry links.

- **Perfect**—Its URL is `http://www.perfect.co.uk`, and it provides a variety of links regarding all areas of the mobile communication industry.

- **wannaWAP**—This global Internet portal for mobile phones (at `http:// www.wannawap.com`) contains a number of WML links. This site allows users to search for WAP and WML sites, as well as submit their own WAP and WML sites.

- **WAP IT OUT**—Its URL is `http://www.wapitout.com`, and it provides one of the best search engines regarding WAP technology.

- **WAPJAG**—Its URL is `http://www.wapjag.com`, and it provides worldwide WAP-links within a well-organized directory.

- **FierceWireless.com**—Its URL is `http://www.fiercewireless.com`, and it is an excellent online newsletter about mobile commerce.

Wireless Services

- **Brainstorm**—Its URL is `http://www.brainstorm.co.uk`, and it is one of Europe's leading-edge wireless applications service providers (WASPs). Brainstorm develops, hosts, and manages applications using SMS, WAP, and GPRS technologies.

- **Caliday**—Its URL is `http://www.caliday.com`, and it provides Web- and WAP-based calendaring applications.

- **envelos**—Its URL is `http://www.envelos.com`, and it develops WAP e-mail accounts that enable people to subscribe for free. Its product is a small Outlook-type application installed onto a wireless device.

- **Macalla**—Its URL is `http://www.macalla.com`, and it is a leading provider of XML and WAP products, as well as e-commerce solutions.

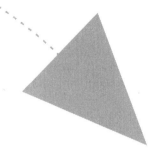

Index

Other Related Titles

The Wi-Fi Experience
Harold Davis and Richard Mansfield
ISBN: 0-7897-2662-9
$29.99 U.S.
$46.99 CAN

Java 2 by Example
Jeff Friesen
ISBN: 0-7897-2593-2
$34.99 U.S./$54.99 CAN

Cascading Style Sheets by Example
Steve Callihan
ISBN: 0-7897-2617-3
$29.99 U.S./$46.99 CAN

Special Edition Using Visual Basic.NET
Brian Siler and Jeff Spotts
ISBN: 0-7897-2572-X
$39.99 U.S./$62.99 CAN

Protect Your Digital Privacy! Survival Skills for the Information Age
Pat McGregor
ISBN: 0-7897-2604-1
$29.99 U.S./$46.99 CAN

Coming Soon:

Special Edition Using HTML and XHTML
Molly Holzschlag
ISBN: 0-7897-2731-5
$39.99 U.S./$62.99 CAN
May 2002

TechTV's Wireless Networking
Les Freed
ISBN: 0-7897-2655-6
$24.99 U.S./$38.99 CAN
June 2002

Special Edition Using Pocket PCs
Michael Morrison
ISBN: 0-7897-2749-8
$34.99 U.S./$54.99 CAN
May 2002

Palm Development
Clayton Crooks
ISBN: 0-7897-2649-1
$29.99 U.S./$46.99 CAN
April 2002

Visual Basic .NET by Example
Gabriel Oancea and Bob Donald
ISBN: 0-7897-2583-5
$39.99 U.S.
$62.99 CAN

Special Edition Using JavaScript
Paul McFedries
ISBN: 0-7897-2576-2
$39.99 U.S.
$62.99 CAN

www.quecorp.com

All prices are subject to change.